KENTUCKY'S
CIVIL WAR BATTLEFIELDS

KENTUCKY'S
CIVIL WAR BATTLEFIELDS

A GUIDE TO THEIR HISTORY AND PRESERVATION

RANDY BISHOP

PELICAN PUBLISHING COMPANY
Gretna 2012

The word "Pelican" and the depiction of a pelican are
trademarks of Pelican Publishing Company, Inc., and are
registered in the U.S. Patent and Trademark Office.

Library of Congress Cataloging-in-Publication Data

Bishop, Randy.
  Kentucky's Civil War battlefields : a guide to their history and
preservation / by Randy Bishop.
    p. cm.
  Includes bibliographical references and index.
  ISBN 978-1-4556-1607-7 (hardcover : alk. paper) — ISBN 978-1-
4556-1608-4 (e-book) 1. Kentucky—History—Civil War, 1861-1865.
2. United States—History—Civil War, 1861-1865—Campaigns. 3.
Kentucky—History, Military—19th century. 4. United States—History—
Civil War, 1861-1865—Battlefields—Conservation and restoration.
5. Battlefields—Conservation and restoration—Kentucky. 6. Historic
preservation—Kentucky. I. Title.
  E472.9.B57 2012
  976.9'03—dc23
                                        2011046817

Jacket painting: Raid on the L & N *by John Paul Strain © 2005*

Printed in the United States of America

Published by Pelican Publishing Company, Inc.
1000 Burmaster Street, Gretna, Louisiana 70053

*In memory of my brothers-in-law:
David Whaley and Mike Bell*

CONTENTS

PREFACE

The Bluegrass State of Kentucky found itself in a unique situation during the early days of the American Civil War. While most of its fellow states committed themselves to the service of either the United States or the Confederate Government, Kentucky attempted to remain neutral during the great conflict. With its people as divided as possible about which "side" to adhere to, Kentucky managed to avoid declaring its allegiance, despite the fact that untold numbers of its citizens perished defending its soil or while fighting in other locations across the North and South.

The purpose of this manuscript is to examine the battles that occurred within the borders of the state attempting to avoid losing its sons and daughters to bloodshed. From the smaller sites, such as Ivy Mountain, to the well-preserved and greatly interpreted fields of Perryville, Richmond, and Mill Springs, the book will attempt to conduct an overview of the battles that the Civil War Sites Advisory Commission has deemed as having some significance on the outcome of the war. In addition, the level of preservation or absence thereof, at the time of publication, will be noted.

With this in mind, it is my hope that those individuals reading the text will be able to both gain the mindset of the warriors of long ago and gain an appreciation and understanding of the concept of viewing the sites as they appear today.

ACKNOWLEDGEMENTS

Most attempts to begin, much less complete, a manuscript of any significant length would be impossible if not for the assistance, input, and support of numerous multitalented and cooperative individuals. In recognizing this, it is suitable to make mention of most of the people who made this study a possibility and greatly aided its completion. Before indulging upon this task, I must first apologize to any person, group, or entity omitted. Doing so is a careless oversight on my part and in no way is an attempt to minimize his or her valuable contributions.

John Paul Strain allowed the use of his outstanding and unequaled artwork to grace the cover. Likewise, Dave Roth, editor of *Blue and Gray Magazine*, provided outstanding maps that enhance the understanding of most of the battles in this work. Without the skills of these men, the appearance of the book would be lacking some degree of completeness.

Untold individuals allowed the use of photographs from their family archives. So as to not delete the individuals whose ancestors are contained within and to adhere to the guidelines of the publisher, I have made notice of them with the respective picture. To each of these contributors a sincere thank you is certainly warranted.

Also, I have to give a special thank you to Phillip Seyfrit of the Richmond Battlefield, Kurt Holman of Perryville, and Gilbert Wilson from Mill Springs for their willingness to review the chapters related to the outstanding battle sites where they work. Such selflessness has, more importantly, allowed these three areas of hallowed ground to rise to the forefront in the state of Kentucky. For their input and suggestions, I am deeply indebted.

Lastly, I have to thank three people who make it possible for each and every one of my projects to evolve from an idea to the finished product. My wife Sharon, my navigator on numerous battlefield visits; Jay, my grown son, who is there to lend his dry humor and give encouragement; and Ben, my teenager, who, like his big brother, is a wonderful companion and source of happiness. From spending an entire fall break trekking around most of the Kentucky battle sites in near-record rainfall to braving the others in extreme heat, they are the most attentive and caring family a man could ask for. I fail to see how they do it, but I love them for their support of "the old man."

INTRODUCTION

Neutrality. In a perfect, utopian-like world, remaining neutral when surrounded by adversity would be the ultimate goal of any noble individual. This was the apparent intention of Kentucky governor Beriah Magoffin during the early months of the American Civil War. Despite the courtship on the part of both Confederate- and Union-biased citizens and government representatives, Magoffin attempted to avoid declaring the allegiance of his state and its citizens; although, history has regularly recorded that he held a strong pro-Confederate stance.

One month after the bombardment of Fort Sumter, the Kentucky legislature officially proclaimed the state's neutrality. Ironically, both the Confederate president, Jefferson Davis, and his U.S. counterpart, Abraham Lincoln, had been born in the Bluegrass State and, in turn, exemplified the growing division of sentiments within the state's borders. Governor Magoffin firmly declined Lincoln's request for four regiments of troops. Magoffin replied to the executive plea, stating that he would "furnish no troops for the wicked purpose of subduing" people whom he termed as Kentucky's fellow Southerners. Subsequently, Davis's similar call for one Kentucky regiment to join the Confederate cause was turned down due to Magoffin's self-proclaimed lack of power to grant such.

Proponents from each side of the struggle continued to maintain hope for Kentucky to offer its assistance, and Lincoln reportedly acknowledged the state's high value, saying that while he hoped God was on his side, he had to have Kentucky's support in order to win the war. Lincoln allegedly stated, "I think to lose Kentucky is nearly the same as to lose the whole game." Ironically, Lincoln had failed to carry Kentucky's popular vote in the 1860 presidential election months earlier, as less than 1,400 Kentuckians had cast votes for their native son.[1]

The division Kentucky experienced was not only confined to her general populace, but it was also felt in the legislative bodies. The state's house of representatives was largely pro-Southern, while the senate held a pro-Union stance. This division becomes clear when viewing two resolutions presented in the early days of the war. One called for the disapproval of Lincoln's "coercing" Kentucky to obey the U.S. government. Another proclaimed that Kentuckians would join "their brethren of the South" to prevent an invasion of the South "at all hazards." The former unanimously passed the house while the latter met the overwhelming approval of 87 to 6. The Kentucky senate defeated both resolutions. As Governor Magoffin became convinced that a U.S. invasion of Kentucky was inevitable, he attempted no less than three times to secure funds to purchase weapons to defend the state. However, the general assembly refused to even address the issue.[2]

It has been expressed that should the three states of Kentucky, Missouri, and Maryland have joined the Confederacy, the nation's number of horses and mules would have increased some 40 percent, its white population would have increased by 45 percent, and its manufacturing capability would have grown by 80 percent. Specifically, Kentucky had the third-largest white population among pro-slave states, giving the area the added asset of potential military manpower. Added to this was the fact that Kentucky's border with Ohio, Indiana, and Illinois consisted of the Ohio River, the all-important east-west flowing waterway. Given these facts, it becomes clearer as to Lincoln's concern over the control of his home state.[3]

Kentucky was similar to Maryland and Missouri in that they were all border states, slave-holding entities that, for the time being, retained membership in the United States. Kentucky,

Maryland, and Missouri were filled with pro-secessionists, leading to fears for Lincoln and his preservation of the union. Western Kentucky's farmers relied upon slave labor a great deal, but their fellow statesmen in the eastern mountainous region saw little need for implementation of what abolitionist Frederick Douglass called the "peculiar institution" of slavery. The oft-noted Hatfield-McCoy feud and other lesser-known disagreements and family divisions mirrored the divisiveness of the war and its components.

Various resolutions from Magoffin and/or the Kentucky legislature eventually seemed to place Kentucky in a pro-Union stance, but by war's end approximately 40,000 Kentuckians volunteered their services to the Confederacy. This statistic frequently invoked Northerners' comprehension of Kentucky as a "rebel state." Exemplifying the state's uneasy peace, some 90,000 Kentuckians joined the service of the United States in its war effort.[4]

Kentucky's name, interpreted from Cherokee, means "dark and bloody ground." The attempts at establishing and maintaining neutrality are to be judged by others; however, there can be little argument that in the years 1861 to 1865 the Cherokee definition for Kentucky was clearly demonstrated. In 1862, Governor Magoffin resigned after his "public policy of strict armed neutrality," forbidding either the Confederacy or the United States to enter his state, and the failure to "force their evacuation when they did" led to an outcry for his removal. Some four hundred engagements of varying sizes bloodied the soil of Kentucky and robbed it and other states, North and South alike, of thousands of their finest young citizens.[5]

To this point military engagements had taken place in areas that literally surrounded Kentucky. Thus, the American Civil War, as the esteemed historian Bruce Catton wrote, "was incomplete. It had two ends and no middle. . . . Once the war broke into Kentucky it could begin to develop its full potential."[6] The battles that inevitably lay ahead soon appeared in Kentucky's southeastern section and quickly spread across the state. Sadly, the presence of the hostilities would cease only when the war itself reached its conclusion.

The intent and purpose of this book is to conduct an overview of a portion of these battles, primarily those regularly regarded as individually having an impact on the outcome of the war. The overview of each battle is combined with the success or failure of preservation efforts at the respective battlefield. The battles included are largely based upon a list the Civil War Sites Advisory Commission produced in a multi-year study and are, therefore, not a group the author randomly composed. These commission-noted sites are: Barbourville, Camp Wildcat, Cynthiana, Ivy Mountain, Middle Creek, Mill Springs, Munfordville, Paducah, Perryville, Richmond, and Rowlett's Station. In addition, the relevance of an additional battle at Sacramento, Kentucky, and the recent success in respect to the preservation efforts at that site has warranted its inclusion in the text. Thus, the latter provides the minor "waver" from the Civil War Sites Advisory Commission list.

Let the journey begin.

CHAPTER ONE

BARBOURVILLE

September 18, 1861

"The charge was made...and the enemy completely routed."
—*Richmond Dispatch* October 2, 1861

The division between pro-Union Kentuckians and their secessionist peers eventually led to the first bloodshed in the state on September 18, 1861. A literal tug-of-war between the two forces had warranted the establishment of Union recruiting and training camps, and the subsequent Confederate response was an effort to thwart the effect of the activity. As a result, the settlement of Barbourville, known as Barboursville at the time of the war, would earn a place in the annals of Kentucky's Civil War history. Although the number of casualties was relatively small and the battle provided little impact upon the struggle between the United States and the Confederate States of America, the conflict deems coverage as the first battle within the borders of Kentucky and the designation as one of the Civil War Sites Advisory Commission's "most significant and endangered"[1] battlefields from the war.

The town of Barbourville, located near the Wilderness Road and just twenty-five miles north of the Cumberland Gap, is usually regarded as owing its settlement to Dr. Thomas Walker. This Kentucky pioneer was a practicing physician as well as a surveyor and an agent for the Loyal Land Company of Virginia. Walker erected a cabin approximately six miles southeast of present-day Barbourville, near a bend of the Cumberland River. In 1795 Richard Ballinger established a tavern in the vicinity, and a few years later James Barbour donated land for the development of a town. The resulting village survived and was designated as Knox County's county seat in 1800.[2]

More famous individuals, such as Daniel Boone, followed Walker's expedition and the area continued to grow, eventually producing a series of state leaders for Kentucky, Missouri, and Texas. The town's nickname "Home of Governors" denoted its rich contribution to the maturation of the United States. As a result, Barbourville became one of the most important cities in Kentucky.[3]

Barbourville's aforementioned location near the Cumberland Gap drew the attention of the opposing armies as soon as the war began in 1861. Despite its declaration of neutrality, Kentucky saw its borders crossed by Union and Confederate men alike. Barbourville, situated in eastern Kentucky and a short distance north of the pro-Union section of East Tennessee, became an early point of contention in the military events.

East Tennesseans' strong stand to remain in the U.S. had literally separated it from its two sister sections to the west. Both Middle and West Tennessee were, from an economic standpoint, more agriculturally based and therefore possessed stronger sentiments in favor of the preservation of slavery. Because of East Tennessee's heavy stance on remaining in the Union, Andrew Johnson was able to remain in Washington, D.C.; he was the only Southern Congressman to do so. The circumstances in East Tennessee had not gone unnoticed in the United States capital as Abraham Lincoln openly stated that he saw the importance of the region and likewise sought its retention of membership in the Union.

In July of 1861, U.S. naval lieutenant William "Bull" Nelson, a native Kentuckian, was given the assignment of establishing a camp in Kentucky for the purpose of recruiting and training Union-minded men of the Bluegrass State to assist in the efforts to secure East Tennessee, its neighbor to the south. The resulting camp was located a short distance east of Danville, Kentucky, and lay approximately halfway between Danville and Richmond, along an east-west line. A Danville-area farmer named Richard Robinson provided the land for the camp that was given the designation Camp Dick Robinson. The farmer was known as "an extensive mule dealer and stock raiser" whose pro-Union stance "incurred the malignant enmity of not only his secession neighbors, but of leading secessionists of the state."[4]

Located six miles from Lancaster and only eight miles from Nicholasville, the Robinson farm held great accessibility for the Union cause. Nicholasville "was a southern terminus of the Kentucky Central Railroad, connecting it with Cincinnati." Lexington, another major city in the state, was only twelve miles north of the agricultural base.[5]

The Robinson farm included more than 1,800 acres that Dick Robinson gained through his marriage to the daughter of William Hoskins, Sr. A mansion of some twelve rooms graced the property that was proclaimed as being "one of the very best and richest tracts of land in the Bluegrass" and that the presence of a "never-failing spring . . . furnish[ed] an absolute inexhaustible flow of water."[6]

A *New York Times* article published in November of 1861 reported that Mr. Robinson sold $22,000 worth of mules to the Confederacy and did so by extending them credit. He had mortgaged his estate to make the initial purchase himself. When the Confederate government failed to pay the debt they owed, Robinson found it necessary to rent his farm. The U.S. government complied for some $33,000, a handsome profit and sizeable return on Robinson's investment.[7]

The presence of Camp Dick Robinson infuriated Kentucky governor Beriah Magoffin, who left no doubt that he wanted the facility shut down. In August, Magoffin wrote Pres. Abraham Lincoln noting that Magoffin desired "the removal from the limits of Kentucky of the military force now organized, and in camp within said state." The request for the camp's removal drew a response from Lincoln that he "acted upon the urgent solicitation of many Kentuckians" and "must respectfully decline" such action.[8]

Confederate leadership responded to the situation in Kentucky by placing recently promoted Brig. Gen. Felix Kirk Zollicoffer in command of soldiers in East Tennessee. Deeply admired and respected among his troops, Zollicoffer soon received an assignment from Gen. Albert Sidney Johnston to negate the growing threat from the increasing Union presence in Kentucky. Zollicoffer's significance in the events of the coming months could not have possibly been foreseen.

In spite of their similar leadership roles in the opposing armies, Nelson and Zollicoffer were distinct in a number of ways. Nelson's nickname of "Bull" exemplified his flamboyant personality and physical size. Political connections undoubtedly played a significant role in Nelson's appointment, related to Camp Dick Robinson. His brother, Thomas, was a Lincoln-appointee serving as minister to Chile and likely helped secure Bull's new leadership role and a promotion to brigadier general.[9]

Zollicoffer's troops regularly referred to him in affectionate terms, such as "Pap." Nelson was a U.S. officer in his mid-thirties while his Confederate counterpart was approaching the half-century mark. Zollicoffer was also a former newspaper editor and U.S. Representative from Tennessee. Their differences ended though with their similar determination to eliminate the other, or his cohorts, from establishing a firm foothold with the confines of Kentucky.[10]

East Tennesseans who were sympathetic to the Union were not forced to simply rely upon others to fight for them. In fact, the loyalists willing and able to cross the Kentucky state line were given the opportunity to join their fellow Unionists in the effort to suppress the Confederate "rebellion." The base of operations for this opportunity was another loyalist camp named for the Tennessee state senator serving in Washington, D.C., Andrew Johnson.

Camp Andy Johnson was established through the determination of Dr. R. T. Tuggle. In early August, Lt. Samuel P. Carter, a native East Tennessean and U.S. Naval Academy graduate, completed a journey of several months, arrived at the camp, and assumed his role as its commander. Upon doing so, Carter moved Camp

Andy Johnson from its original location near the Barbourville town square to a site approximately two miles east of the settlement. By the middle of the month, Carter had assembled some eight hundred Tennessee loyalists to form the 1st East Tennessee Infantry Regiment.[11]

Groups such as those established at Camp Andy Johnson and destined for pro-Union service were called Home Guard units. Their counterparts, determined to serve the Confederate cause, were known as State Guards. As the nation became more divided and violence erupted, Kentucky reflected this divisiveness in many ways. One of these was through the establishment of Confederate recruitment and training camps that opposed the earlier camps such as Johnson and Robinson.

A military chess match evolved as the opposing armies sought to gain control of several locations across the ever-decreasing neutral land of Kentucky. Confederate leaders Brig. Gen. Simon Bolivar Buckners well as Maj. Gen. Leonidas Polk moved into the Bluegrass State while Union groups established similar positions at other key sites. Tensions mounted as the time neared for the players in this real-life strategic game readied for a more forceful display of military might.

By mid-September, Union forces occupied Paducah in Northwestern Kentucky and Elizabethton in the North-central portion of the state. In addition to these soldiers, the Home Guard members stationed at Camp Dick Robinson had enabled the Union army to gain a solid foothold across the state. Total U.S. troop strength in Kentucky topped 20,000 as the state continued to declare its neutrality and—thus far—avoid bloodshed within its borders.[12]

Zollicoffer held the view that the Cumberland Gap would serve as the primary entry for a Kentucky Unionist invasion of Tennessee. He notified officials in Richmond that reliable sources had informed him of forces numbering in the thousands "threatening to force a passage through the mountains into East Tennessee." In turn, the Confederate general grew determined to eliminate the ability of the Kentucky Unionists to initiate actions in Tennessee.[13]

To more effectively facilitate his plan of defending against Union aggression, General Zollicoffer moved across the Cumberland Gap and entered the southeastern section of Kentucky. Zollicoffer had his men establish Camp Buckner during the second week of September.[14] From this location the Confederates could closely monitor Union activity in the area.

One Confederate wrote that an encampment near Camp Buckner was located "on high, steep, and rough ground" where soldiers determined it was necessary "to tie themselves in bed at night to keep from rolling out." Zollicoffer's command consisted of the 11th, 17th, 19th, and 20th Tennessee Infantry Regiments as well as two cavalry companies of Benjamin Branner's 4th Tennessee Battalion. This group of "the most completely exhausted set of men imaginable" entered camp on the Rufus Moss farm a short distance from the junction of Clear Creek and the Cumberland River.[15]

A Confederate recalled that a "monotonous routine of military duties" became commonplace at Camp Buckner in addition to what another declared was a siege from "measles, diarrhea, and all the diseases camp life is heir to." A lack of food and forage hampered the campers and added to the poor conditions. Undoubtedly, earlier encounters with residents some ten miles from Camp Buckner were present in the Confederates' minds. The contrasting observations of an abundance of "mountain girls, nearly all brunettes, with long dark, uncombed hair" and bare feet to that of "long-legged, long haired men with long squirrel rifles ever ready to shoot a rebel"[16] provide insight into the situation at hand for non-native soldiers.

The arrival of Rutledge's Tennessee Battery and the 15th Mississippi Infantry Regiment placed the number of Confederates in the vicinity of Camp Buckner at approximately 5,000. Although the amount of troops was significant, Zollicoffer appeared threatened by the Federals gathered and training at Camp Andy Johnson, less than twenty miles north of the Cumberland Ford.[17] The issue of this perceived threat would soon lead to the first confrontation on Kentucky soil.

From Knoxville, Tennessee, Zollicoffer sent orders for Col. Joel Allen Battle of the 20th Tennessee to advance north on September

18 with the assignment of neutralizing the training efforts at Camp Andy Johnson. Colonel Battle's face was graced with a thick white mustache and beard, the presence of which earned Battle the nickname "Grandpa" among his command. Battle's force of some eight hundred men was comprised of two companies from the earlier noted Branner's Cavalry battalion as well as portions of the 11th, 17th, 19th, and 20th Tennessee Infantry Regiments. One historian has proposed that these companies were chosen because they were among the most well armed men present at Camp Buckner. Although it appears uncertain as to the exact number of Federal troops Zollicoffer believed were stationed at Camp Andy Johnson, one individual reported an estimate as high as six hundred.[18]

Zollicoffer was unaware of the serious lack of supplies and sufficient weapons at Camp Andy Johnson. Almost all of the 1,000 Union soldiers who had spent the majority of the last month at Camp Andy Johnson had relocated eighty miles away to Camp Dick Robinson where ample provisions did exist. Various sources record the number of Home Guard members remaining at Camp Andy Johnson to have ranged anywhere between a reported "small . . . unit" and Zollicoffer's official recording of three hundred. Historian Kenneth A. Hafendorfer stated, "there probably was at least 150 Home Guards" at the camp.[19]

On September 18 a detachment of Confederate cavalry companies from Branner's Battalion and under the leadership of captains John Rowan and A. C. Plumlee left the Cumberland Ford and moved north toward Camp Andy Johnson. Eight infantry companies followed the cavalry as the latter reached the area of Barbourville before sundown. With the arrival of darkness, a reported fifty members from Plumlee's command approached the bridge that spanned Little Richland Creek.[20]

The advancing Confederates encountered members of the Home Guard positioned at the bridge. Reportedly, the Confederates fired the first shots and the Home Guards replied in a like manner. One of the Confederate accounts countered this recollection of the series of events as the soldier recalled, "We went rather cautiously until their pickets fired on us. . . . We charged along the road, not knowing where the men were stationed . . . within a quarter of a mile of Barbourville . . . we were fired on from the wood 50 or 75 yards from the road."[21]

A member of the Home Guard noted that when the Confederates caught sight of the Home Guard, members the Confederates opened fire. A Barbourville resident remarked, "There were some thirty of the Home Guard guarding the bridge; the seceshers [pro-secessionists] fired at them."[22]

Another participant recorded that the Confederates retreated at the same instant that the Home Guard left the scene. Discrepancies exist in relation to the number of casualties inflicted, as the Home Guard reported no losses and three Confederates wounded. The Confederates denied any losses while claiming to have killed a member of the Home Guard and inflicted minor wounds. By "about 1 or 2 a.m." the fighting was reportedly over.[23] However, the action of September 18 was merely a prelude of what was to come the following day.

Col. Joel Battle and his detachment of Confederate infantry arrived at the outskirts of Barbourville at approximately 6 a.m. on September 19, Battle's fiftieth birthday. The infantrymen had covered several miles in their approach upon Barbourville. Capt. Dick McCann of the Cheatham Rifles recalled the presence of anti-secessionism was extremely strong. McCann wrote that in the suburbs of Barbourville the "atmosphere is foul with the stench of Unionism," and that he witnessed, "every house decorated with that old flag." After being informed of the skirmish that took place a few hours earlier, Battle determined that the entire force of cavalry, not a mere group of fifty, should advance toward the town. Battle's eight infantry companies were to bring up the rear.[24]

A Confederate noted, "The morning was very foggy and we were not able to distinguish a man one hundred yards off." Another stated that the thickness of the fog negated seeing anything over a distance of thirty feet. Ormond Beatty was an area educator and served as the weather observer for the town of Barbourville. He recorded that the rains of the previous night had helped create the fog on the morning of September 19 and that the temperature at 7 a.m. was 70 degrees. The foggy conditions would soon be eradicated as the temperature rose to 85 by 2 p.m.[25]

A member of the Confederate force approaching the town reminisced, "a lane leads to the town, over a bridge, crossing the ravine to the left and right of the road. On our right was a field of luxuriant corn . . . on our left stubble fields."[26]

An estimated three hundred members of the Confederate force approached the bridge spanning Little Richland Creek. As few as twenty-one Home Guard members protected the approach to the bridge and had likely participated in removing the planks of the structure. As least one Barbourville resident claimed that his fellow townspeople had anticipated the morning return of the Confederates and ripped the floorboards from the bridge frame. With the cross planks gone, the bridge could only be traversed along the "sleepers," the section of the bridge used to support the cross planks.[27] Otherwise, the Confederates would have to enter the creek in order to successfully reach their goal.

The exact sequence of events that followed is filled with conflicting recollections. One citizen of Barbourville recalled that when the three hundred Confederate cavalrymen arrived, they fired upon the Home Guard. A period newspaper article written by a Confederate participant indicated the Home Guard fired the first shots of the day. He wrote, "When we had approached to within about thirty yards of the bridge, the enemy, concealed in the ravine, behind fences, in the corn-field, and under the bridge, commenced a brisk fire."[28]

Lt. Robert Davis Powell, 19th Tennessee Infantry, had volunteered to accompany Capt. John Rowan's cavalry squadron in its approach upon Barbourville. Powell gained permission to join the expedition, secured a horse, and rode with the advance guard. The young officer secured a horse and rode with the advance Confederate guard. In his mid-thirties, Powell was an attorney who had never been married.[29]

J. P. Coffin recalled the events of the Confederate arrival in noting, "When the front rank of the advanced guard had gotten within about thirty steps of the bridge and saw in the early dawn that the floor had been taken up, they hesitated for a moment, and just then the enemy gave us their first volley, and Lieut. Powel [sic], who was riding at my right, fell forward and to his left, striking the neck of my horse and falling to the ground."[30]

It is a generally regarded fact that Powell holds the unfortunate distinction of being the first Confederate officer killed in action in Kentucky. He is also considered to be the first Confederate officer killed outside of the Virginia borders. In the ensuing events, Pvt. John Hendrickson, a member of the pro-Union Barboursville Home Guard, was also killed. His death secured the town's place in history as the sight of Kentucky's first armed struggle that resulted in the death of a soldier from both armies.[31]

The Confederates followed orders from Captain Rowan as one company moved to the right and another to the left of the road. Several of the men in gray heard Colonel Battle give the command to "clear the way for the artillery." Another interpretation of the order was, "let the artillery come forward." The fact of the matter was that the nearest Confederate artillery was at Cumberland Ford, some eighteen miles away. However, the call for artillery yielded the desired effect upon the Home Guard as the steadfast twenty-one members, who refused to abandon their position during the initial contact and had twice beaten back the Confederate attacks, began fleeing their defensive positions.[32]

The Home Guard retreat was described in a *Richmond Dispatch* article in early October. The article stated that part of the Home Guard detachment was silenced with a few pistol shots and that a subsequent charge was made upon their position. The writer recalled, "The charge was made, the corn field cleared, and the enemy completely routed. The infantry . . . gave them the farewell shot."[33]

Another Confederate wrote, "Our men were running up and down the gulley [sic] trying to get over to the enemy. When they made way, so that the infantry could fire a few charges, the enemy ran."[34]

A Knox County resident wrote of the action and the Confederates negotiating a ditch to gain an advantage on the Home Guard. The writer noted, "the [Confederate] cavalry . . . went back, crossed the gut back about one-fourth of mile, made their way around, came up the town, and . . . upon the rear of the Home Guards, intending to surround them. When [the Home Guard] . . . saw that, they escaped . . . one was shot through the ear and one through the top of the shoulder."[35]

One Confederate recollection offered humorous insight in relation to the Home Guards' resistance. Statements providing credence to the stubbornness of the defenders' fighting noted "A hostile bullet emptied my canteen of a very good article of peach brandy, leaving me otherwise unwounded as I charged across the stringers of a bridge from which the planks had been removed. Here I saw my brother's cavalry company . . . emptying their revolvers at the enemy."[36]

For all practical purposes, the battle of Barbourville ended with the retreat of the Home Guard. The Confederates moved to Camp Andrew Johnson where they took possession of supplies, weapons, and ammunition. The raiders then destroyed the camp before returning to Barbourville.

Related events are preserved in an article published a week after the battle. The writer recorded, "When they [Confederates] took possession of the town they destroyed a great amount of property and . . . were reveling upon the spoils of victory. . . . Men, women, and Negroes are all fleeing in the direction of Camp Robinson."[37]

An inaccurate account of the Confederate casualties gave the number as some thirty killed and twelve mortally wounded. This same report stated that the attacking force loaded a wagon "with their dead, and the blood was strewn all along the road from the wagon for miles." Zollicoffer, in his official report, listed Lt. Powell as the only death yet noted that one of the additional four soldiers who were wounded was mortally wounded. The Confederate commander also proclaimed that his soldiers had killed twelve members of the Home Guard and captured two. He was unable to provide an estimate of the wounded Home Guardsmen.[38]

Barbourville has grown a great deal since the battle and modern structures have been built on a large amount of the land where fighting took place in September of 1861. There are three historical markers on the north side of town and one of these, state marker 518, is related to the action of that fateful day. From a negative standpoint, it is positioned at a dangerous and busy intersection, making it difficult to reach, read, and interpret. Additionally, a Civil War Sites Advisory Commission Report on the Nation's Civil War Battlefields studied approximately 940 acres and summarized the condition of the Barbourville battlefield as "landscape and terrain have been altered beyond recognition."[39]

Debate exists about the exact location Camp Andrew Johnson occupied, but Union College is often regarded to be located on the site. The institute of higher learning was founded in 1879 and is one of the oldest in the region.[40] Aside from these facts, several positive aspects exist in relation to the preservation efforts at Barbourville.

On September 12, 2008 the Barbourville Civil War Interpretive Park was dedicated near the intersection of Cumberland Avenue and Daniel Boone Drive. This outstanding one-quarter-acre memorial to those who fought in Kentucky's first battle will, in the words of historian Joseph E. Brent, make "it difficult for citizens and visitors alike to be uninformed about" the battle of Barbourville.[41] The initial impact of viewing this memorial is positive and arouses curiosity to seek additional information in relation to the contents of the signage and other aspects of the attractive site.

Several groups working together enabled this dream to become a reality and preserve the memory of the battle and its participants. Fundraising products and a grant greatly helped this multi-year dream to come true. A land donation from Curry Oil Company as well as an equipment and labor donation from William and Rhonda Roach of Compliance Industrial LLC to clear a building from the site was combined with the efforts of other entities to create the park. Among those who added to the construction of the site were the Barbourville Tourism Commission, the City of Barbourville, Renaissance on Main Street, and Congressman Harold Rogers. The Southern and Eastern Kentucky Tourism Development Association, the Knox County Chamber of Commerce, and the Knox Historical Museum are also to be commended for their efforts. No less important to the project were the Knox County Area Technology Center, Corey Patrick Jones of Berea College, Mudpuppy & Waterdog, Inc., and Union College.[42]

Two informative and easy-to-access kiosks, each consisting of three panels, enable readers to gain an understanding of the battle while standing on some of the actual ground where the military action took place. Benches and a gazebo provide locations for rest and reflection for park visitors. Area buildings contain murals that add to the reverence for each soldier who long ago offered his best in defense of the cause he so unselfishly and willingly served. In addition to the kiosks, individuals entering the park are able to view a miniature replica of the bridge that spanned the gulch on the outskirts of town. Flags, a cannon, and memorials add to the impressive location.

More insight into the area's history can be gained by visiting the Knox Historical Museum, established in 1987 in Barbourville. A series of themed rooms focuses on various aspects of the rich heritage Knox County possesses. The building is located on the corner of Liberty Street and Daniel Boone Drive. Additional information can be gained by calling 606-546-4300. In addition, the Knox County Public Library, located on Knox Street, contains research material on local and state history. The facility is open every day except Sunday and hours of operation vary. More information is attainable at 606-546-5339. Dr. Thomas Walker State Park is open year round and is situated near the Cumberland River and memorializes the settler who arrived in the area seventeen years ahead of noted explorer Daniel Boone. The park's phone number is 606-546-4400.

A successful and active means of preservation of the Battle

of Barbourville is the annual reenactment. Ray Adkins founded this event, which usually occurs in mid-September and includes campsite and battle action. In its first decade of existence, the reenactment has grown to include several hundred participants. Contacting the museum above will provide interested parties with additional and up-to-date information.

The modern city of Barbourville contains a population of approximately 3,600 people. As with many towns across the nation, Barbourville could greatly benefit from the economic opportunities offered in taking advantage of the park and resources the area offers. The groundwork for both preservation and monetary gains has been laid. The willingness and continued devotion of interested townspeople to properly utilize these will determine the success of the efforts previously enacted.

These headstones honoring two of the casualties of the battle of Barbourville, the first combat deaths in Kentucky, are located in the Barbourville Civil War Interpretive Park. (Photo by author)

The Barbourville Civil War Interpretive Park. (Photo by author)

These markers are virtually stacked to the side of a busy highway outside of Barbourville. (Photo by author)

Lt. Robert D. Powel (Powell) was the first Confederate killed outside of Virginia. (Courtesy of Lt. Robert D. Powel, S.C.V., Camp #1817)

CHAPTER TWO

WILDCAT MOUNTAIN OR CAMP WILDCAT
Also known as Rockcastle Heights and London Heights

October 21, 1861

"The mountainsides seemed to be vomiting fire."
—Lt. Castillo Barfield, C.S.A.

After their September victory at Barbourville, Brig. Gen. Felix Zollicoffer's Confederates moved to Camp Buckner and began to fortify that position against a possible Federal attack. Almost immediately Zollicoffer began to question his own decision and informed General Johnston of this in writing, "I think it far from being as strong as I imagined. . . . It will be difficult to prevent the turning of this position if the enemy should have strategy. The country in advance is so hostile it is difficult to obtain any information." Zollicoffer soon proposed a new strategy to Johnston as he stated, "It is probable our best defense of East Tennessee is an onward movement towards those who threaten invasion."[1] This revelation on Zollicoffer's part would soon lead to an attack upon a newly established military installation located in the mountainous terrain near London, Kentucky.

With the Wilderness Road holding the key to the control of the southeastern end of Kentucky, its safety became an issue for both sides of the struggle for Southern independence. It has been noted that Confederate officials were fearful of the possibility of Union recruits being used to invade East Tennessee, while United States officials held a concern that the Confederate presence could eventually lead to the control of Kentucky and the Ohio River. Col. Theophilus Toulmin Garrard, the grandson of a former Kentucky governor, a Mexican War veteran, and a legislator in his own right, was given the task organizing an infantry regiment that would soon be used to protect the Federal interests. In less than two months from the time of his assignment, Garrard had enlisted approximately 1,000 men and obtained the necessary supplies for them. Garrard's 7th Kentucky Infantry Regiment was ordered to fortify a camp some three miles from the Rockcastle River.[2] This camp became known as Camp Wildcat.

Various sources cite different reasons for the origin of the camp's name. A member of the 14th Ohio recalled that the area was so named due to the wild cats that once inhabited the area. Another suggested that the wild and rugged area was justification enough for the designation. The latter recorded that, "The scenery is grand, and the way becomes more rugged at every step," yet he soon held a different perspective of the area. The man, a regimental chaplain, wrote, "There is nothing different in the name . . . but the term 'Wild Cat' is said to be exceedingly appropriate. Until recently, these high knobs and these awful ravines were the undisturbed haunts of all sorts of wild animals. The scenery is all that the most enthusiastic admirer of nature could wish."[3]

A reporter noted on his visit to Camp Wildcat that the surrounding area was "the roughest country upon which the sun shines. It is up hill and down dale, over rocks and through bogs. . . . It must have been the creation of some of nature's journeymen, for surely the mother of all good things never made such an abortion."[4] It was in this type of terrain that Garrard prepared for the defense against the invasion that Zollicoffer was planning.

On October 6, 1861 General Zollicoffer informed Gen. Albert Sidney Johnston of his intentions, saying that he planned to "move forward and attack them instantly," but a lack of proper supplies hindered the move to do so. Zollicoffer noted that he currently possessed only five days' rations and judged he "could not properly advance with less than 10."[5]

The interesting aspect of Zollicoffer's statement is that area residents were complaining about his troops' pillaging of the area after a September 29 skirmish at Laurel Bridge. There, the Home Guard camp was destroyed and the Confederates confiscated 8,000 cartridges, 3 kegs of powder, 25 pairs of shoes, 25,000 caps, 6 salt barrels, and 2 wagons and their teams, as well as 3 horses. At the Goose Creek Salt Works, the men in gray had allegedly confiscated various types of game as well as cattle while procuring blankets, quilts, and other material from the home of a judge.[6]

It was mid-October before Zollicoffer obtained the supplies he desired in order to begin his advancement upon the Federal position. With more than 5,700 men he had an impressive fighting force, but all indications are that he lacked proper knowledge of the exact number of troops Garrard had at his disposal.

Zollicoffer's column was slowed in its progress from the onset. On Tuesday October 17, the group encountered rain early in the morning and the deluge continued throughout the day. Pvt. Richard Hancock, of Lt. Col. Frank McNairy's Cavalry Battalion, described the day's trek, "The road, which was already bad enough, was made still worse by its raining that day. . . . We camped for the night about where the head of the columns had bivouacked the night previous."[7]

That same day Colonel Garrard received news from two messengers that Zollicoffer was nine miles from London and moving in the direction of Garrard's position. In turn, Garrard pleaded with Brig. Gen. George H. Thomas, his newly appointed superior. Garrard sent a note to Thomas saying, "I must have aid here tomorrow . . . they [Confederates] have some 6,000 [troops]." Garrard had earlier proclaimed that he would abandon Camp Wildcat if he did not receive more troops and added, "I have no idea of having my men butchered up here" while outnumbered six to one.[8]

Adding to the seriousness of the situation at hand, Garrard had to face the fact that illness was devastating his ranks. Water had been scarce at Camp Dick Robinson where the occupants of Camp Wildcat had had to retrieve water from as far as three miles away.

Now Garrard only had nine hundred soldiers on hand and some three hundred of those "gallant fellows lay wasting with dysentery and measles."[9] In addition, Zollicoffer's force of more than 5,400 was slowly but steadily moving in the direction of Camp Wildcat.

Brig. Gen. Albin Francisco Schoepf was General Thomas's choice to take over command of Camp Wildcat. Schoepf was a Hungarian who was evidently intended to shore up the defenses at Wildcat and brace for the Confederate attack. A Federal sergeant described Schoepf as "a fine looking man, rather youthful looking for the position, and clean shaven, with the exception of a long waxed moustache parted in the middle, which gave him, notwithstanding his pleasant manner, a fierce, warlike appearance." Despite the tenacity of Schoepf's appearance, his complete assumption of command is questionable as one Northern paper proclaimed, "The General being totally unacquainted with the position, deferred to the advice of his colonels, and they conducted action according to their judgment."[10]

Zollicoffer's plan for an immediate Confederate attack grew two weeks old. Anxiousness had begun to take effect upon the men in gray and discontent sat in with many of the troops. An officer in the 20th Tennessee evaluated the situation in writing, "In a country wild and rugged and sixty miles from our camp, and a hundred or more from the 'provision provider', under a general, who, though cool, sagacious, brave and skillful, was not acquainted with the country, nor the enemy, nor familiar with their system of cowardly mountain warfare; tired, hungry, and wanting sleep; it was not at all surprising that a gloom pervaded the entire column, and made every soldier silent and thoughtful."[11]

The mood of many soldiers in the Confederate column changed on the afternoon of October 20, when they viewed the arrival of Federal reinforcements at Camp Wildcat. The Confederates had come in view of the hills near Wildcat Mountain when they were halted as members of the general's staff peered toward the hills. Lt. Albert Roberts, Company A, 20th Tennessee, inquired as to the reason for the cessation of the march, and Zollicoffer handed him his glass for a view of the action in the distance. "I could distinctly see the bayonets of a moving column, glistening in the light of the sun. . . . Instead of evacuating, then, the enemy was determined to meet us. I at once concluded they must be stronger than we had first imagined."[12] Information given to the Confederates had listed the number of defenders as approaching 1,500.

In fact, reinforcements had been entering the confines of Camp Wildcat from the moment word had reached Camp Dick Robinson that only six hundred effectives were braced for the Confederate offensive. A member of the 14th Ohio wrote, "It touched our hearts to hear of this little band being surrounded."[13] The total Federal force would eventually approach 7,000 and presented a much more difficult task for Zollicoffer's 5,400 troops.

Adding to the difficulties the Confederates faced, and undoubtedly affecting their fighting spirits, was the vast amount of obstacles they encountered on the march toward the Federal camp. Creating what one source described as "a masterly defense against the approaching enemy," Colonel Garrard had his soldiers cut trees bordering the Wilderness Road. The timber was felled into the thoroughfare for an estimated two miles,[14] necessitating the Confederates literally cut their way into the Wildcat defenses.

Unfortunately for the Federal reinforcements, they encountered similar problems themselves. A member of the 14th Ohio recalled that as he and others headed to Wildcat, they embarked upon the task of attempting "to fill up mud holes with fence rails so that our boys would not have to go ankle deep in the mud."[15]

Near 4 p.m. on October 20, Lt. Col. William Brazelton's Cavalry Battalion, serving as the vanguard of Zollicoffer's attacking force, came in contact with Federal pickets. Reportedly, the Confederates raised their hats as a signal to the men and the word "Union" was the response. This action resulted in Brazelton's cavalrymen firing a volley into the group of Federals from the 1st Kentucky Cavalry, killing Pvt. James Mariman and wounding the group's captain. The gunfire hurried members of the 15th Mississippi and 20th Tennessee to the scene that the Federal pickets had quickly abandoned. The sight of the dead man, the first such incident for many of Zollicoffer's men, caused them to walk on the opposite side of the road from where Mariman's body lay.[16]

The Confederate cavalry advanced toward Wildcat, but their movement slowed when the retreating Federal pickets regrouped "faster than they went" and poured shots into Brazelton's men. Lt. Col. Frank McNairy's cavalrymen arrived to reinforce Brazelton as the sun set on the scene.[17]

A witness recalled the event in writing, "McNairy's cavalry were ordered forward. . . . Away they went, dashing through the leaves, and cornstalks and crack! crack! went a dozen rifles right amongst them. Our boys gave an answering cheer and charged after them madly, even dismounting from the horses and firing their guns and revolvers into the bushes that skirted the road . . . I could hear distinctly the enemy's drums sounding the alarm in the distance, and I knew the Abolitionists were rallying behind their breastworks."[18]

In fact, the Federal rally was created when a "horseman came dashing up, and reported that he belonged to the outside picket post; that . . . the enemy came upon them by surprise . . . and he alone was left to tell the tale." An additional group of Federal cavalrymen were ordered "500 yards beyond the infantry post . . . down the mountain [that] had been blocked with fallen timber. . . . In one place it was so steep that we dismounted and lead our horses. . . . On reaching [our post] we found ourselves in open moonlight, with a dense, dark woods in our front."[19]

The contact of the night gave way to preparations for the battle to come the next morning. In turn, the men of the opposing armies soon settled in to rest through the uneasy night. Federal campfires used fence rails as fuel and somewhat eased the cold as men nervously awaited dawn. A member of the 17th Ohio noted that only the "star-lit dome" covered his comrades and himself as they made "earth's green carpet our couch." Confederates attempted to sleep in campsites where no fires were allowed, causing one to proclaim the night felt as "cold as the North Pole."[20] For the time being, at least, peace again prevailed on Wildcat Mountain.

On the morning of October 21, Zollicoffer telegraphed Gen.

Albert Sidney Johnston who was in Bowling Green, Kentucky. Zollicoffer stated that he would discover the strength of the Federal position using "two regiments and some cavalry" in an attempt to determine the value of an all-out assault. Johnston recorded that while he was aware of thousands of reinforcements arriving at Wildcat he had "no means of adding to Zollicoffer's force . . . important as I think it."[21]

Areas with names such as the Hazel Patch, Happy Hollow, and Round Hill awaited the men of both armies as the morning of October 21 arrived. At 7 a.m. the temperature was a cool 52 degrees and a dense fog covered the area where bloodshed and gunfire would soon become prevalent. [22] The fog served as a camouflage for the last-minute preparations of both armies as the Federal defenders moved into position and the Confederates continued clearing the felled trees and began negotiating the ravines and heights of the mountains they faced.

As the fog cleared, the Confederates moved across Happy Hollow and toward the nearby higher ground where Capt. Philos Stratton commanded a company of the 7th Kentucky Infantry Regiment that was serving as pickets. Lt. Albert Roberts, Company A, 20th Tennessee, remarked that as he and his fellow Confederates began scaling the hills, the gunfire from Stratton's troops became significant. "The angry bullets of the enemy . . . buzzing uncomfortably close to our ears as our progress through the woods . . . exposed our persons to their aim. I was struck with the long range of the enemy's guns and great force" with which they knocked bark and twigs from the trees.[23]

Zollicoffer determined that the well-rested 11th Tennessee Infantry Regiment, under the command of Col. James Rains, would be used to probe the Federal lines. In order to gauge the strength of the defenses on Wildcat Mountain, Rains led his men through Happy Hollow and into John's Hollow near 8:30 a.m. The two hollows ran perpendicular to one another and sat southeast of Camp Wildcat. Artillery support for Rains was to come from a battery of Lt. Eugene Falconnet, although in actuality the battery fired only two or three shots prior to being silenced.[24]

From a position on Round Hill, an eminence located northeast of John's Hollow, a Federal officer, Col. John Coburn of the 33rd Indiana, watched the Confederate deployment. He stated, "They were in large numbers and were over half an hour in passing by an open space in the woods, when they formed again in line." Another witness gave a less intimidating evaluation of the Confederates in writing that they were "badly dressed . . . some wearing old jeans coats and pants, others summer clothing."[25]

Rains's Confederates soon sighted four companies from the 33rd Indiana, who were sent forward as skirmishers. Colonel Coburn reported that in less than 20 minutes from the time he had ordered companies D, E, G, and I forward, "the rebels, who were concealed in the woods, commenced firing. At almost the first fire Private McFerran, of Company A, was killed." In fact, McFerran was shot just minutes into his first battle, having served approximately one month in the military.[26]

The Confederate reinforcements of six companies from the 17th Tennessee advanced on Round Hill and Colonel Coburn recalled that the action had devastating effects upon the Federal troops. Gunfire and minimal artillery fire caused the 1st Kentucky Cavalry Regiment to "waver and retreat" as reportedly did members of the Kentucky Home Guard.[27]

However, as occurred in numerous similar situations in various battles throughout the war, the retreating force was able to reform and counterattack. Colonel Coburn remarked that the Kentuckians "were soon rallied and formed again in order and fought with good spirit. Too much praise cannot be given to the brave Captain Hauser, who continued fighting at the head of his men" despite having a finger shot off during the fray.[28]

On the eastern side of Round Hill, confusion set in as noon approached. Col. Tazewell Newman of the 17th Tennessee progressed up the eastern spur of Round Hill. Newman reported, "Upon reaching a point within eighty yards of the heights, we discovered a number of men ascending the heights and entering the fortifications, but supposing these men to be a portion of Colonel Rains' command, I did not order them to be fired upon. At this point we received a heavy volley of rifles and musketry."[29]

The troops Newman believed to be Confederates actually belonged to Company E of the 33rd Indiana. Under the command of Capt. Isaac Hendricks, the group had moved in order to better defend against the advancing Confederates. They had waited until the Confederates were within seventy-five yards of the Federal breastworks before "the Indiana boys sprang from their shelter and poured their fire with unceasing vigor upon them."[30]

The true identification of the alleged Confederates became clear and the result was a tremendous exchange of gunfire between the two foes. Confederate Lt. Castillo Barfield, Company I, 11th Tennessee proclaimed that, "the firing on both sides resembled one universal volcanic eruption. . . . The mountainsides seemed to be vomiting fire."[31]

U.S. cannons arrived on the field and seemed to have a more adverse effect upon the Confederates than did the minimal and inaccurate shots of the Confederate artillery. While the Confederate shells reportedly missed their proposed targets altogether, the six guns of Capt. Wiliam Standart's battery had devastating results on the Confederates. Evidently caught by surprise in relation to the existence of the Federal guns, Zollicoffer's troops were shocked. There was a response shot from Falconnet's battery, but with little effect. One Confederate recalled, "Nothing could be heard but the booming of cannon. . . . The firing was so heavy that we had to fall back." The retreat was likely encouraged when a shell from Standart's battery hit the carriage of the Confederate artillery and rendered it useless.[32]

General Schoepf proposed that the artillery only required a few rounds being fired before the Confederates determined that retreat from the field was the best option. Col. Tazewell Newman stated that after he had reached the fortification and some of his men had entered the works but failed to receive "any support, and being nearly destitute of cartridges, I ordered my command to fall back." Cheers erupted from portions of the Federal lines as the victorious troops realized they had retained ownership of the camp.[33]

Zollicoffer noted his rationale for the decision to abandon additional attempts to take Camp Wildcat in writing, "Having reconnoitered in force under heavy fire for several hours from heights on the right, left, and front, I became satisfied that it could not be carried otherwise than by immense exposure if at all. The enemy received large re-enforcements. . . . The country is so poor we had exhausted the forage on the road for 15 miles back in twenty-four hours. Our subsistence is nearly exhausted." One of Zollicoffer's soldiers added that capturing Camp Wildcat "was a perfect impossibility."[34]

The natural defensive position that Zollicoffer declared as being "almost inaccessible" had survived three Confederate charges. Perhaps most significant in the Confederate failure to take possession of Camp Wildcat was the simple aspect of timing. Had the attack come one day earlier, the results would have likely been different as Zollicoffer's force would have significantly outnumbered the Federal defenders and the last minute defenses would have been nonexistent. One reporter summed this up in writing that the "attack was unsuccessful, simply because it came 24 hours too late."[35]

Lt. Albert Roberts of the 20th Tennessee explained in the *Nashville Banner* issue of October 30, 1861 that Camp Wildcat was "a Federal stronghold in the Rock Castle cliffs between Little Rock Castle and Big Rock Castle rivers." Roberts added that the reason for the Confederate loss was that the Federal troops "were too cowardly to meet us face to face, but cunningly endeavored to seduce us into an ambuscade where they were strongly fortified and where they might have cut us literally to pieces, had it not been for their cowardice and the caution and prudence of our gallant leader."[36]

Zollicoffer's troops left Wildcat Mountain for a camp on the Little Rockcastle River late in the afternoon, and his troops marched some eighteen miles before establishing their camp around midnight. There, they spent a cold, wet night without the Confederate surgeons, who remained at the battlefield until the next night caring for the wounded. Likewise, the Federal troops attempted to rest in the chilly damp conditions they faced. Additionally, preparations were made for a presumed Confederate return. An Indiana defender of Round Hill reminisced, "During the night we fortified our hill with a strong embankment all around the summit and a deep rifle pit in addition."[37]

In the days following the battle, the inevitable care for the wounded and burial of the dead began. The thick woods occupying the area around Camp Wildcat minimized the effectiveness of gunfire in the struggle, benefiting both armies with low numbers of casualties. In addition, smoothbore muskets were prevalent weapons of choice. These two factors likely minimized the number of dead and wounded, which was less than one percent for both sides, yet those struck were nonetheless unconcerned about the lack of a large number of individuals needing medical attention.[38]

The regimental chaplain of the 14th Ohio recalled that he witnessed the sick of both sides being cared for in caves located on Wildcat Mountain. One of his most vivid memories of the care for the wounded involved his assistance to one Dr. Daniels, who had been appointed brigade surgeon. The chaplain stated, "I was able to render some assistance and helped to extract with my own hand a ball nearly one inch long from the side of a poor Kentucky soldier. I have it in my possession."[39]

Colonel Coburn reported that some thirty Confederates received care near one of the cabins in Happy Hollow. At the field hospital, Coburn witnessed amputated limbs and pieces of flesh that attested to the action of medical personnel. Coburn remembered, "It is sorrowful to see scores of fine young men lying strewed around groaning and gasping with pain and many cold in death."[40]

Decades after the war, a veteran of the battle provided a graphic, if not exaggerated, account. He noted, "seeing fellows lying there with their heads shot off, brains scattered all around. It was a terrible sight."[41]

Lt. Albert Roberts, Company A, 20th Tennessee, recalled that as he was leaving the field during the Confederate retreat, he witnessed

Dr. Callender holding a Minnie ball that he had just removed from a soldier's head. Roberts wrote, "the ball having passed through the gun-stock, bending the barrel and had entered his cheek . . . was cut out from the back part of his head . . . with its jagged and broken edge [the ball] was about the ugliest think I ever saw go through a man's head and not kill him."[42]

The actual number of casualties is difficult to determine as sources vary on the associated figures. General Zollicoffer reported fifty-three casualties with eleven Confederate soldiers killed and another forty-two wounded or missing from approximately 2,000 actively involved soldiers of the Confederates present. Col. Tazewell Newman gave the number of casualties among the men in gray as eleven killed and thirty-four wounded for a total of forty-five. Using regimental and company records, historian Kenneth A. Hafendorfer ascertained fifty-two Confederate losses from figures of eleven killed, one mortally wounded, and forty wounded. Zollicoffer's foe, Brigadier General Schoepf, estimated Confederate losses "at 30 killed with a large wounded list, the latter taken off the field . . . except 3, which were brought into our camp and properly cared for; one since died." Schoepf later over-estimated Confederate deaths of 100.[43]

While Zollicoffer offered no estimation of Federal losses, he did report that twenty-one Federal prisoners were taken in addition to "about 100 guns, and 4 horses." Brigadier General Schoepf reported the day after the battle that the U.S. casualties were 4 killed and 18 wounded. Historian Kenneth A. Hafendorfer, in using Federal regimental and company records, reached a total of five deaths and twenty-two wounded. Of the Federal soldiers present at Wildcat, only some 1,600 saw action that day. Sadly, diseases such as measles took a heavy toll on the Federal soldiers after the battle. Twelve of the twenty-one Federal prisoners Zollicoffer reported taking succumbed to disease within six months of their capture. The 33rd Indiana, the Hoosier heroes of Round Hill, later renamed in their honor, lost an additional fifty plus men to various illnesses soon after the battle and several hundred others became gravely ill in the weeks following the action on Wildcat Mountain.[44]

The eyewitness statements and varied casualty numbers attest to one statement a Federal soldier provided. The words of Lt. George W. Daniel, 7th Kentucky Infantry Regiment, praised his comrades and the Confederate veterans alike. Daniel wrote, "While the Battle of Wild Cat was small, it was . . . a hard fought battle."[45]

The battle of Wildcat Mountain will be remembered as the first Union victory in the state of Kentucky. Additionally, the battlefield marks the first time that regular troops were engaged in battle in the Bluegrass State.[46]

A modern visit to Camp Wildcat reveals a remote location filled with beautiful scenery, not unlike that which the veterans of the battle encountered in the fall of 1861. In fact, a 2008 revised study of the area determined that the "land use is little changed" since the time of the battle. It is to be noted though that, as the Camp Wildcat Preservation Foundation acknowledges, the vast majority of the battleground acreage has been used as timber-cutting sites on numerous occasions.[47] The battlefield is well marked and contains partially asphalted roads, but a complete visit to the site will necessitate driving on a single-lane gravel road and/or walking along a graveled trail to Infantry Ridge. Additional trails to key locations on the battlefield are currently underway. Mountain trenches occupied during the battle can be viewed and interpretive signs, both at a trailhead gazebo and along the trail itself, provide visitors with a wealth of information about the battle. Sadly, the signs of the battle have disappeared on the farmlands located at the mountain's base.

Some 433 acres of the land associated with Camp Wildcat have been set aside for preservation, with 150 of those acres accessible to the public. The Daniel Boone National Forest and the Wildcat Mountain Civil War Battlefield share management areas for the site and both brochures and living-history programs have been utilized in recent years to add to the public interpretation of and familiarity with the battlefield. In addition, the Laurel County Fiscal Court, the Kentucky Heritage Council, the USDA Forest Service—Daniel Boone National Forest, the Civil War Preservation Trust, and the

Camp Wildcat Preservation Foundation have combined efforts to help protect this area of hallowed ground.[48]

The primary group responsible for the preservation of the Camp Wildcat battlefield is the Camp Wildcat Preservation Foundation, "incorporated on May 26, 1994 with the major goals of preserving, protecting, and interpreting" the related battlefield. This outstanding organization has a variety of merchandise available for sale, the profits of which are used to benefit the battlefield. Various membership levels are also available for a range of costs. Information related to membership, merchandise, or meeting location and times can be acquired by contacting Mr. James Cass at 606-864-9776. The organization's Web site is *wildcatbattlefield.org* and additional contact information includes writing the Camp Wildcat Preservation Foundation at 223 Morgan Street, London, Kentucky, 40741.

Among the worthwhile projects the Foundation has engaged in are the purchase of more than 260 acres of land containing trenches and other remnants of the battle. Another 20-acre tract that served as the Confederate camp for the battle is now used as the site of the annual reenactment of the battle that is conducted the third weekend of October through the joint effort of the Foundation and the Laurel Home Guard.

Traveling on Interstate 75, interested individuals can take exit 49, the Livingston exit, to reach Wildcat Mountain. Travel east 0.6 miles on 909 and then south onto U.S. 25. Drive just 0.7 miles until reaching Hazel Patch Road on the left. Signs can be easily followed from this point and will enable a deeper first-hand study of one of the preservation success stories in the Bluegrass State. Additional information regarding directions and traveling conditions can be gained from visiting their Web site at *campwildcatpreservationfoundation.org* or by calling either the Camp Wildcat Civil War Battlefield at 606-864-9776, the USDA Forest Service, London District at 606-864-4163, or the London Tourism Commission at 800-348-0095. (*fs.fed.us*; *trailsrus.com*; *civilwardiscoverytrail.org*; all accessed September 7, 2009)

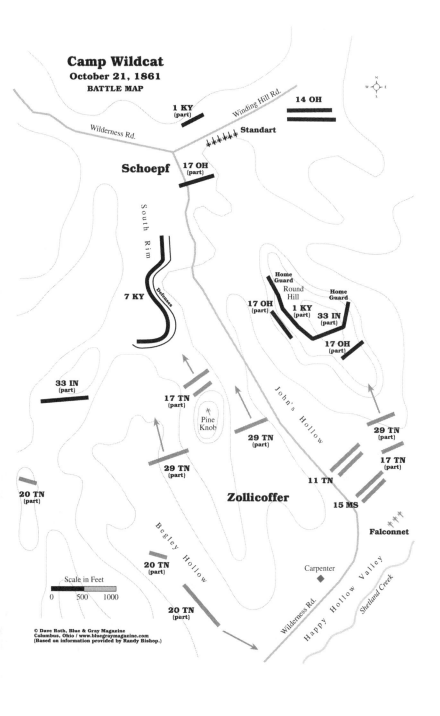

Camp Wildcat
October 21, 1861
BATTLE MAP

This monument was dedicated in 2008 and notes the location of the Confederate encampment of October 1861. (Photo by author)

This gazebo is located near the mountain trailhead and contains several interpretive panels related to the battle. (Photo by author)

Several trenches are distinguishable atop the mountain, and visitors are urged to avoid entering them in order to preserve them for future generations. (Photo by author)

CHAPTER THREE

IVY MOUNTAIN
(Ivy Creek, or Ivy Narrows)

November 8, 1861

"The skirmish was very sharp"
—Brig. Gen. William "Bull" Nelson

The battles at Barbourville and Wildcat Mountain had resulted in bloodshed on the soil of the Bluegrass State despite numerous parties' previous efforts to maintain the state's neutrality. Similarly, the battle to gain the advantage in the recruitment of soldiers for the Confederate and Federal efforts alike was proving no less strategic in nature. As had taken place following the action at Barbourville and as was the catalyst for the Wildcat Mountain engagement, the intention to thwart enemy recruiting efforts in Kentucky would again lead to casualties in the home state of Jefferson Davis and Abraham Lincoln, the presidents of the two warring nations. The activities led to the state's third major struggle, this one at a location known as Ivy Mountain.

Confederate recruitment activities centered in Floyd, Morgan, and Bath counties reaped benefits with the October 1861 formation of the 5th Kentucky Infantry, also referred to as the Army of Eastern Kentucky. Among the regimental officers were Lt. Col. Hiram Hawkins, Circuit Court Judge W. H. Burns, Col. John S. Williams, and Capt. Andrew Jackson May. The May family's farm, according to legend, contained a meadow that served as the site of the regiment's organization.[1]

The members of the 5th Kentucky were noted in a periodical of the time to be a group of "raw-boned, brave mountaineers" who held a determination "to drive out the hordes of King Lincoln, who have dared to invade the sacred soil of Kentucky."[2]

A Confederate officer added that the 5th Kentucky, also known as the Ragmuffin Regiment, was comprised almost completely of mountain men who were "trained to hardships, and armed with long rifles." He also proclaimed this regiment to be "one of the finest corps of soldiers ever enlisted in the army."[3] With this mindset, the Confederates prepared for any opportunity to carry out their goal.

In opposition to the 5th Kentucky's infantrymen who served the Confederate cause, another group of Kentuckians, under the leadership of Col. Charles A. Marshall, answered Brig. Gen. William "Bull" Nelson's plea for volunteers to serve the Union. Marshall, the nephew of U.S. Supreme Court Chief Justice John Marshall, would lead these volunteers, later to be known as the 16th Kentucky Regiment, into battle in the coming weeks.[4]

Under orders from Gen. William Tecumseh Sherman, Brigadier General Nelson gathered forces to break up the Confederate training camp at Prestonsburg. At 5 a.m. on November 8, 1861, Nelson led the 2nd, 21st, and 59th Ohio Regiments, Battery D of the 1st Ohio Light Artillery, and Colonel Marshall's volunteers toward Pikeville, Kentucky.[5]

In an attempt to "turn or cut them [rebels] off," Nelson dispatched another group to make a march of some forty miles by John's Creek and to the left of Pikeville. At 11 a.m. on November 7, Col. Joshua Sill of the 33rd Ohio left Louisa, Kentucky, with a detachment of Ohio and Kentucky infantry, mounted troops, and a section of artillery, on the quest for Confederate trainees.[6]

Col. John S. Williams had reported that the Confederate troops he was assisting in training at Prestonsburg were "badly clad and badly armed, with not a knapsack, haversack, or canteen." Another participant added, "The army was not only badly clothed, but in general badly armed. Many of the men had only shot-guns and squirrel rifles . . . General Lee wrote that owing to the scarcity of arms he was having pikes made" and offered those to Marshall.

The condition of the troops, each soldier with only two rounds of ammunition, had already necessitated a move to Pikeville to replenish his supplies.[7] With the simultaneous advance of Nelson and Sill's forces, the stage was set for certain military action.

Capt. Andrew Jackson May undertook the task of delaying Nelson's advance upon the Confederate position. May deployed his troops on farmland that his father-in-law, Samuel Davidson, owned. Colonel May had just three hundred men at his disposal; these included men from companies B, C, and D of the 1st Battalion Kentucky Mounted Rifles and companies A and C of the 5th Kentucky Infantry.[8] Their leader's familiarity with the landscape and the advantage of a surprise attack would enable the remaining Confederates to safely evacuate Pikeville.

A clear sky and southwest breeze combined, enabling the temperature to reach the low 70s just after noon. Five preceding days of warm, dry weather had caused area roads to become dusty, inhibiting vision along the road at the base of Ivy Mountain.[9] Conditions appeared favorable for May's command, lying in ambush as Nelson's Federals approached.

At 1 p.m. Nelson's column advanced along a thoroughfare that was only seven feet wide and was cut some twenty-five-feet above the river. Nelson stated, "The ridge descends in a rapid curve and very sharp to the creek . . . where it makes a complete elbow."[10]

May's detachment of Confederates was positioned near the "elbow," prepared for the attack. Nelson reported that May's selection of the site was advantageous as "the mountain is highest along the river and very precipitous and thickly covered with timber and undergrowth."[11]

Reportedly responding to a signal shot from May's pistol, the Confederates sent a violent volley into the Federal column when the latter reached the sharp bend, or elbow, in the road. Colonel Marshall's battalion of Kentucky Unionists was at the head of the Federal column and received the brunt of the Confederate fire.[12]

General Nelson reported the incident in writing, "The mountain-side was blue with puffs of smoke and not an enemy to be seen.

The first discharge killed 4 and wounded 13 of Marshall's men."[13]

Colonel Williams noted the action from the Confederate perspective by stating, "The bluecoats were received by 250 rifles and shot-guns in point-blank range. The Yankees were thrown back, unable to see the Confederates in their front, but pressed forward again with the same result."[14]

In response to the Confederate ambush, General Nelson ordered a counterattack in the direction of the blue smoke. The 2nd Ohio advanced behind Colonel Harris and took a position on the face of the mountain. The 21st Ohio reached the defile and, "Col. . . . Norton . . . led his men up the northern ridge of the mountain."[15]

Norton's troops deployed on the face and crest of the northern ridge. As they moved toward the Confederate position, two cannon were placed in the road and "opened upon" the Confederates. General Nelson praised the efforts of his command, many of whom were previously untested in combat. However, Nelson did note in his official report that the movement of his men in blue, "owing to the steepness of the mountain . . . required time."[16]

Confederate infantrymen on the opposite side of the "narrow, deep, and swift" river poured shots into Nelson's command. General Nelson noted that the effectiveness of the fire was minimal, although it "annoyed us." A shot directed from the Confederate line on the mountain struck Captain Berryhill of the 2nd Ohio, yet the cross-river firing remained largely ineffective.[17]

After an estimated hour and twenty minutes of action, which General Nelson testified as being a "very sharp skirmish," the Confederates abandoned their position. General Nelson reported that the "Rebels fled, leaving a number of killed and wounded on the ground and 6 prisoners unhurt."[18]

Colonel Williams rationalized his decision for his Confederates to retreat in writing, "We had only about 300 men. The enemy had not less than 1,500—most probably 2,000—with six pieces of artillery. They were at first checked but on account of their great superiority of numbers they were able to outflank us, and our force was compelled to fall back."[19]

A Federal attempt to follow the Confederate retreat met obstacles from both man-made and natural causes. Trees cut across the road toward Pound Gap and numerous burned bridges yielded the desired effect as the men in gray made good on the plan to enter the safety of Virginia. During the night, cold weather arrived and rain began falling. Nelson advanced only four miles beyond Ivy Creek before entering camp for the night. Nelson wrote, "I bivouacked 4 miles beyond Ivy Creek. It rained, and the men waded through mud and in a heavy rain all the day of the 9th, the march being heavy and slow on account of the trees across the roads and the necessity of repairing the bridges."[20]

Sill, who arrived in time to clash with the Confederate rear guard, and Nelson met at Piketon at 9 a.m. on November 9. After this, Sill recorded comments about the hunger his troops experienced in saying, "Troops are very hungry. All that we can get is beef. There is a mill here, which we will set in motion today, and get plenty of corn meal."[21]

Casualty figures remain uncertain for the battle of Ivy Mountain. Nelson reported that his troops encountered thirty-two dead Confederates and that the Federal losses were six killed and twenty-four wounded. However, Col. John S. Williams noted the Confederate casualties as "10 killed and 7 or 8 wounded." Williams stated that, in relation to the Federal casualties, "The enemy's loss was heavy—could not have been less than 150 killed and a large number wounded, for the road was strewn with men and horses."[22]

Colonel Williams was glad to acknowledge the tenacity of the Federals, but gave little credit to them for their apparent victory. He wrote, "The enemy is perfectly equipped, with plenty of artillery. They are well instructed and fight with courage. We have nothing in the world upon our side but bravery. The disparity in the loss was due alone to our position."[23]

Further hardships awaited the Confederate veterans of the clash at Ivy Mountain. Traveling was slow as wagons struggled to cover a few miles each day. It was written, "the scanty rations and great hardships made hundreds of the men sick . . . measles and mumps broke out in the camps, and many died from these diseases and from exposure."[24]

The Ivy Mountain battlefield is in a despicable state of preservation. A 2008 National Park Service study categorized the site as one in which "landscape and terrain have been altered beyond recognition." In fact, only one acre from a core battlefield of almost 260 acres has been permanently preserved.[25] Sadly, the disheartening news does not end with this fact.

In 1971 U.S. Highway 23, the primary roadway between Pikeville and Prestonsburg was widened. This act resulted in the excavation of the side of the mountain, destroying the battlefield. Near the mouth of Ivy Creek, along the highway, a battlefield monument was erected to memorialize the action that took place on November 8, 1861. The fourteen-foot tall obelisk marks the approximate location of the lost field near Ivel, Kentucky. To reach the site, visitors can take exit 191 from Interstate 64 and travel south on Highway 23 approximately forty-three miles to the monument at Ivel. Another site in nearby Prestonsburg, Kentucky is the Samuel May House. The residence was used as a Confederate recruiting post during the war and is recorded as being the site where the 5th Kentucky Infantry was organized.

The Ivy Mountain battlefield is, for all practical purposes, gone forever. Future generations will have to be blessed with a keen sense of imagination to gain even a basic understanding of the terrain the soldiers faced during the late 1861 battle. However, as Americans tend to rise to the occasion and readily face challenges, the site at Ivy Mountain may one day have its remaining acres properly preserved and interpreted for the benefit of Civil War enthusiasts yet to come.

This obelisk and pair of interpretive markers serve as the only reminders of the location of the battle of Ivy Mountain. (Photo by author)

The obelisk and markers with the remnants of Ivy Mountain in the background. (Photo by author)

This creek served as one of the namesakes for the battle. (Photo by author)

CHAPTER FOUR

ROWLETT'S STATION

December 17, 1861

"I never saw men fall as they did."

—Mark L. Evans, C.S.A.

Although the December 1861 battle at Rowlett's Station was relatively short in duration, the buildup for the conflict was rather lengthy. The plans for a bridge spanning the Green River were several years old when the completion of the structure actually took place. Eventually, the bridge became the focal point of military action and provided the area around Munfordville, Kentucky, with a high amount of significance to both the U.S. and Confederate armies for the duration of the war. The first of two bloody struggles for the possession of the Green River Bridge pitted a group of pro-Union German soldiers against a much larger Confederate force largely composed of cavalry. The story of this battle and of the bridge, which has continued to be used into the twenty-first century, is one of historic and preservation importance.

As with many antebellum towns and cities across the nation, Munfordville, Kentucky, owed a large amount of its success to a railroad in the area. The Louisville & Nashville Railroad linked with similar lines, enabling the transporting of materials between the Great Lakes and the Gulf of Mexico. In addition, the railroad became the only one to completely intersect Kentucky in a north-south direction.[1] A major obstacle for the construction of the line had been the Green River, located near Munfordville.

Under the direction of the celebrated German engineer Albert Fink, the two-year construction of the structure was completed in the summer of 1859 at a cost of $265,000. Hailed by *Harper's Weekly* as a source of "national pride and eulogy," the railroad bridge also served as a source of local boasting. John W. Key, a stonemason from nearby Woodsonville, contributed greatly to the development of four massive, stone piers that supported the tracks.[2]

The February 15, 1860 issue of *Harper's Weekly* estimated that the bridge stood approximately 120 feet above the river at low tide. In addition, the article reported that more than 10,000 cubic yards of masonry were used in the piers and abutments, 2,500 cubic feet of timber was needed for the joist on the rails, and more than 381,000 pounds of wrought iron and 638,000 pounds of cast iron comprised the bridge that was more than 1,100 feet in length.[3]

Needless to say, the bridge held major importance for the two hundred residents of Munfordville. As Hart County's county seat, Munfordville, located about seventy miles south of Louisville, was believed to be prone to feel the impact of armies fighting for control of the bridge. With the onset of the Civil War and recent action in Kentucky, it would only be a matter of time before this belief became reality.

In October of 1861, Confederate Gen. Albert Sidney Johnston issued an order to Brig. Gen. Simon Bolivar Buckner to destroy the Green River Bridge. The purpose of this mission was to eliminate the possibility of a Federal attack upon Bowling Green, Kentucky, before the town could be properly fortified. Buckner's force of five hundred men were stationed at Woodsonville and Munfordville, but were to abandon these towns upon carrying out their mission. However, Buckner was a native Kentuckian as well as a pre-war construction superintendent and held both the bridge and its craftsmanship in high regard. For these reasons, Bucker protested the order, but to no avail. Explosive charges were placed on the two southernmost piers, but Buckner determined that the damage caused to the two southern spans by the explosion on the first pier was significant enough to provide sufficient delay to ensure the protection of Bowling Green and felt there was no reason to detonate the charge on the second pier.[4]

Buckner's action was filled with irony and repercussions. John Key, the stonemason who had provided the supervision of the construction of the bridge's piers, was the individual who, along with his two sons, oversaw the placement of the explosives. Key's sons had also provided their expertise in the construction of the masonry on the bridge. In spite of Buckner's reluctance to completely carry out Johnston's order, the Louisville and Nashville Railroad sued him for damages. In addition, Northern reporters lambasted Buckner for his destructive act.[5]

On December 9, 1861, one month after assuming command of the U.S. Department of the Ohio, Maj. Gen. Don Carlos Buell detailed the 6th Brigade from Brig. Gen. Alexander M. McCook's Second Division to Munfordville. This brigade was under the command of Brig. Gen. R. W. Johnston and included troops of the all-German 32nd Indiana Regiment. A regiment led by Lt. Col. Louis von Trebra from the 32nd Indiana was ordered to secure the bridge site while a crew under Albert Fink, the German engineer who figured so heavily into the design and construction of the bridge, attempted to repair the structure.[6]

At four o'clock on the afternoon of December 10, 1861, the 32nd Indiana arrived in Munfordville. Accompanying the 32nd Indiana were the remaining regiments in Johnston's 6th Brigade. These regiments included the 39th Indiana and the 15th and 49th Indiana.[7]

The 32nd Indiana Regiment owed its existence to Col. August Willich, a German immigrant and veteran of the 1848 German Revolution. Willich, born in 1810, had entered the military at a young age and became a lieutenant in the Prussian artillery at eighteen. Described as "tall and dignified," Willich had immigrated to the United States and had enlisted as a private in the Union army just thirteen days after the April 1861 bombardment of Fort

Sumter. Although he was older than many of the more famous northern commanders, such as Sherman, Grant, McClellan, and Sheridan, Willich overcame the age factor, as he gained prominence by leading younger troops in bayonet charges. General Rosecrans noted that Willich's actions were of the type "often read about but seldom seen."[8]

Also known as the First German, the 32nd Indiana was mustered into service on a three-year term in August 1861. True to their heritage, the troops of the 32nd were drilled primarily in German. Less than four months later, the group composed of German immigrants and German descendants found themselves given the task of serving as pickets and providing protection for those men involved in repairing the southern spans of the Green River bridge.[9]

Willich's regiment not only detached two companies to serve as pickets approximately one and a half miles from the southern end of the bridge, but all of the carpenters from the 32nd Indiana were selected to begin construction on a pontoon bridge to be used for additional troops to cross the river. By December 16 two pontoons had been completed, one near the Green River bridge and another located east of the bridge. The first was recorded as consisting of wagon bodies; the second contained wagons atop a strong wooden substructure. The latter utilized planks to speed crossings of the Louisville-Nashville Turnpike. The 32nd Indiana used these bridges to place half of their companies on the south side of the bridge and the other half held in reserve on the north side.[10]

Colonel Willich, in his post-battle account, praised Lt. Pietzuch and his work crew "who by their unceasing efforts succeeded in constructing a bridge across Green River with the poor tools and scanty material furnished them in incredibly short time."[11] The weather was obviously partially to credit for the timely manner in which the bridge was reconstructed.

The mid-December 1861 weather was beautiful in the Munfordville area and had enabled the construction crews to make excellent progress on the bridge repairs. One Federal infantryman wrote his wife, "The weather is magnificent. The most beautiful Indian summer I have ever seen and has been for the last 3 weeks. I can look out of my tent door and see for miles in every direction. Hills some of them as wild and rugged as nature left them . . . I love to gaze for hours upon sights . . . naturally grand and glorious."[12]

Another blue-clad infantryman wrote that the weather was, "exceedingly beautiful" and that he determined the temperature was "astonishingly warm for this season of the year." Official reports confirm this soldier's recollections in noting that the morning temperature on December 17 was 33 degrees and had risen to 61 degrees by 2 p.m.[13]

A Confederate force led by Brig. Gen. Thomas Hindman and consisting of approximately 1,100 infantrymen, 4 cannon, and 250 cavalrymen used the warm weather to their advantage and began moving from their camp at Cave City toward Woodsonville. The 2nd and 6th Arkansas, the 1st Arkansas Battalion, and the Texas Rangers joined the four-piece battery of Capt. Charles Swett to form an impressive Confederate fighting force. Leaving at 8 a.m. on the morning of the seventeenth, the group intended to destroy a portion of the railroad in the Green River area from the vicinity of Woodsonville southward to hamper Federal troop movements in the area. The column moved within two and a half miles of Woodsonville before halting. There, Major Phifer's cavalry took a position on the Confederate left with Hindman at the center and Texas Rangers to Hindman's right, left, and front.[14]

The Rangers' depleated ranks were recovering from a recent onset of measles. While in Nashville, the group of "undeveloped boys, scarcely from the leading string of mothers" was stricken with such a severe epidemic that, at one point in November, only 78 of the group's 1,002 troops were able to answer roll call. The efforts of Nashville citizens whose "hospitals . . . and many private houses were filled with the sick and dying" enabled most of the afflicted soldiers to gradually recover. One patient reminisced that he "was kept alive by the best of nursing and attention of the good ladies of Nashville who . . . nursed the sick night and day." Another veteran recalled that, "the fire of patriotism burned as brightly and as beautiful as ever" and that the young men returned to duty as soon as they recovered from the horrible disease.[15]

Before the recent onset of warm temperatures, the weather the Rangers had endured was brutal, to say the least. One of the Rangers wrote of the conditions, "The cold is intolerable." The lack of the proper number of men to serve on picket duty caused those who were well enough to perform their duties to do so in the extreme conditions. A member of Company F of the Rangers remarked, "It was not uncommon for men to be compelled to stand picket in the snow several inches deep for four hours at a time and then be relieved for two hours and be put in again for four hours."[16] The Rangers survived such situations and soon found themselves in the midst of what would become known as the battle of Rowlett's Station.

Once Hindman's deployment orders were carried out and no Federal troops or pickets were discovered, the Confederate brigadier moved forward until the right side of his line reached the railroad. The advancement had brought the men in gray within three-quarters of a mile of the Green River and allowed all but the cavalry on the extreme right to remain concealed. Two artillery pieces were placed on a hill belonging to a Mrs. Lewis and the other two were positioned across the railroad on an eminence known as East Hill. The former rise would also be known as Terry Hill after the battle.[17]

Further Confederate deployment placed a company of Rangers, under the command of Maj. C. W. Phifer, on Rowlett's Knob where the group would be able to observe the Federal troops. With a "strip of timber [that] bordered the river parallel to the line" they held, the Confederate cavalry maintained what appeared to be a strong position.[18] It appeared to the Confederates that they held the upper hand, in respect to the position they occupied and given the belief that the element of surprise was with them.

Meanwhile, U.S. Colonel Willich was at the headquarters of Gen. Lovelle Rosseau at Bacon Creek, a situation that placed Lt.

Col. Henry von Treba in command of approximately 420 soldiers in the 32nd Indiana.[19] In Willich's absence, von Treba would have the daunting task of coordinating Federal efforts against any Confederate advance upon the bridge as well as the troops and workers assigned to the area nearby. The test of von Treba's leadership would not be long in coming, as the stage was set for the battle of Rowlett's Station.

Between noon and one o'clock, the men of Company B of the 32nd Indiana became the recipients of the Confederate advance. A Federal infantryman wrote that, "having just finished our dinner of hard crackers and coffee, we were alarmed by the sound of musketry a short distance across the river." Pickets of the Hoosier regiment moved into the timber at the base of the ridge that extended east and west of the railroad. Confederate cavalry skirmishers fired upon members of Company B under the leadership of Capt. Jacob Glass. The immediate response to the Confederate fire was for Glass to send a patrol forward and fire a volley in their direction. This move initially proved successful as the Confederates were driven back and Glass sent his troops forward. However, large numbers of Confederate infantry arrived as reinforcements and Glass found he and his company were "obliged to retreat."[20]

The initial exchange of fire ceased for approximately thirty minutes and Confederate Brig. Gen. Thomas C. Hindman used the situation to locate "a suitable place" to establish a point of ambush. Hindman turned over command to Col. Benjamin Franklin Terry, commander of the Texas Rangers, also known as the 8th Texas Cavalry. Hindman instructed Terry to "decoy the enemy up the hill" where Hindman would spring a trap and use a combination artillery and infantry to strike the Federal troops. The latter would be out of range of their artillery support and at the mercy of the Confederates.[21]

Before Hindman was capable of returning to his command, he heard the Confederate column firing and realized the action had begun again. Lieutenant Colonel von Treba had ordered three additional companies forward to support Company B on the

Federal right; two other companies from the regiment were sent to the aid of Company C, located on the Federal left. An official report noted "Companies E and H and a few men of Company D" were held in reserve, under the command of Major Schnackenberg.[22] Within minutes those units held in reserved would be needed to maintain the Federal line.

Terry was reported to have informed Captain C. S. Ferrell, "You will take command of your own company and the four others in your rear, and move to the right of the railway to the hay ricks and fodder stacks, in the field. I will take the first five companies . . . to the left of the railway until I reach the cabins in the field on that side of the cut in the railway . . . Every man will do his duty, as a Texan knows how, in the hour of danger, and in the patriotic discharge of his duty to his state, his country and his mother."[23]

At this point of the battle "under infernal yelling" and approaching with "lighting speed," an estimated seventy-five Rangers, with Terry leading, charged the Federal position. The initial advance moved within 20 yards of the Union line. The men in blue then "opened a destructive fire" on the advancing Confederates. Lt. Max Sachs, a German-Jewish immigrant and a member of the 32nd Indiana, "left his covered position" in an effort to hasten a Confederate withdrawal, but soon found himself surrounded by a large number of Rangers. Captain Schwarz of Company D, 32nd Indiana, recalled that Sachs moved forward with Company C "into a open field . . . dangerously exposed themselves to the fierce and gallant attack of the rebel cavalry." A group of Rangers demanded that Sachs surrender his sword and his troops, but Sachs refused. Upon the third denial of the request, Sachs began a last ditch effort to drive the Confederates from his position. Sachs, reportedly shot as many as ten times with "about twenty buckshot in the abdomen," and three of his command fell in the successful effort to drive back the Confederates.[24]

However, Colonel Willich was critical of Sachs's actions that led to his death as he noted that Sachs "gave way too much to his courage and advanced too hastily and too soon, which caused our mourning over his loss and that of several brave soldiers."[25]

Like the death of many heroes of the American Civil War, Sachs's had varied accounts. One of those stated, "Sachs . . . left his covered position . . . was surrounded by about fifty Rangers . . . and defended himself till he fell, with three of his men." Misspelling Sachs's name, another account proclaimed, "Lieut. Saxe, of Cincinnati . . . killed a man with two revolvers, but was finally killed, receiving nine bullets." Capt. William Sievers wrote a letter to a Louisville newspaper adding, "Lt. Max Sachs died in my arms." The thirty-five-year-old officer, born in Fraustadt, Prussia, was buried in section A of K. K. Adath Israel Cemetery in Cincinnati.[26]

After falling back briefly, the Rangers advanced again and struck between companies C and I, penetrating the Federal ranks in what one Federal officer recalled "in force upon my right and center." Another Federal officer remarked that the Rangers "again rallied and made another most desperate attack upon" companies C and I. Lt. Peter Cappell led Company H of the 32nd Indiana forward and plugged the hole in the Federal line as Confederate cannon fire hit the position of the reserves from companies D and E in an attempt to eliminate additional reinforcements from negating additional punctures.[27]

In the early stages of the action, Colonel Terry, the beloved leader of the Rangers, "fell dead, having received a [shot] in the chin and coming out in the back of his head." A witness recalled, "Col. Terry raised his hat and waved it, and shouted, 'Charge, my brave boys, charge!'" The soldier recalled, "The boys raised the yell, and every one dashed ahead upon the bright bayonets and right in the face of a hail of bullets . . . I never saw men fall as they did. One tried to run his bayonet into me, but was shot."[28]

During the charge, according to one Confederate, "Col. Terry made a desperate charge . . . and fell dead . . . I have the honor to know that I shot the Dutchman's brains out that killed him. I emptied my six shooters in the crowd, and saw several fall dead."[29]

Recalling Col. Terry's death, a reporter wrote, "Seven shots were deliberately fired at him, one shot taking effect in his neck and producing instant death, another in his theigh [sic], and a third killed his horse . . . a fourth killed the horse of a comrade."[30]

A. L. Steele, a member of Terry's command, wrote that Terry's death site was approximately two hundred yards northwest of the bridge. Steele was reportedly present when Terry's remains were recovered and subsequently removed via an ambulance. The ambulance moved the body to a train station from which point it was eventually transported to Texas. It was noted that Terry's admiration among his troops was unequaled and that he "enjoyed the unlimited confidence and love of his men" and that his loss was "a great calamity to" the Confederacy.[31]

Another Confederate added, "Col. Terry, always in the front, discovered a nest of five of the enemy . . . He fired and killed two of them. The other three fired simultaneously. One shot killed his charger. Another . . . him. He fell headlong from his horse, without a groan or a moan. He was killed instantly, the ball piercing his windpipe and penetrating the lower part of the brain. At the same time [other Confederates] rode up and dispatched the remaining three. The man who killed Col. Terry was a huge raw-boned German, well dressed, and armed with a fine Belgian musket."[32]

The Texas cavalrymen were able to fire "their six-shooters with great effect, as they proceeded, killing numbers on either side of the fence, and scattering them to the right and left." Several witnesses, Federal and Confederate alike, recalled the Rangers emptying their pistols, dropping back, reappearing, and doing the same again. One reporter wrote that each Ranger "was equipped with a pair of revolvers and a shot gun. They did not . . . budge one inch until they had each . . . fired 14 shots."[33] With the use of such military techniques, the Rangers were regularly regarded as an impressive and effective fighting unit.

An estimated fifty Federal troops from Company G of the 32nd Indiana employed a technique of their own, known as the hollow square. This means of defense was used in Europe and developed during a time when weapons were far less accurate and lacked the range of Civil War muskets. Its use at Rowlett's Station is the first recorded implementation of the strategy during the horrific war and was estimated to have repelled three Confederate charges. The hollow square created a violent situation. As one witness remarked, during the Ranger's assaults on the Federal position, "The Rangers came so close they were lifted off their horses by the German bayonets. Some of the Germans used their rifles as clubs." Hand-to-hand fighting became the norm as "the struggle [grew] fiercer and hotter." It was noted that during the hand-to-hand struggle, the Rangers retreated and the Germans followed in what was described as "one of the most desperate fights of the war. It was hand-to-hand from first to last." A witness reported, "Seldom is there seen such fighting." Another stated that Germans and Rangers "mingled dying groans" across the field.[34]

Confederate artillery opened on Lieutenant Colonel von Treba's men, but the effects were later recalled with mixed results. A Federal soldier wrote, "Few were hurt by the artillery fire. The only injuries sustained were from splinters from trees and fences." A Confederate reminisced, "batteries opened from our bluff. Germans slowly, but unwillingly, retired to the woods."[35]

In response, Union guns opened fire upon the Confederates. The chaplain of the 15th Ohio stated that Federal reinforcements hurried to the aid of their comrades, who "found themselves in a net," while "Cotter's batteries opened." A member of the 1st Wisconsin added, "soon after the battery begun to play, we . . . were called out . . . and started for the battlefield. . . . We had to go about 3/4 of a mile . . . we had the mortification to see the enemy on the retreat."[36]

The news of Terry's death spread throughout the Confederate ranks. The knowledge of this disaster, coupled with the Federal reinforcements and artillery, brought about an end to the battle of Rowlett's Station, approximately one and a half hours after it began.[37] The task of gathering and caring for the wounded and burying the dead became the major effort for those fortunate enough to survive the battle to fight another day.

The morning after the battle, an announcement was made

that Confederates were approaching the Federal lines near the area where the 39th Indiana had relieved the battle-weary 32nd Indiana. However, there would be no fighting on that day. Under a flag of truce, Major Phifer met with Federal Col. Thomas J. Harrison seeking permission to bury the Confederate dead.[38] The request was graciously granted, and the grisly work began.

Willich complimented his adversaries in his official report in stating, "The noble conduct of some surgeons of the rebels I cannot pass with silence, although I am unable to give their names. They dressed the wounds of 3 of our men and sent them back to us in a farmer's wagon."[39] The humanity of this act overshadowed some of the carnage that existed on the field.

Evidence of the ferocity of the battle exists in a description from the chaplain of the 15th Ohio. The man recorded that he saw one man with an ear shot off and another missing the bridge of his nose. Other soldiers' wounds were described as four or five in the arms, a similar number in the legs, four chest wounds, one with an abdomen wound, and a soldier with buckshot in his side.[40]

In his official report, Brigadier General Hindman listed the Confederate losses as four killed and ten wounded. Eighty percent of the Confederate casualties came from the Texas Rangers; the remaining twenty percent were members of the 1st Arkansas Battalion.[41] The most celebrated of the Confederate casualties was Colonel Terry of the Rangers.

Both houses of the Kentucky Legislature voted unanimously to adjourn at 10 a.m. on December 18 "to proceed to the Louisville depot and join the procession which accompanied the remains" of Colonel Terry. A witness to the procession wrote that it "consisted of several companies of infantry and a squadron of cavalry, the Senate and House of Representatives of the Tennessee Legislature, the Masonic fraternity and citizens in carriage and on foot. Members of Col. Terry's own Regiment acted as pallbearers. The hearse was draped in the flag of the Confederate States, and one of his horses was led in the rear of the hearse. It was a most solemn and impressive spectacle and drew tears from many eyes."[42]

Colonel Willich listed the Federal losses as eleven killed, twenty-two wounded, and five missing. From the 32nd Indiana, the dead included 1st Lt. Max Sachs, Sgt. William Statts, and a host of privates. Among the dead was seventeen-year-old Pvt. George Burkhardt, born in Kieselbach, Saxony; nineteen-year-old Pvt. John Fellerman, born in Menzen, Hannover; eighteen-year-old Charles Knab from Munchberg, Bavaria; and twenty-seven-year-old Daniel Schmidt who was born in Grabowa, Prussia.[43] The battle, often regarded as minor in the eyes of many, certainly had international ramifications.

As a gesture of memorializing his comrades killed in action at Rowlett's Station, in January of 1862 Pvt. August Bloedner of Company F, 32nd Indiana used a large piece of limestone to serve as a marker for the thirteen men, slightly more than the original official report, who were victims of the battle. The men were originally buried on a hill near the bridge they died defending. The remains of Schmidt and Sachs were moved to Cincinnati in December of 1861. In June of 1867 the remains of the rest of the soldiers, as well as the monument, were moved to Louisville's Cave Hill National Cemetery. The graves are in Section C of the cemetery.[44]

The monument's inscription, written in German, contained the names, birth dates, and locations of all of the members of the 32nd Indiana killed at Rowlett's Station. Intricate carvings of an eagle and flags also graced the memorial. The text on the memorial stated, "Here rest the first martyrs of the 32nd, the first German regiment of Indiana. They were fighting nobly in defense of the free Constitution of the United States of America. They fell on the 17th day of December, 1861, in the battle at Rowlett's Station, in which one regiment of Texas Rangers, two regiments of infantry, and six pieces of rebel artillery, in all over three thousand men, were defeated by five hundred German soldiers."[45] Obviously, the number of participants was greatly exaggerated.

In respect to the preservation of the battle of Rowlett's Station, the Bloedner Monument is one of the most recent success stories.

Reportedly the oldest Civil War monument in the United States, the monument has suffered a large amount of deterioration since its carving. More than half of its original inscriptions had been lost due to the effects of pollution and weather that battered the monument for more than 145 years. On December 17, 2008, the 147th anniversary of the battle of Rowlett's Station, the monument was removed from Cave Hill National Cemetery to receive conservation efforts at the University of Louisville. The 3,500 pound limestone monument is approximately three and a half feet high, one foot deep, and five feet long. Once the project is complete, the monument will be displayed in a public facility.[46]

The Federal victims of the battle at Rowlett's Station rest in Cave Hill National Cemetery, a four-acre plot in the northwest corner of Cave Hill Cemetery.[47] These soldiers are a fraction of more than 6,000 people buried in the complex. To reach the cemetery, take Interstate 65 to the Broadway exit to Baxter Avenue. The cemetery is located at 701 Baxter Avenue in Louisville and is open from 8 a.m. to 4:45 p.m. all days except federal holidays. Additional information can be gained by calling 502-893-3852.

As for the battlefield itself, only 47 acres of the estimated 900 acres are accessible to the public. A one-half-mile walking trail, interpretive signs, and a Web site related to the battle have been the major positives in relation to the preservation of the site. Recent developments seem to indicate additional land will be added. An official of the preservation movement proclaimed, "We secured 46 acres where the 32nd did its bloodiest work, and salvaged a small area . . . pointed out to me as the site of Col. Terry's death."[48]

The Texas Historical Commission dedicated one of its signature Sunset Red granite monuments on December 17, 2008. The monument was dedicated on the 147th anniversary of the battle and honors Col. Terry and the Texas Rangers. Donations from Texas members of the Civil War Preservation Trust largely made the monument possible, although a number of other individuals contributed to the structure.[49]

Other signage and information related to the battle of Rowlett's

Station include state marker 606 located on US 31-E. Another marker, 1504, is located two miles south of Munfordville on US 31-W. A visit to the area should include a stop at the Hart County Historical Museum, located at 109 Main Street in downtown Munfordville, Kentucky. The museum is open from 9 a.m. to 4 p.m. Monday through Friday and on Saturday from 8 a.m. to 4 p.m. The museum can be contacted by calling 270-524-0101. The historical society can be reached at the same number for additional information related to the annual September reenactment of battles that took place in and around Munfordville.

With the battle at Rowlett's Station and the battle of Munfordville being so closely related, it is difficult to distinguish many of the aspects of preservation. However, while the support of research is high in relation to Rowlett's Station, the simple review of the amount of land not currently set aside for preservation shows that much remains to be done in order to secure this Kentucky site. Failure to do so may relegate this battlefield to the "second class level" it has received in the past and eliminate the potential that it holds.

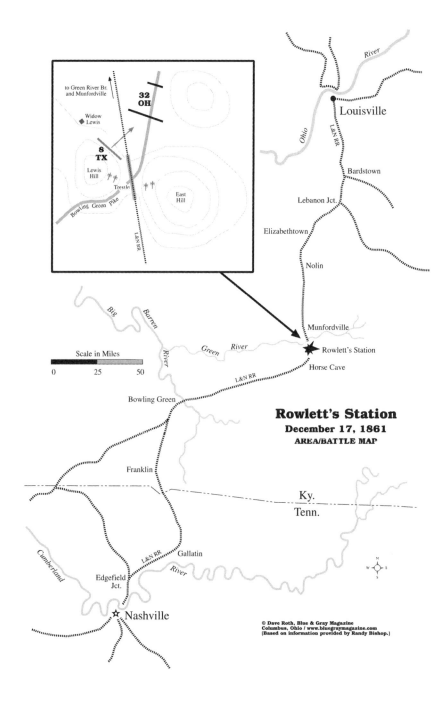

to Green River Br. and Munfordville

32 OH

Widow Lewis

8 TX

Lewis Hill

Trestle

East Hill

Bowling Green Pike

L&N RR

River

Ohio

L&N RR

Louisville

Bardstown

Lebanon Jct.

Elizabethtown

Nolin

Big

Barren

Green River

River

Munfordville

Rowlett's Station

Horse Cave

Scale in Miles

0   25   50

L&N RR

Bowling Green

Rowlett's Station
December 17, 1861
AREA/BATTLE MAP

Franklin

Ky.
Tenn.

Cumberland

L&N RR

Gallatin

River

Edgefield Jct.

Nashville

N
W · E
S

The Texas Memorial, dedicated in 2008, memorializes the contributions of Terry's Texas Rangers. (Photo by author)

This highway marker is located some 400 yards east of Colonel Terry's death site. (Photo by author)

CHAPTER FIVE

SACRAMENTO

December 28, 1861

"They seemed only to look for security in flight."
— Lt. Col. Nathan Bedford Forrest

As Christmas of 1861 approached and bitter winter weather set in, Lt. Col. Nathan Bedford Forrest supervised his Confederate cavalrymen at building winter huts in Hopkinsville, Kentucky. A member of Forrest's command noted construction was completed just before the holiday and that, "The whole command [was] very comfortably fixed with good floored tents and good beds." To the troopers' advantage, the commissary department was reported to be "most abundantly supplied." Unfortunately, not all was bliss as various diseases, primarily measles, struck the camp. In addition, word of possible Federal movements "looking to an advance upon the Confederate lines in Kentucky," led to the assignment of Forrest's battalion to conduct a cavalry reconnaissance "for the definite ascertainment of the military situation."[1]

The Federal group rumored to be advancing into Confederate territory was a detachment of the 5th Division, Army of the Ohio. The brigadier general in command of the division was Thomas L. Crittenden, a native Kentuckian whose family was the epitome of the division the nation experienced. One son, Thomas, was a Federal brigadier general; another, George, was a general in the Confederate military. Having gained his promotion in September,

Brig. Gen. Thomas Crittenden arrived at Calhoon, Kentucky, at approximately the same time Forrest had moved to Hopkinsville. Crittenden established his headquarters at the Griffith-Franklin home, built in 1854 and purchased five years later by W. W. Franklin.[2]

On the morning of December 26, Forrest led approximately 250 men from Hopkinsville toward the Green River. Attending the future "Wizard of the Saddle" were detachments from six companies and a group of twenty-five Kentuckians. The trek in the direction of Greenville was slow as the group was hampered in attempting to negotiate roads "deep with mud and rough with ice." Reportedly, intermittent freezing rain and snow mixed to increase the miserable conditions of the day.[3]

The Confederates left the Greenville Road approximately four miles from Hopkinsville and made their way toward Rochester. On December 27, the group reached Greenville where they spent the night. As news of the presence of Federal troops circulated, Forrest felt it necessary to send Adam R. Johnson and Robert Martin to scout the area. On the morning of December 28, 1861, two additional commands joined Forrest and "volunteered to accompany him." The addition of these two units provided Forrest with some three hundred troopers at his disposal.[4]

Having made no contact with the Federals he was dispatched to locate, Forrest determined it most beneficial to extend the "march to the vicinity of Rumsey." The command "moved forward in one column, with advance guard under Captain Meriwether and rear under Captain McLemore." Forrest led the main column while Major Kelly's troops occupied the middle and those of Lieutenant Colonel Starnes trailed. After traveling eight miles down the Rumsey Road, Forrest received word from the earlier dispatched scouting duo of Johnson and Martin that five hundred Federals had left their base at Calhoun and were approaching Rumsey.[5]

Originally known as Fort Vienna, Calhoon's name was changed in 1852 in honor of John Calhoon, not to be confused with John C. Calhoun of Jacksonian Era fame. Two years later the town became the county seat of the recently formed McLean County. In the early 1900s the name was changed to Calhoun and the town has been known as such from that point forward. More significantly, in the months following the attack on Fort Sumter, one of the first military bases in Kentucky was established at Calhoun and became known as Camp Calhoun.[6]

In late September of 1861, large numbers of soldiers poured into Camp Calhoun. The total eventually reached somewhere between 5,000 and 7,000 troops who shared the small town with approximately "500 disconcerted private citizens." Diseases ran rampant as companies regularly had half of their enlistments sick. Many succumbed to the variety of maladies that attacked the camp.[7]

One of the units that diseases devastated at Camp Calhoun was the 31st Indiana Infantry Regiment. Mustered into service in September of 1861, the group arrived at Calhoun in November of the same year. While little is recorded of the time the 31st spent at Camp Calhoun, the regimental historian, John Thomas Smith, recalled that the unit was "thoroughly drilled" during their stay. In addition, Smith noted that the 31st was "assailed with disease. Measles, mumps, malarial fever and rheumatism were, in a manner, epidemic, and many fell victim." The number of deaths may have been higher, but at least fifty members of the 31st Indiana are recorded as dying during the regiment's stay at Calhoun.[8]

One of the tasks assigned to the Federal troops at Calhoun was to secure the area around the lock and dam on the Green River. The structures and the river served as integral parts of the line for Federal troop and supply movements and warranted a great deal of attention. On the morning of December 28, 1861, Federal Maj. Eli Murray, only eighteen years old, was given the assignment to take a 168-man scouting party of companies A, B, C, and D of the 3rd Kentucky Cavalry Regiment from Calhoun and reconnoiter the nearby area of Sacramento, Kentucky.[9]

The town of Sacramento was located nine miles south of Calhoun and had once been known as Cross Roads. John Vickers and his son-in-law John Bender had left the area in search of riches during the California Gold Rush, but they returned when the harsh reality of their inability to locate gold sank in. The village where they lived was surveyed in 1854 and a new name, based upon Vickers's suggestion, was given: Sacramento.[10] Murray's scouting party neared the village of Sacramento from the north, unaware that Forrest's Confederates were approaching from the south.

Forrest's three hundred troopers were almost out of control as the enthusiasm over the possibility of fighting filled their bodies. In their biography of Forrest, Thomas Jordan and J. P. Pryor stated that the news of the close proximity of the Federals "quickly communicated among the men, exhilarated them perceptibly, notwithstanding the fatigues of their long march; and with one impulse the whole command moved ahead, at an accelerated gait, which was soon increased to a gallop."[11]

A participant also recalled that the possibility of fighting created an atmosphere in which "it was impossible to repress jubilant and defiant shouts, which reached the height of enthusiasm as the women from the houses waved us forward."[12]

In his official report of the battle, Forrest noted that as his command neared Sacramento, "an unexpected volunteer in the person of a Kentucky belle" a "beautiful young lady" approached him and smiled with her "united tresses, floating in the breeze, infused nerve into my arm and kindled knightly chivalry into my heart."[13]

The young lady was Mollie Morehead, the eighteen-year-old daughter of Hugh N. Morehead, a farmer and slave-owner who lived approximately 1½ miles north of Sacramento. Mollie and Betsy, her sister, had been on an errand near Sacramento Hill and, on their way home, passed a column of Federal soldiers. Betsy had gone to warn her father of the presence of the men in blue while Mollie sought out the Confederates in the direction of Greenville. The young lady rode with Forrest's cavalrymen for a short distance until Forrest asked her to abandon the group for the sake of her safety.[14]

A report of the time stated that Miss Morehead, "Deeply

sympathizing with the cause . . . and excited by the scene, waving her hat in the air . . . urged the Confederates to 'hurry up' and rode back at a gallop for several hundred yards at the side of Colonel Forrest, before she was induced to return."[15]

Approximately one mile south of Sacramento, Forrest's advance party came in sight of Maj. Eli Murray's scouting party as the latter watered their horses. It was theorized that the Federals were "in doubt whether friends or foes" were approaching, but when Forrest grabbed a Maynard rifle from one of his men he "settled all doubt . . . by firing a shot at them."[16] The battle of Sacramento, Kentucky, had begun.

Murray's scouts returned fire at Forrest's troops and then retreated in order to join the bulk of the Federal force positioned on a "wooded ridge close by." Likewise, Forrest's entire command was not at his disposal as the fast pace of the approach had resulted in the unfortunate dispersion of the cavalrymen. It was noted that, "the command had become somewhat scattered" due to the fact that at least ten miles had been covered "at a canter or full gallop." The Confederate commander ordered the gray-clad warriors forward with directions to avoid firing until they were in range of the Federals.[17]

A period historian wrote that the gathering Confederate force of some 175 men galloped forward only a short distance before they discovered the men in blue "deployed in a line across and on either side of the highway in a heavy grove" where their position was determined to be "highly advantageous and sheltered." The distance separating the foes was estimated to be approximately two hundred yards.[18]

From this distance, the Federals "opened a sharp fire" that was also noted as "a distressing fire." At a distance of some eighty yards, the Confederates returned three rounds of fire before Forrest again determined that he lacked the proper troop strength, as he proclaimed that his men "were not up in sufficient numbers," to advance and "pursue them with success" and ordered his men to fall back. A Confederate participant recalled that Forrest "quickly dismounted his men and held the enemy in check until his command came up."[19]

The Federal troops appeared "to be forming for a charge," apparently under the impression that Forrest's Confederates were retreating. Meanwhile, the Confederate stragglers were arriving and Forrest "dismounted a number of men with Sharp's Carbines and Maynard rifles to act as sharpshooters." At that point Forrest first employed a technique that would eventually become his military trademark. "Posting his men on horseback in a position of least exposure," Forrest "ordered a flank movement" as Major Kelly and thirty men moved to the right while Colonel Starnes and sixty others assumed a position on the left. Forrest would lead "detachments from the companies under . . . [Forrest's] command, still mounted" in a charge on the Federal center.[20]

Kelly and Starnes appeared from their concealed points of advancement, and Forrest seized the moment to order a charge. A Confederate private recalled that Forrest forcefully spoke to his bugler and said, "Blow the charge, Isham." The soldier added, "With that, we raised the yell and away we went."[21]

A period historian wrote that the Confederate troopers followed Forrest's order, "each seemingly bent on keeping up with their leader." Forrest stood up in his stirrups with "his saber in the left hand [and] looked a foot taller than any of his men."[22]

During the Confederate charge that was carried out "with no semblance of formation" and "with an animating shout and all possible spirit and resolution," Forrest's troopers continued forward "in the face of a sharp fire" from the Federal position. Reportedly, the ground was beginning to thaw by this time of the day and the Confederates "were soon covered with mud from head to foot." Capt. J. C. Blanton, commander of Company C in Forrest's regiment, proclaimed that after the regiment formed they "drove the blue coats pell mell through the village." The men in blue found themselves "threatened on both flanks, and assailed in . . . desperate fashion from the front" and their ranks broke "in utter confusion" and began to retreat "in a disorderly flight at full speed." The latter action occurred in spite of "a few gallant" Federal officers who provided "zealous efforts" to hold the position. Forrest, who had advanced "down directly on the centre" of the Federal line, in addition to Starnes and Capt. C. E. Meriwether overtook the rearmost fleeing Federals who began surrendering or falling "at close range with saber thrust or pistol shot" as the fighting neared the village of Sacramento.[23]

In the early phase of the charge, the Confederates suffered a disastrous loss when Captain Meriwether was shot through the brain. Forrest noted in his official report that Meriwether, who was recalled as being the "Confederate guide of the expedition," unfortunately "fell in front of the engagement." It was also mentioned in a period writing that Meriwether was at Forrest's side when the fatal incident occurred.[24]

Just north of Sacramento, the contact between the two foes evolved into a hand-to-hand struggle. Forrest reported that "when the best mounted men" of his troopers arrived, the fighting became vicious. Forrest added, "There commenced a promiscuous saber slaughter" of the soldiers in the Federal rear. The level of this bloodshed was noted to have been high, as the Union soldiers supposedly left "their bleeding and wounded strewn along the whole route" and that the road was "thickly dotted with the wounded and slain" men in blue.[25] However, not all of the casualties inflicted were to be credited to the Confederates.

Forrest found himself "assailed from all sides" and in a position where little help was present as his horse had "carried him somewhat in advance of any of his men." Federal Capt. Albert G. Bacon fired a shot at Forrest, but the Federal officer narrowly missed. By some accounts Forrest returned fire and engaged in a saber fight with Bacon. In Forrest's official report, he stated that Bacon was "run through with saber thrusts."[26]

Jordan and Pryor noted that Forrest shot Bacon after the latter's shot "passed through his collar." Then Forrest, who was assaulted by a tandem of Federal officers, found Bacon still making a "show of battle, obliging him to run his saber through" the Federal officer.

Allegedly, Confederates took liberties with Bacon's corpse and "stripped him of his watch and rifled his pockets." In all, the series of events led to a bullet passing through Forrest's coat collar, Forrest shooting one enlisted Federal and an officer, and the Confederate colonel striking another officer with a sword.[27]

The incident holds significance as it led to Forrest killing his first man in hand-to-hand combat during the war. By war's end, similar situations would increase the number of Forrest's victims to approximately thirty.[28]

At that point, Pvt. W. H. Terry, "one of the foremost of the Southern troopers" and a member of McLemore's company, joined Forrest's side. Terry placed his horse between Forrest's and the one belonging to Federal Capt. Arthur N. Davis "who was endeavoring to reach the Confederate chieftain . . . Forrest rushed at Davis . . . in the hope of saving Terry, but was a second too late" as Davis inflicted "a fatal saber wound" upon Terry. Confederate B. L. Ridley recalled it was the only time he saw a hand-to-hand struggle with sabers.[29]

Forrest's horse struck that of Davis and both animals and their riders "fell in a heap." Jordan and Pryor, the preeminent historians of Forrest, proclaimed that two horses collided with that of Forrest while the two animals, "Riderless . . . knocked each other over at the bottom of a short, abrupt hillock, where . . . Forrest . . . came in contact with them and horse and rider were thrown prone to the earth . . . [Forrest] falling headlong some twenty feet in advance of the heap."[30]

It was also reported, "The Federal officer struck the ground with such velocity that his shoulder was dislocated, rendering him incapable of further resistance." Forrest noted that the injury resulted in Davis surrendering "as my prisoner." Aside from the bruises and "severe shock" from the fall, Forrest was uninjured.[31]

Similar to Forrest, Starnes found himself in what was noted as "a battle royal of his own." Starnes fired the last ball from his pistol and threw the empty weapon at a fleeing Federal officer. A period historian recalled that the hurled pistol "struck and bounded off with no other effect than to speed the parting guest."[32]

Forrest reported, "The enemy, without officers, threw down their arms and depended alone upon the speed of their horses." Some of the Federal soldiers turned to attempt to make a stand, but, "Of the squadron which turned to offer battle, none escaped."[33]

It was duly noted that Forrest and a small group of "his best mounted men" were able to ride into the "thick . . . stream of panic-struck fugitives" and demand surrender. However, "no heed was given by the terrified fugitives to the repeated demands of surrender and offers of safety made them. They seemed only to look for security in flight."[34]

Major Kelley then arrived at Forrest's side. Recalling the moment years later, Kelley wrote, "Forrest seemed in desperate mood and very much excited. His face was flushed till it looked like a painted warrior, and his eyes, usually mild in expression, glared like those of a panther about to spring upon its prey. He looked as little like the Forrest of the mess-table as the storm of December resembles the quiet of June."[35]

Another Confederate officer explained that Forrest looked "so fierce . . . he was almost equally dangerous to friend or foe . . . that excitement neither paralyzed nor mislead his magnificent military genius."[36]

Despite his appearance and attitude, Forrest allowed his rationale to rule. He felt confident that the horses that were not worn out would be fully capable of catching the Federals in retreat and, in turn, run "through every one they came up with." However, Forrest was also keenly aware of the fact that his troopers' horses were largely tired from the recent lengthy ride and that the Federal horses "were much fresher." Therefore, Forrest determined that additional pursuit would be unproductive and felt it best "to call off the chase."[37]

One Confederate officer recalled that the fight had "lasted but a very short time," while another remarked that fifteen minutes would have been a reasonable projection of the battle's duration. One historical record referred to the battle as a "brave and brief work soon ended."[38]

After ceasing their pursuit of the Federal troops, Forrest's Confederates returned to the location of the intense fighting of minutes earlier. In his official report, Forrest recalled that his men witnessed large numbers of men in blue "dead and wounded in every direction. Those who were able to be moved we placed wagons."[39]

In a humanitarian effort, the wounded Federal enlisted were made as comfortable as possible and the officers were taken to a nearby farm house where the residents were "applied . . . to take care of them." The Confederate troops returned to Greenville where they spent the night of December 28 and arrived at their camp in Hopkinsville the next day.[40]

At least one Confederate recalled that the move to Hopkinsville was celebratory as "great piles of biscuits, fried chicken, and ham were brought into the picket posts by the citizens, and the best part of it was that the girls generally brought it to us and remained to see us eat and hear what we had to say."[41]

Confirming Forrest's claim that the Federal wounded were cared for in the best manner possible, Brig. Gen. Thomas L. Crittenden noted that as many as half a dozen men were "so badly wounded that we could not bring them in. They are in good quarters and will be well cared for."[42]

Although Forrest estimated sixty-five Federal troops were killed and another thirty-five were wounded and taken prisoners, Crittenden noted the actual number as eight killed. Crittenden likewise overestimated the Confederate killed as five and that three "wagon loads of dead and wounded" were taken from the field. In contrast, Forrest reported his losses as two killed and three wounded.[43]

One of the Confederate casualties was reportedly the victim of friendly fire. James Hammer, a member of Forrest's cavalry, wrote to his family and stated that the wounded soldier, a Mexican War veteran, wore a blue military coat, not too different from those issued to the Federal soldiers. Hammer wrote, "We were all mixed up together and one of our men took him for a Yankee . . . sad misfortune as he is a good man."[44]

Among the more severely wounded Federals was Capt. Arthur N. Davis. The officer held the distinction of killing Pvt. William H. Terry of the 8th Tennessee, the only enlisted man in gray to fall at Sacramento. However, the fall that Davis subsequently suffered while combating Forrest caused a shoulder injury that failed to heal properly. Following a prisoner-of-war term of almost eight months, Davis was released. In April of 1863, the wounded officer was given a surgeon's certificate of disability and he resigned. A civilian recalled seeing another wounded Federal private, Edward Baker, the day after the battle. The citizen wrote, "He was badly wounded; shot in the legs, arms, and body, and was absolutely helpless."[45]

Another wounded Federal soldier was nineteen-year-old C. A. McCulloch. A pistol ball punctured the young cavalryman's right lung, but the trooper managed to stay in the saddle. During the Federal retreat, McCulloch was wounded again when a saber was thrust into his left side and penetrated his bowels. The loss of blood caused McCulloch to fall from his saddle. Through the medical care of a local doctor and an unidentified family, McCulloch survived, despite a period of "protracted suffering." In October of 1862 McCulloch was discharged and "enjoyed better health than could be expected."[46]

Under orders from Crittenden, Col. James S. Jackson brought the 3rd Kentucky Cavalry to Sacramento in an effort to provide relief for Murray's patrol. The *Louisville Democrat* reported that nine citizens of Sacramento were taken captive in response to their anti-Federal actions. Allegedly, the citizens "engaged in shooting" Federal soldiers as they passed through the town. Among those arrested was Sheriff Lucas who was described as "a very violent rebel."[47]

The reaction toward the Federal troops was reportedly extremely different than that the Confederates received. A veteran in Forrest's cavalry recalled that as the men in gray passed through Sacramento, "Every window and door was full of excited people waving their handkerchiefs."[48]

The battle of Sacramento, though not as well known as many others that took place within the borders of the Bluegrass State, is the subject of several noteworthy facts. Most significantly, the battle was the first in which Nathan Bedford Forrest commanded troops in action. Brig. Gen. Charles Clark wrote that Forrest, "a brave and chivalrous gentleman," acted with "skill, courage, and energy" and was "entitled to the highest praise" as "one of the best officers of his rank in the service." Clark could have been no more correct in his analysis of the future Confederate military great.[49]

Capt. J. C. Blanton praised both Forrest and Maj. D. C. Kelly in writing, "This battle had a splendid effect in our regiment, causing men and officers to confide in and respect each other. We were convinced that Forrest and Kelly were wise selections for our leaders."[50]

Forrest was in the company of three other future generals at Sacramento. Adam Johnson, one of the Confederate scouts at Sacramento, later commanded a brigade under cavalryman John Hunt Morgan; Lt. Col. James Starnes, who lead the 8th Tennessee at Sacramento, rose to the rank of brigadier general under Forrest. On the Federal side, Eli Murray, the eighteen-year-old major whose patrol holds the distinction of becoming Forrest's first defeated enemy, was brevetted brigadier general less than a month prior to the end of the war.[51]

Sadly, Mary Susan "Mollie" Morehead, the young lady who risked her personal safety to warn Forrest's troops of the location of Murray's patrol, lived less than a decade after the battle of Sacramento. The year after the Civil War ended Morehead married Dr. George E. Stowers, a dentist. On March 29, 1870, the then-twenty-seven year-old Mollie Stowers died during childbirth. She and her infant son are buried in the Cumberland Presbyterian Cemetery in Sacramento.[52]

The cemetery is one of ten stops on the Battle of Sacramento Driving Tour. The others include the Greenville-Muhlenberg County Courthouse, a building that stands on the spot where Forrest assembled his troops prior to the trip to Sacramento; the location where Forrest encountered his scouts, Garst's pond; as well as the battlefield and village of Sacramento. The location of the saber battle, the Calhoun lock and dam, as well as Crittenden's headquarters are among the remaining sites on the tour. While the stops are clearly marked, all visitors are cautioned to be aware of the hills and curves frequenting the narrow road that allows access to the tour stops. In addition, some of the stops necessitate parking a short distance from the respective site and crossing Highway 181 to properly visit and interpret the battlefield location. A free brochure related to the driving tour can be obtained at the Sacramento City Hall at 218 West 3rd Street. The phone number is 270-736-5274, or a visit to battleofsac.com will provide the necessary information to participate in the tour.

Although there is no library in Sacramento, a wealth of information is available at those of two nearby communities. The Livermore Community Library located at 116 East 2nd Street is housed in a building constructed in the 1880s and is open Monday through Friday from 10 a.m. to 5 p.m. The McLean County Historical and Genealogy Museum at 540 Main Street in Calhoun is only open Monday and Friday, but can be contacted at 270-273-9760 to set up an appointment.

A twenty-eight-stop driving tour is also available in Calhoun. Numerous stops on the tour are related to the battle of Sacramento and include the John Calhoon Cemetery, the Camp Calhoon Cemetery, and antebellum homes. There is also a walking tour of Calhoun available, which allows visitors to see Crittenden's headquarters, a home known as the Griffith-Franklin House. Additional information related to the tour is available form the McLean County History and Genealogy Museum.

In 2002, the city of Sacramento and McLean County completed a $520,000 purchase of land where the battle of Sacramento took place. The annual reenactment of the Battle of Sacramento is held the third weekend of May on the actual site of the most significant ground of the struggle. The sixty-five acre battlefield is located at the intersection of Kentucky state highways 81 and

85.[53] Typically, Friday is dedicated to area students while Saturday includes a parade, tea, battle, cavalry competition, and an evening ball. Prior to the Sunday afternoon battle, a morning worship service is held. The event is the largest cavalry reenactment in the state and has evolved into a major event in the area, with thousands of reenactors participating. The Battle of Sacramento Committee, chaired by Wendell Miller, conducts the reenactment with the city of Sacramento and the McLean County Fiscal Court combining efforts to ensure an accurate and enjoyable event. The Web site battleofsac.com can be visited for additional information or interested parties can call affiliated parties at 270-781-6858 or 270-736-2254.

A major advantage that Sacramento holds in relation to preservation is that the population of the town is significantly below 1,000. Therefore, the area has yet to be subjected to the process of urbanization or commercialization. With the groundwork firmly established and no visible threats in sight for the immediate future, Sacramento holds bright promise for the issue of preservation.

Battle of
Sacramento
December 28, 1861
MOVEMENT MAP

Scale in Miles

0   5   10

© Dave Roth, Blue & Gray Magazine
Columbus, Ohio / www.bluegraymagazine.com
(Based on Brian Steel Wills' *A Battle from the
Start: The Life of Nathan Bedford Forrest*,
and information provided by Randy Bishop.)

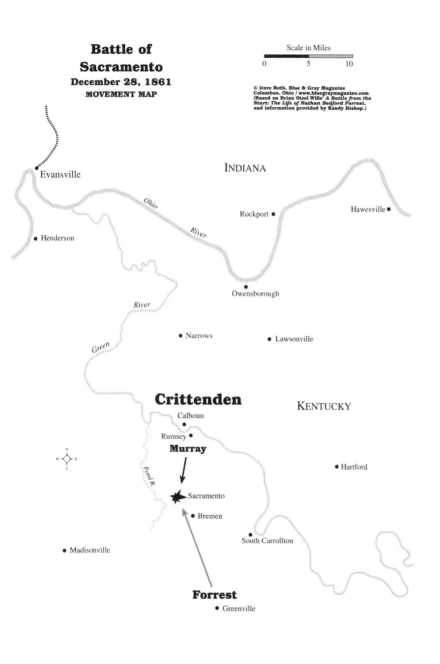

INDIANA

Evansville

Ohio

Rockport

Hawesville

Henderson

River

Owensborough

River

Narrows

Lawsonville

Green

Crittenden

KENTUCKY

Calhoun

Rumsey

Murray

Pond R.

Hartford

Sacramento

Bremen

South Carrollton

Madisonville

Forrest

Greenville

A typical marker on the Sacramento driving tour. (Photo by author)

This is indicative of the well-preserved portion of the Sacramento battlefield. (Photo by author)

The driving tour contains locations that are difficult to negotiate as indicated in this tour stop for the battlefield. (Photo by author)

The grave of Mary "Mollie" Morehead Stowers, the young lady who warned Forrest of the presence of Federal troops. (Photo by author)

CHAPTER SIX

MIDDLE CREEK

January 10, 1862

"Three discharges of artillery put the cavalry to flight."
—Brig. Gen. Humphrey Marshall, C.S.A.

In March of 1881, James Abram Garfield took the oath of office as president of the United States. Similar to a large number of both his predecessors and successors, Garfield owed a great deal of his future political clout and level of support to the fame associated with his successful military career. At the age of thirty-one, Garfield had been promoted to the rank of brigadier general, a rank he achieved largely in part for his performance against a numerically superior Confederate force encountered at the battle of Middle Creek. The action at this site, located near the town of Prestonsburg, Kentucky, admittedly became a major catalyst for James Garfield and eventually placed his name into the national political arena.

Some twenty years before his ascension to the leadership role of the nation he helped defend in the extremely bloody American Civil War, Garfield held the rank of colonel in the United States Army. On December 17, 1861, Gen. Don Carlos Buell, commanding the Department of the Ohio, of which Kentucky was a member state, ordered Garfield and his 42nd Ohio Volunteer Infantry to move into the Big Sandy Valley and rid the region of Confederate troops. On the 23rd of that month, Garfield moved his forces from the town of Louisa toward Confederates under the command of Brig. Gen. Humphrey Marshall, a West Point graduate, former lawyer, Congressman, and politically appointed officer, then camped at Prestonsburg.[1]

Marshall's tenure at Prestonsburg had begun on November 1, 1861 when the Confederate government ordered Marshall to relieve Col. John S. Williams, commander of the troops at that location. Colonel Williams had organized the 5th Kentucky Regiment, also known as the "Ragmuffin Regiment," earlier that fall, as well as a mounted rifle battalion from Central Kentucky. The 5th Kentucky was primarily composed of "hardy, raw boned, brave mountaineers," trained to hardships, and armed with long rifles, while the latter group consisted of "young men of education and fortune."[2]

In addition, the 29th and 54th Virginia Regiments and a battery of four artillery pieces became Marshall's responsibility. Marshall's estimation of the number of troops at his disposal varied from 1,800 to 3,000, yet one of his subordinates viewed the force as "very small, considering the interests involved" and in relation to the objectives "to be attained."[3]

The same officer projected an estimate of "several thousand men" being required to ensure a successful Confederate occupation and protection of eastern Kentucky. However, a request from Brigadier General Marshall to Jefferson Davis, proclaiming that Marshall was "sorely pressed on every side," received an explanation that no reinforcements were available.[4]

The lack of reinforcements was not the only problem Marshall's troops confronted during the "very severe winter" of 1861-62. Edward O. Guerrant, Marshall's assistant adjutant general , recalled the situation in an article written two decades later. Guerrant wrote, "Marshall's men were poorly clad, and many . . . were nearly naked. One regiment had 350 bare-footed men and not over 100 blankets for 700 men." Fortunately, an attempt was made to lessen the severity of this situation when Gen. Albert Sidney Johnston ordered 1,000 hats, pairs of shoes, and suits of clothes sent to Whitesburg, a town south of Prestonsburg. Unfortunately, the uniforms were cotton rather than wool.[5]

As if the lack of reinforcements and proper clothing were not enough, "The army was . . . in general badly armed," as shot guns and squirrel rifles were common weapons in possession of Marshall's Confederates. Reportedly, a representative of the Confederate War Department wrote that "owing to the scarcity of arms he was having pikes made." Marshall's unarmed troops were to use the pikes as their weapons.[6]

The area around Prestonsburg "lay in the Cumberland Mountains, along the sources of the Big Sandy River" and was noted as thinly settled. One Confederate remarked that the region was also poor and wild. The soldier wrote that the area contained roads that were frequently "rendered impassable by the high waters" and were literally ruined as wagons, artillery, and cavalry used them. Marshall reported that, at times, his wagons found it difficult to travel four miles a day. A Confederate artillery captain stated that it took him three days to move his battery sixteen miles along primitive roads in the area.[7]

Lastly, as in numerous settings during the course of the war, diseases ran rampant at Prestonsburg, located more than one hundred miles from the nearest supply base at Abingdon, Virginia. A rebel survivor of the dismal conditions wrote, "An unusual amount of rain fell, drenching the unprotected soldiers, most of them raw recruits, and keeping the roads deep and the waters high. This first winter was the worst of the war, and the scanty rations and great hardships made hundreds of the men sick. In addition, cases of measles and mumps abounded in the camps, and many soldiers died from these diseases and from exposure. The command at Prestonsburg . . . for weeks . . . subsisted upon mountain beef and parched corn. These privations General Marshall shared, giving up his tent to the sick and wounded, and sleeping beneath a wagon."[8]

Meanwhile, Colonel Garfield's December 23 exodus from Louisa was hampered in attempting to negotiate the muddy roads previously noted. In fact, it took two days for Garfield's baggage train to travel three miles. A large number of his wagons were dismantled and placed on boats to be transported to Garfield's destination. Some of the empty wagons were transported on push-boats and steamboats.[9]

Moving the supplies Garfield's troops needed for the upcoming action was no small task as the command contained approximately 2,000 men. In addition to the 18th Brigade, Garfield had more than half a dozen units at his disposal. These included the 42nd Ohio, the 1st Squadron Ohio Cavalry, the 14th Kentucky, the 22nd Kentucky, 6 companies of the 2nd Virginia Cavalry, the 40th Ohio, and three hundred men of the 1st Kentucky Cavalry. Despite the deplorable road conditions and the presence of additional hardships, Garfield was within six miles of Paintsville on January 6.[10]

The previous day Brigadier General Marshall had moved from his position on Hager Hill, the original location he had chosen as the site for a battle against the Federal troops. Marshall's move was the result of the receipt of reports that Col. Jonathan Cranor and his command of the 40th Ohio Infantry Regiment, accompanied by as many as four hundred cavalrymen, were advancing from Salyersville. In addition, scouts notified Marshall that Garfield and his troops were approaching.[11]

Reportedly all of Marshall's company commanders had signed a letter proclaiming that they believed they were to "accomplish no good result this winter" and felt it in the best interest of the Confederate cause to abandon the position. Sickness, poor rations, and inhospitable area residents combined to cause Marshall to forego the planned Hager Hill defensive. In the subsequent days, Garfield's cavalry fought with Marshall's rear guard at Jenny's Creek, Garfield gained control of Paintsville, and the future president arrived at Marshall's abandoned position on Hager Hill.[12]

Marshall had determined to move his forces from Hager Hill along the Prestonsburg Road and the Mount Sterling-Pound Gap Road to what he determined to be a strong defensive position at "the forks of Middle Creek, where he awaited the approach of the Federal forces." Intentions often encounter difficulties, and Marshall's plan was no exception. He wrote of the conditions of the road that was once a series of Native American trails, "I found the roads nearly impassable. With great labor my battery was moved six miles . . . my wagons could not move four miles. It was the second day before I passed . . . from Salyersville to Prestonsburg."[13]

It has been explained that Marshall believed he held several advantages in possessing the land around the forks of Middle Creek. Primarily, he would be able to intercept Cranor's command if it moved eastward on the Pound Gap Road or the troops of Garfield, moving westward on the same road, would fall into a formidable trap. In a worst-case scenario, Marshall saw the roadway as an escape route if he were to be defeated; the thoroughfare could be used as a route into Central Kentucky should victory be his blessing. Additionally, the lack of proper equipment could be overcome with the excellent defensive position the Middle Creek valley provided the cold and hungry Confederates.[14]

Upon his arrival at a high ridge located to the south of Middle Creek, Marshall deployed his troops while he established his command post near his four cannon. Six and twelve-pound 1841 smooth bore artillery pieces, manned by sixty artillerymen under the command of Capt. William C. Jeffress, were "placed in a gorge of the left fork of Middle Creek," while the heights and spurs to the right of the creek served as the placement for the 29th Virginia Infantry and 5th Kentucky Infantry Regiments along with a detachment of the Kentucky Battalion of Mounted Riflemen. Trigg's 54th Virginia Infantry took a position on a height covering the battery while three cavalry companies from the 1st Kentucky were held in reserve. Two additional cavalry companies were dismounted and located across Middle Creek "on a height commanding the valley." Holliday's company of cavalry served as the supply train guard. Marshall estimated his strength at 1,500, but modern sources have noted the total number of Confederates at Middle Creek may have approached 2,000.[15]

Having "slept on their arms," Garfield's Federals, according to his report, left their camp some two miles from Prestonsburg at 4 a.m. on January 10 and were approximately 1,100 in number. However, totals ranging from 900 to 1,700 have also been proposed.

Regardless of these discrepancies, it is a generally agreed-upon fact that contact took place between 8 a.m. and 10 a.m. that same day on land belonging to the Fitzpatrick family.[16]

Colonel Garfield established his command post on a high ridge known as Graveyard Point. From that location, he could easily observe "the plain and all the hills" and what Marshall declared to be a slow advance of the Federal troops. Marshall's pickets and Garfield's skirmishers fought against each other approximately one-half mile from the mouth of Middle Creek, a fact that caused Garfield to envision a trap and to send his personal escort into the valley to draw fire from the Confederates. Garfield felt this would enable him to determine the location and strength of the men in gray. Capt. Ezekiel Clay's 1st Kentucky Mounted Rifles fired upon Garfield's escort, fulfilling Garfield's intended purpose for the group and escalating the action at Middle Creek. [17]

As noon approached, Garfield ordered a cavalry charge with infantry support. Marshall's assistant adjutant declared that the Confederate artillery put "the cavalry to the flight, and it appeared no more during the engagement." Marshall declared, "Three discharges of artillery put the cavalry to flight, and if they did anything more during the day it was done on foot." Garfield's troops would, in fact, do much more as they "dismounted and fought on foot, as the ground was not suitable for cavalry operations."[18]

It has been proposed that the Confederate artillery was largely ineffective due to the advanced age and condition of the shells. The shells were reportedly twenty years old and had been stored in the Nottoway County, Virginia, arsenal where the gunpowder inside them had become damp. These facts caused the shells to be "useless except as metal projectiles." Additionally, a member of the 42nd Ohio Infantry Regiment noted that despite the initial effectiveness of the Confederate artillery, the poor aim of the Confederate gunners caused the shells to bury deeply into the mud and lose the advantage they provided in the early stages of the conflict.[19]

Garfield made three attempts to take the Confederate position, focusing his efforts on the area of Spurlock Branch. One of Marshall's subordinates declared that the three attacks were met with the same unsuccessful results due to the fact that, "The ascent was steep, the top of the mountain was covered with trees and rocks affording good protection to the Confederate forces."[20]

It has also been noted that the Federal troops' clothing almost created disaster for Garfield's warriors. Members of the 14th Kentucky wore sky-blue jackets similar to those the Confederate troops were issued. Reportedly Garfield made a strong pro-Union statement that caused a widespread response of "Hurrah for Jeff Davis," clarifying the membership and stance of the members of the 14th Kentucky.[21]

U.S. Maj. Don Pardee led two companies across the ice-cold waters of Middle Creek and against the position the 29th Virginia and 5th Kentucky held on the right wing of the Confederate line. Capt. F. A. Williams simultaneously moved three companies of the 42nd Ohio toward the 5th Kentucky. One volley from the Confederate guns drove Williams back and led to a Confederate charge that left seven Confederates dead. Although this series of attacks did little to dislodge the Confederates, it did enable Federal troops to move into position to reinforce Pardee, a situation made more beneficial with the arrival of Cranor's 40th Ohio during the heat of the battle. Marshall ordered a six-pounder moved in order to inflict "a fair flank fire at the enemy." The Confederate commander reported, "This soon attracted a hot fire . . . but no further damage than the shooting of one of the artillery horses through the head."[22]

Lt. Col. George W. Monroe used a detachment of some 120 members of the 22nd Kentucky to make a bayonet charge against Confederate sharpshooters located across from Graveyard Point. The charge was a success, causing the front line of Confederates to retreat toward the primary Confederate line. In the process, Pvt. Nelson Boggs, 14th Kentucky, was killed when a Confederate ball passed through his brain.[23]

The intense fire from both Federal and Confederate guns was reportedly deafening, but victory apparently fell to Garfield's Federal troops. Garfield noted that the Confederate troops were, "driven from the slopes at every point," providing support for the rationale that the battle was a Federal victory.[24]

In addition, the Confederates began the process of withdrawal along the left fork of Middle Creek with the approach of darkness near 5 p.m., burning several of their wagons, and, in turn, took three days to travel Martin's Mill, a distance of sixteen miles. There, Marshall secured rations for his men, many of whom had gone more than four days without anything to eat. This situation had reportedly led to Marshall's belief that a literal mutiny could have erupted at any minute, should he have chosen to prolong the stay at Middle Creek.[25]

Classified as both a Federal victory and indecisive, the battle of Middle Creek has been called "a desperate fight" with few casualties. Signage on the battlefield's driving tour notes that although 3,000 men were engaged in battle, a minute percentage of the soldiers were killed. In fact, only fifteen men died as a result of their wounds received at Middle Creek. Aside from the aforementioned death of Pvt. Nelson Boggs of the 14th Kentucky, the Federals suffered two additional deaths at Middle Creek. Those men, privates William Gaudier and Frederick Coffin, members of the 42nd Ohio, died from their wounds days after the battle. Additionally, Garfield reported that only twenty-five Federal soldiers were wounded in the series of charges made upon a relatively strong Confederate position. Modern statistics of the battle state that only eighteen Federal troops were wounded during the action at Middle Creek.[26]

Marshall reported his losses as eleven killed and fifteen wounded while Garfield exaggerated that no less than tewnty-seven dead Confederates were left on the field. The official number of Confederate deaths, according to the Middle Creek battlefield signage, is twelve. The 29th Virginia reportedly suffered half of those deaths with one member of the Kentucky Mounted Rifles and four from the 5th Kentucky also falling at Middle Creek. One unknown Confederate died the day after the battle and is buried in the Gearheart Cemetery near Hueysville.[27]

From a military standpoint, the action at Middle Creek brought an end to the first Confederate attempt to control the Upper Big Sandy River Valley. Due to the success of Garfield and his troops, the conflict is also labeled "the battle that launched a presidency." The National Historic Landmarks Program has noted that Middle Creek is also significant in that it "was an important victory for the Union and brought hope to a disheartened Northern population."[28] With these facts in mind, it is fitting that the battlefield has seen some level of success in relation to preserving the ground on which more than a dozen men died and the catalyst was provided for the rise of an American president.

Today, the battlefield at Middle Creek, the site of the largest battle in eastern Kentucky, has undergone a largely successful preservation campaign. The Fitzpatrick farm, the location of the battle, was owned by the same family since the late 1700s, and has been noted as undergoing "very little change" since the time of the battle. The battlefield has been described as "ridge and valley, hay fields and pasture." A 2008 U.S. Department of the Interior report noted that while "portions of landscape have been altered . . . most essential features remain." While only thirty-three of the 288 acres of the battlefield are classified as unprotected, just ten acres are classified as publicly accessible. Brown direction signs clearly mark the location of the battlefield near the intersection of Kentucky Routes 114 and 404, west of Prestonsburg.[29]

A great deal of this success is due to the work of the Middle Creek National Battlefield Foundation, Inc., an organization founded in 1992 to "honor the memory of the gallant men, both Union and Confederate, who fought and died at Middle Creek." Through the foundation's efforts, a large amount of preservation activities and public interpretation has taken place since 1993. These include a four-mile driving tour that includes stops such as Graveyard Point and the site of Garfield's post-battle headquarters at the Burns or Garfield House, wayside exhibits and signs, and an excellent Web site, middlecreek.org.[30]

Promoted on the Web site and clearly noticeable upon a visit to the battlefield are the efforts that have been used in creating an outstanding set of walking tours and trails. Two distinct trails, each approximately a quarter-mile in length and marked with several interpretive markers, are labeled as the Confederate Loop Trail and the Union Loop Trail. An extensive parking lot borders the trailheads as does a reader-friendly kiosk with four double-sided panels. These conduct a thorough overview of the situation that existed in Kentucky at the time of the Middle Creek battle.[31]

In addition, any visitor to the battlefield will gain a firm foundation of the battle by viewing the additional interpretive signs in the area. The latter is related to the Samuel May House, a Confederate recruiting post, and the May's gristmill, a site the Federal troops raided prior to the battle of Middle Creek. Future plans for the battlefield proper and the area include a visitor's center, a theater, and a library. The Middle Creek National Battlefield Foundation can be contacted for membership purposes, to make donations, or for additional information at P.O. Box 326, Prestonsburg, Kentucky, 41653 or by calling 606-886-1312.[32]

Another noteworthy organization related to the battlefield's preservation and interpretation is the Friends of Middlecreek. This organization was founded in 2008 and has experienced a high level of success. Using an annual reenactment of the battle and "education and community service," the goal is "to promote knowledge of [the] unique position in historic events and how those . . . had a lasting impact on Eastern Kentucky."[33]

The battleground at Middle Creek is certainly an example of preservation success. Perhaps the vision of the Middle Creek National Battlefield Foundation is one that similar organizations should view with envy and practice. Simply stated, the group says of its efforts, "We hope that what we are doing here will inspire visitors from other regions to work to preserve their own Civil War battlefields and historic sites."[34] With the groundwork being successfully laid, the area's potential is basically unlimited. The future will bear witness to the implementation of what has been done thus far.

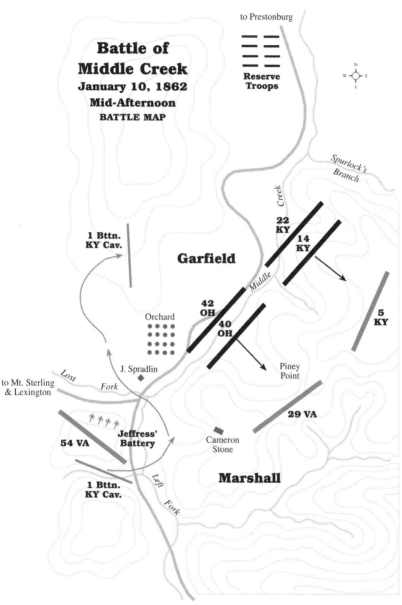

Battle of Middle Creek
January 10, 1862
Mid-Afternoon
BATTLE MAP

to Prestonburg

Reserve Troops

Spurlock's Branch

Creek

1 Bttn. KY Cav.

Garfield

22 KY

14 KY

Middle

5 KY

42 OH

Orchard

40 OH

Piney Point

Lost

J. Spradlin

Fork

to Mt. Sterling & Lexington

29 VA

54 VA

Jeffress' Battery

Cameron Stone

Left

1 Bttn. KY Cav.

Fork

Marshall

to Virginia

© Dave Roth, Blue & Gray Magazine
Columbus, Ohio / www.bluegraymagazine.com
(Based on Confederate General Humphrey Marshall's
map provided by Middle Creek National Battlefield.)

One of the Confederates deaths was Pvt. Stanford Lea Jessee from the 29th Virginia Infantry. The twenty-nine-year-old left behind a wife and five small children. (Courtesy of Gordon B. Jessee)

The location along Middle Creek where Federal artillery was positioned.
(Photo by author)

A marker and set of interpretive panels along the battlefield's perimeter.
(Photo by author)

The Union trail marker sits atop a hill bordering the scenic battlefield.
(Photo by author)

CHAPTER SEVEN

MILL SPRINGS

January 19,1862

"It was a place of carnage and death."
—Pvt. Manly Harris, 2nd Minnesota

Little more than a week after the struggle at Middle Creek, Kentucky, Confederate and Federal forces clashed in a battle that came to be known by the name of Mill Springs. Members of these armies, as well as historians and other interested parties, have assigned a lengthy collection of additional names to the battle, giving it one of the highest, if not the single highest, total for such. These include Logan's Crossroads, Fishing Creek, Beech Grove, Mill Spring, Mills Spring, Mill Creek, Somerset, Cliff Creek, Clifty Creek, Webb's Crossroads, Old Fields, and the Battle of the Cumberland. Dr. Kenneth A. Hafendorfer has submitted that Mill Springs has come to be the most accepted of these names, despite that fact that the battlefield is located ten miles from the springs. An official report from Union Brig. Gen. George Henry Thomas provided this designation and a series of articles in newspapers across the nation, as well as a note of praise from Abraham Lincoln; thus, the name stuck.[1]

The history of Mill Springs appears as early as 1700 when hunters and explorers located a spot "with excellent springs near a waterfall." In 1817 members of the Metcalf family moved into the area and established a spring-fed carding mill for cleaning and combing cotton, wool, or flax fibers. Seven years later fire destroyed the mill, but a gristmill, sawmill, and a variety of other structures were eventually built on the high bluffs of the area. In 1825, John Metcalfe, Jr. became the first postmaster of the newly established post office. The name soon given to the post office's location was Mill Springs, Kentucky.[2]

Brig. Gen. Felix Kirk Zollicoffer arrived in the same area on November 29, 1861, stopping one mile south of Mill Springs. His earlier attempt at probing the interior of Kentucky had been negated at Wildcat Mountain; his hopes were more positive for the second effort. Zollicoffer and his staff established their temporary headquarters on the south side of the Cumberland River at the home of a wealthy farmer named Allen Russell West, a strong pro-Union citizen in a largely pro-Confederate area of Kentucky. In addition to the twenty slaves that occupied various buildings on West's land, five members of the West family resided in the home at the time of Zollicoffer's arrival. The grounds around the residence quickly filled with soldiers and served as a supply depot for the Confederate army. Zollicoffer's superiors were clear in their orders for Zollicoffer's occupation of the area in that he "should occupy a position of observation merely until he should be re-enforced, or his troops be incorporated in the main command."[3]

Within days Union Brig. Gen. Albin Francisco Schoepf, Zollicoffer's foe at Wildcat Mountain, arrived at Camp Goggin, a Federal encampment near Waitsborough and only nine miles upriver from Mill Springs. On December 2, Schoepf reported that he "arrived . . . yesterday, reconnoitered same day and today. This morning the enemy opened fire from three pieces . . . and infantry." In fact, Zollicoffer had noted that a large number of Federal tents "were in full view" and the Confederate artillery "soon shelled them out of their encampment." As a result, according to Zollicoffer, the men in blue were forced to "retire out of sight."[4]

Schoepf estimated the Confederate strength at 2,000 infantry and 1,000 cavalry at the West Farm with another 5,000 Confederates within an additional five miles of "Captain West's farm." Reportedly,

West was known as "Captain" among citizens of the area, despite his questionable former military experience.[5]

Well aware of Zollicoffer's lack of military training and his past tactics, Brigadier General Schoepf stated that he was "apprehensive of the probability of" a Confederate crossing "at Mill Springs" and he noted an area east of the Federal camp could easily serve as a legitimate ford. In response, Schoepf, "detailed two companies of cavalry to that place."[6]

In the following days, numerous incidents occurred between the two armies. Zollicoffer's cavalry pickets drove away their Federal foes on December 3 and captured a small amount of materials including "a pistol, a saddle, and some other trappings."[7]

The following day Confederate cavalry pickets captured two severely wounded officers, a captain and a major, "after a chase of more than a mile." Subsequent Confederate patrols discovered entrenchments in the process of being completed on the banks of Fishing Creek, eleven miles from the current Confederate position, and another set of entrenchments only seven miles from Mill Springs.[8]

A confrontation at the Federal camp near Somerset on December 8 resulted in the killing of an estimated "10 or 12 and capturing 17 prisoners" and the acquisition "a number of muskets, pistols, accouterments, [and] articles of wearing apparel" from the Federal stores, while Zollicoffer reported Confederate losses of only "1 man and 2 horses killed."[9]

Against the suggestion of Confederate Gen. Albert Sidney Johnston, Zollicoffer determined that moving a majority of his command to the north side of the Cumberland River would provide a stronger defensive location. Zollicoffer had previously explained to Johnston, on December 2, that the Cumberland River was "very high" and that he was "building transports to enable me to cross, but I fear there will be several days' delay." However, on December 14 Zollicoffer reported from the north side of the Cumberland that, "On the 5th, 6th, 7th, and 8th, we were employed crossing, by aid of a few boats."[10]

Dr. Kenneth A. Hafendorfer, the author of an extensive study on the Mill Springs Campaign, explained that the move on Zollicoffer's part was not only intended to offer a strong defensive position, but also "with its mere potential of striking a flanking blow, would deter any Federal thoughts of moving a column from the area of Columbia to gain his rear south of the river." Hafendorfer best summarizes Zollicoffer's mindset in stating that the Confederate general was "going to give up a strong defensive position . . . but by moving to the north bank and posing an offensive threat, he believed that he would improve his defensive posture."[11]

The Confederate camp on the north side of the Cumberland was called Beech Grove; another name, Zollie's Den, would be used as well. At Beech Grove, an estimated 800 to 1,000 huts were built according to Zollicoffer's December 20, 1861 order to "protect the forces . . . against inclement weather." Regimental, battalion, and corps commanders met with Confederate engineer Capt. Victor Sheliha and made suggestions "as to the cheapest and most readily constructed style of hut . . . sufficient to protect against bad weather." At that point Sheliha was to "at once employ all the available force and implements that can be spared from the general defense" in the process of constructing the quarters. The units set to occupy the Beech Grove camp were the 16th Alabama, 15th Mississippi, and the 19th, 20th, 25th, and 28th Tennessee Regiments. The 17th and 29th Tennessee Regiments were to maintain a support position at Mill Springs.[12]

Historians throughout the last century and a half have regularly deemed Zollicoffer's move to Beech Grove a poor tactical move due to the fact that the Cumberland River blocked the Confederate route of retreat to the south. Despite this situation, many agree that the construction of the earthworks and cabins at Beech Grove was a feat completed in a quick manner. Zollicoffer informed a fellow officer that hunger should not be an issue at Beech Grove as, "Pork, corn, beef, hay, or fodder, horses . . . are abundant and cheap here . . . the supply of flour will be good."[13]

Members of Confederate regiments provided proof of Zollicoffer's statement in writing that they were "living fat" and that they were "well fixed in our mess for a while." The bountiful supply of food likely aided in the timely construction of the hundreds of huts, each able to house at least four men. The log cabins contained walls that were well chinked and dug some three feet into the ground. For extra comfort, each contained a chimney. The size of the cabins varied, as did the amenities; glass windows, as well as wooden floors, were not scarce.[14]

Beech Grove, located on a peninsula and directly across the river from Mill Springs, allegedly gained its name from local citizens. Zollicoffer's perceived strength of its defensive position was largely due to the fact that it was situated between White Oak Creek on the west and the Cumberland River on the east. The banks of the Cumberland in the area were some three hundred feet high, eliminating all approaches except from the north. Beech Grove peninsula's north-end defenses consisted of fortifications that ran more than half a mile and were arranged "so that 5 or 6 regiments can defend the entire line of that side." One of the Confederates stationed at Beech Grove estimated, "from the breastworks to the point in the bend of the river is about one mile . . . breastworks extend around the point of the bend leaving a narrow strip of land . . . entirely protected by the hill."[15]

Union Brig. Gen. Don Carlos Buell determined that the Confederate position should be attacked in a timely manner, and he ordered Brig. Gen. George Thomas to move forward and force the Confederates back across the Cumberland. Thomas left Lebanon on New Year's Eve with the Second Brigade, two regiments of Colonel McCook's brigade, Kinney's artillery, and a detachment of Wolford's cavalry in tow.[16] It would be up to these units and those soon to join them, to attack the Confederates stationed at Mill Springs.

Pvt. Morgan Parker of the 1st Michigan Engineers and Mechanics remarked how the large, heavily loaded Federal wagons "cut the roads down so that they were impassable after the first two or three regiments had passed." With the situation at hand, Parker and his fellow mechanics began using picks, shovels, spades, and mechanical tools as they "cut new roads, fixed and repaired old one, built crossings . . . pushed wagons through the mud with our hands, and held them up in deep ruts and on steep hillsides . . . repaired wagons when broken, shod horses and mules when needed . . . leaving some of the heaviest loads behind."[17]

Another Federal soldier, Mastin Dashiel of the 3rd Indiana Cavalry, was in his mid-forties when the Civil War started. He joined Capt. Graham's Company of the Indiana Mounted Volunteers, determined to serve his country. In his letter that appeared in the February 6, 1862 issue of the Indianapolis *Daily Journal,* Dashiel wrote that the approach to Mill Springs and the subsequent occupation of the area provided "some of Graham's squadron an opportunity to look slightly into 'Dixie', and to there behold some of its deluded soldiers, who profess to be fighting for their rights."[18]

On the Confederate side, Maj. Gen. George Crittenden arrived at Mill Springs on January 3, 1862. Crittenden was surprised to find that General Zollicoffer maintained a position on the north side of the Cumberland. Crittenden recalled that Zollicoffer was, "hoping to be able to convince me that it would be better to remain on the right bank, he had postponed crossing until, by a rise in the river, it had become impossible to do so . . . I was dissatisfied."[19]

Crittenden believed that an attack against the advancing Federal troops would be more advantageous than to await the arrival of the full Union force from within the Confederate earthworks at Mill Springs. Lt. Albert Roberts of the 20th Tennessee served as a correspondent for the *Memphis Daily Avalanche* at Mill Springs. Roberts wrote, "Crittenden had information . . . that the enemy was concentrating large forces around his position at Mill Springs, with the evident determination to cut off his supplies and starve out our little army." Roberts felt that it was Crittenden's mindset to take the attack to the Federals as he wrote, "General C. concluded . . . to fight the enemy . . . and, if possible, drive them back."[20]

David Anderson Deaderick, a member of Confederate Lt. Col. Benjamin Branner's 4th Battalion, Tennessee Cavalry, recalled the situation of the time. Deaderick wrote, "On the 18th of Jany., 1862, order came . . . to prepare two days rations and hold ourselves in readiness to move at any moment. It was understood . . . that 6 or 7 thousand Federals had crossed Fishing Creek, and we were going to meet them after being in camp for so long a time without doing much fighting."[21]

Historical writings on the battle of Mill Springs note that Crittenden actually believed that no more than 2,000 Federal troops were at Logan's Crossroads and should prove little opposition for the 4,500 Confederates at Crittenden's disposal. Capt. Albert Marks of the 17th Tennessee analyzed the orders given and determined, "Crittenden's adopted plan was for the regiments to assail the enemy as soon as he was reached, without an effort to form a general line."[22]

Another Confederate wrote, "We were ordered to cook two days rations . . . and towards evening we received orders to march at 12 o'clock . . . in the direction of Fishing Creek."[23]

One historian noted that the rains of recent days had had a serious effect upon Fishing Creek, a tributary of the Cumberland. He wrote, "Owing to continuous rains, this mountainous stream had become so increased as to be impossible of fording."[24]

The effects of the rains would have major repercussions upon troop movements and the military actions that lay ahead. Zollicoffer's Confederates, under orders from Crittenden, moved north from Beech Grove near midnight as a gentle rain fell. As the men in gray marched throughout the night in an ever-increasing rain, their Federal counterparts fared no better.[25]

Pvt. James Baker, a member of the 1st Ohio Light Artillery, remarked that he and his comrades were without tents during the rainy night of January 18-19, although some were able to find shelter with others who were more fortunate.[26]

Another Federal artilleryman, Pvt. Joseph G. Durfee, 9th Ohio Battery, recalled that he and his fellow battery members "lay all night in the rain" and that the next morning they "were a sorry set of boys."[27]

Infantryman Lt. Oliver Eckels of the 31st Ohio added, "It commenced raining . . . and rained hard all night . . . both regiments laid out in the rain without anything to shelter them from the dashing rain . . . nothing under them but the wet ground, and nothing over them but one blanket."[28]

Recalling the Confederate march, Lt. Albert Roberts of the 20th Tennessee Infantry wrote, "the roads were in wretched condition for the task we had before us, the dust being reduced to the consistency of mush, sometimes knee-deep, and in many places almost impassable."[29]

Roberts detailed the march in noting, "At midnight we started . . . the most cheerless and disagreeable night I have ever experienced, to attack an enemy . . . Long before we reached the vicinity of the enemy, our troops were completely fagged out, from the great difficulty of dragging themselves through the thick, heavy slush, in almost Egyptian darkness. Before daylight a cold rain commenced falling, which saturated our clothing and rendered progress still more difficult and disagreeable."[30]

Another Confederate, Pvt. Spencer Talley of the 28th Tennessee, recalled that he joined his comrades in tearing down some of the roadside fences and burning them to keep warm. Talley added, "The night was very cold and it had been raining, sleeting, or snowing all night."[31]

Despite having to endure a march through varying forms of precipitation, the Confederates trudged forward. The lead units, cavalrymen belonging to captains Willis Bledsoe and Quincy Sanders, reached the area of Timmy's Branch near 6 a.m. on the 19th. Timmy's Branch, "a shallow tributary of Clifty Creek," intersected the Mill Springs road approximately two miles from Logan's Crossroads.[32]

Some twenty men of Sgt. George Thrasher's command of the 1st Kentucky were positioned at the location and, through the dark and foggy morning, the Federal pickets heard the approaching Confederates. Reportedly, a challenge of "Halt! Who goes there?" was shouted from the pickets. At that point a shot was fired, though sources contradict about which side fired first.[33] The battle of Mill Springs had begun.

A quick exchange of fire resulted in the Federal pickets retrieving their horses and moving up the Mill Springs Road toward the Federal camps. Sergeant Thrasher set up a defensive position near a cabin located approximately one-quarter of a mile north of Timmy's Branch. Thrasher then sent word that an undetermined number of Confederates were in the vicinity.[34]

Hearing the shots, Zollicoffer ordered the 15th Mississippi Infantry and 19th Tennessee Infantry Regiments forward. Another exchange of fire occurred when members of these units reached Thrasher's position near Timmy's Branch.[35]

Crittenden reported that as the Confederate infantrymen reached the cabin, the well-positioned pickets delivered deadly volleys into the ranks of the men in gray. He wrote, "From this house and woods in the rear of it quite a brisk firing opened upon the head of the column."[36]

With the arrival of sunlight, the Federal pickets became fully aware of the strength of the enemy they faced. A contested retreat began as fighting continued across wooded areas and land known as "Old Fields" among the residents of the area. The land reportedly belonged to the local Burton families. The series of small fields had seen little use in recent times and, as a result, were regularly dotted with underbrush or fenced in with remnants of corn and other crops. Additionally, a thirty-five-foot-tall hill in the area lay approximately 1¼ miles south of Logan's Crossroads and, due to the family surname that bore prominence in the area, was called Burton's Hill.[37]

William L. Burton, the ten-year-old son of one of the area's namesakes, recalled the ensuing events in an article published decades after the war. William wrote, "about daylight . . . up comes the Rebel pickets . . . They hadn't gone far when a musket cracked and one of them tumbled down in the mud . . . They had run square into a Yankee outpost . . . puffs of smoke came up from where the Yankees were shooting; up the road a piece . . . some Rebels came up the road but they spread out in the thickets and pretty soon here come Zolly a-riding his horse . . . he was a fine looking man."[38]

In the Federal camp Col. Mahlon Manson received a courier who informed him of the Confederate attack to the south. Manson hurriedly ordered additional Federal units forward. Among them was the 4th Kentucky, under the command of Col. Speed Fry. The 4th Kentucky formed rapidly and, "Fry led them at double-quick in the direction of the firing." With no orders to do so and lacking specific directions from anyone, Fry chose a position behind a fence with woods to the rear and an open field to his front. The right side of Fry's line stood near the Mill Springs Road. A company of the 10th Indiana and fragments of the Federal picket rallied at Fry's position and prepared for the Confederate attack.[39]

A member of the 10th Indiana Infantry Regiment wrote in *Harper's Weekly* that the battle came as a surprise to the members of his camp. The young man stated, "At six o'clock Sunday morning Captain Perkins came in and reported every thing was quiet. Hardly had he got away from the tent when one of Wolford's cavalry rode up and said our pickets were firing."[40]

Fry's troops witnessed the Confederates advancing "from the shelter of woodland on the opposite side" of the open field. A ravine ran through the open field to Fry's front and a large number of Confederates used the cut to gain a strong position. The ravine was described in relation to Fry's position as "heading near the road on his right, with steep sides in his front, but sloping gradually beyond" the Federal left.[41]

The Confederates used the ravine to move within a short distance of the Federal line at the fence before they "delivered their fire." A Federal soldier wrote that Fry "was at once subjected to a severe attack." According to this same witness, Fry had earlier climbed atop the fence and "in stentorian tones denounced them [the Confederate troops] as dastards, and defied them to stand up on their feet and come forward like men."[42]

The Confederate advance stalled just short of flanking the Federal right. Apparently the inexperience of the majority of the soldiers combined with simple fatigue and the low level of visibility created by fog and black-powder smoke to create confusion that temporarily halted the Confederate attack.

The battle of Mill Springs was approximately one hour into its duration when the feelings of its premature conclusion, brought about by the momentary silence, appeared. The dampness of the weather had a devastating effect upon the Confederate flint-locks that performed best in dry conditions, as they required a spark to ignite the black powder. A Federal soldier estimated that as many as two-thirds of Crittenden's soldiers were armed with flint-locks, "common rifles and shot-guns."[43]

Pvt. James L. Cooper of the 20th Tennessee testified to this situation in writing, "The rain was descending in torrents and our flint lock muskets were in bad condition; not one in three would fire." Cooper recalled that after his gun went off the first time during the action of the battle, he "wiped the pan and primed a dozen times" and was unable to get the weapon to fire again.[44]

Lt. Albert Roberts, also a member of the 20th Tennessee, remarked on the situation. "For three quarters of an hour [the battle] as one incessant, deafening rattle of small arms . . . it commenced raining, and the priming in the pans of our muskets became wet and the pieces refused to fire. In this the enemy had a fearful advantage in their percussion lock rifles . . . We were in a fearful strait, with guns rendered utterly useless by the rain, and no supporting regiment coming to our assistance."[45]

Ironically, Colonel Fry, as well as General Zollicoffer, used the lull in the fighting to ride to the Federal right to scout the situation at hand. Fry reportedly desired a better understanding of the Confederate flanking movement in that sector of the battlefield. Zollicoffer had apparently become convinced that the soldiers possessing properly-firing guns may have been firing into other Confederate ranks.[46] The ensuing events would have a deadly effect for the Confederate high command.

Zollicoffer and a small group of aides rode to the front to evaluate the situation. The officers attending Zollicoffer were Lt. Henry

Fogg, Lt. Evan Shields, and Sgt. Maj. Henry Ewing. Zollicoffer proceeded forward despite the alleged pleas of numerous parties to avoid doing so from a safety perspective.[47]

One early twentieth century historian recalled, "Zollicoffer . . . rode forward to inspect the position of the enemy and ascertain the situation, it being impossible to see clearly through the gloom and rain . . . By mistake he passed his own line and around the flank of the 4th Kentucky Infantry" under Fry's command. [48] Fry moved toward the same location as Zollicoffer and a tragically chance meeting took place.

More than twenty years after the incident, Fry recorded a report of the events. Fry wrote,

> In order to ascertain more certainly the exact state of affairs, the firing having ceased, I rode from the right of my regiment . . . to the fence behind which we had been fighting, and, discovering no enemy in that direction, I turned my horse and rode slowly back to the place I had just left. As I neared the road I saw an officer riding slowly down the road . . . within twenty paces of the right of my regiment. His uniform was concealed except the extremities of his pantaloons, which I observed were of the color worn by Federal officers, by a long green overcoat. His near approach to my regiment, his calm manner, my close proximity to him, indeed everything I saw led me to believe he was a Federal officer belonging to one of the regiments just arriving . . . I did not hesitate to ride up to his side so closely that our knees touched. He was calm, self-possessed and dignified in manner. He said to me, 'We must not shoot our own men,' to which I responded, 'Of course not; I would not do so intentionally,' then turning his eyes to his left and pointing in the same direction he said, 'those are our men.' I could not see the men from my position, but I supposed they were there. I immediately moved off to the right of my regiment, perhaps some fifteen or twenty paces from the spot on which I met him. His language convinced me more than ever that he was a federal officer. How it is that he did not discover that I was one I cannot tell, as my uniform was entirely exposed to view, having on nothing to conceal it. As soon as I reached my regiment, I paused, turning my horse a little to the left, and across the road,

looked back to see what was going on, when, to my great surprise, another officer whom I had not seen rode out from behind a tree near the place of my meeting with the first officer, and, with pistol in hand, leveled it directly at me, fired, and paused for a moment, doubtless to observe the effect of his shot. Instead of striking the object at which it was aimed, the ball struck my horse just above the hipbone making a flesh wound. I immediately drew my Colt's revolver from the holster, and was about to fire, when he retreated behind a tree. Not until this time was I aware that I had been in conversation with an officer of the opposing army. In an instant the thought flashed across my mind that the officer with whom I had met and conversed had attempted to draw me into the snare of death or secure my capture by a false representation of his position, and feeling thus, I aimed at him and fired.[49]

The officer who fired at Fry was Lieutenant Fogg, who reportedly yelled, "General, It's the enemy," before firing. Fry's responding shot struck Zollicoffer in the left hip, while nearby members of Fry's command, the 4th Kentucky, fired at Fogg, mortally wounding him. Zollicoffer was also hit by a number of other shots, one of which was a wound to the chest.[50]

One period historian recorded that the fatal shot to Zollicoffer's breast was a pistol shot while two other musket balls inflicted other injuries. Another account in *Harper's Weekly* confirmed three wounds, but proposed that the fatal shot "was from an Enfield rifle." Various accounts of Zollicoffer's last words were written, one of which noted that he proclaimed, "Go on . . . my brave boys. I am killed." Regardless of what, if any, statement he uttered, Zollicoffer died moments after being struck. Lt. Evan Shields stepped from his horse and attempted to retrieve Zollicoffer's body, but was shot in both hips. Shields, like Fogg, succumbed to his wounds, leaving Ewing as the sole member of those attending Zollicoffer to return to the safety of the Confederate lines.[51]

Despite claims to the contrary, the exact identity of the individual who killed Zollicoffer is unknown. Capt. William H. Honnell of the 1st Kentucky Cavalry stated that Fry fired the fatal shot and thus gave Fry the title of "slayer of Gen. Zollicoffer."[52] However, practically as many self-proclaimed and legitimate witnesses denounce Fry as the man who slew Zollicoffer as say he delivered the projectile. In addition, a variety of stories abound regarding what, if any, possessions and types of relics were taken from Zollicoffer's body following his death.

Pvt. Thomas C. Potter of the 1st Ohio Battery made the claim that he was within a short distance of Zollicoffer "when he fell and cut three buttons from his coat." Potter's statement was made in a letter written to his sister less than a week after the battle.[53]

Lemuel F. Drake, chaplain of the 31st Ohio Infantry, wrote to his hometown newspaper, the *Perry County Weekly* of New Lexington, Ohio, about witnessing Zollicoffer's body. Although the 31st Ohio did not participate in the battle, it arrived on the field as reinforcements on the night of January 19. Drake explained, "I saw Zollicoffer, the rebel General . . . cold in death, stretched out on a board in a tent. He was about six feet tall, and well built. One of the finest heads I ever saw upon the shoulders of any man . . . The South . . . lost one of their bravest and best generals."[54]

Chaplain William H. Honnell of the 1st Kentucky Cavalry admitted to cutting a white oak stick from the area near Zollicoffer's death as a souvenir. Honnell "noticed that it had five bullet marks and clots of blood on it." He also acknowledged the rumors surrounding the defacing of Zollicoffer's body.[55]

Honnell remarked in an 1894 essay, "It was charged by the Confederates that the body of Gen. Zollicoffer was terribly outraged on the battlefield, pulling out his hair, etc. The facts of the case are these . . . some of the privates, out of mere thoughtlessness, not thinking how bad it looked, tore his clothes in order to produce souvenirs of the noted general; but . . . his body was removed from the field, nicely laid out, and a guard placed over him. Nobody but the guard was even allowed to uncover his face for those who wished to see him. There was a ruffled place in his hair on one side of his head, which appeared as if a lock of hair had been plucked out, but it did not disfigure his looks." Honnell also claimed to have joined other soldiers in moving Zollicoffer's lifeless body "from near the road, back toward the fence line."[56]

A series of letters in the early 1900s addressed a Minnesota resident who claimed to have a bracelet that one of the post-mortem relic-seekers took from Zollicoffer's body. Mrs. Octavia Zollicoffer Bond, a daughter of the late general, graciously acknowledged the Northern lady's request to hear from one of Zollicoffer's family members in writing, "Thanking those who would restore the bracelet, the daughters of General Zollicoffer beg to say . . . it is not credible that their father wore such an ornament. Notably simple in dress, he never wore at any time either a ring, gold shirt button, or scarf pin, the only adornment of his scrupulously neat attire being a watch and chain." Mrs. Bond continued to explain other "articles" allegedly taken from her father's body, "the false teeth, said to have been taken from his mouth . . . the epaulets from his shoulders, and the pistols and field glass from his saddle . . . His teeth were all natural and quite sound . . . the epaulets were not genuine."[57]

Mrs. Bond held her father in high esteem, and Gen. Bennett Young also spoke highly of the deceased general. In a speech given a few years after the battle, Young commented, "There was always something pathetic to me in the death of General Zollicoffer. He had been a brilliant statesman, a versatile scholar, and an excellent soldier. He was possessed of great wisdom, endowed with the highest degree of courage, and on the battlefield was calm and collected . . . I doubt not that in the passing instant of consciousness, when death stared him in the face, when probably he realized that the end was at hand, his last prayer and thought was for heaven's care over the . . . children . . . who in their home on the banks of the Cumberland, near Nashville, were all unconscious of the tremendous sacrifice a nation's cause was demanding of their noble and chivalrous father."[58]

Perhaps the highest praise and admiration for Zollicoffer came from a Southerner who wrote an article for *Confederate Veteran* in 1907. Margaret Boyles concluded her exposé in noting, "He was among the first who laid down their lives, but his influence lived. His nobility, courage, and purity shaped other men's lives, gave them ideals for action, inspired them to noble deeds. He lived again in the lives of his devoted men. He shall ever live as one of the heroes of our South."[59]

Although Zollicoffer's death had lasting effects on an untold number of individuals in the civilian and military sectors of the nation for years to come, the immediate impact upon the Confederate troops at Mill Springs can not be underestimated. A member of the 19th Tennessee, Capt. Carrick Heiskell, stated that he and other members of his regiment saw Zollicoffer fall. Evidently, at least partially in reaction to Zollicoffer's death, the 19th Tennessee, in Crittenden's words, "broke its line and gave back" in what William Worsham of the 19th Tennessee declared was "in some disorder." The retreat was likely hastened with the arrival of additional Federal ammunition, providing the men in blue with an additional advantage over the retreating and poorly armed Confederates. The men of the 4th Kentucky fired at the retreating Confederates until they were out of range, at which time silence again fell upon the Mill Springs battlefield. Col. Robert Kelly of the 4th Kentucky added, "The fall of Zollicoffer and the sharp fighting that followed caused two of his regiments to retreat in confusion."[60]

General Crittenden ordered Brig. Gen. William Carroll forward in an effort to "sustain the gallant Fifteenth Mississippi" in a charge that was in the process of being initiated. Carroll reported, "I accordingly ordered Colonel Murray's regiment to move forward to the foot of the hill and take shelter behind a rail fence and some surrounding timber. In a few minutes the chivalrous Mississippians gallantly charged and were driving the enemy rapidly before them."[61]

The men of the 15th Mississippi moved forward with the rebel yell filling the air. Unfortunately, the men of the Magnolia State were walking into an utter ambush. Pvt. Charles Frierson of the 15th Mississippi remarked that the Federals "got out in the timber and fired on us heavily in the open field. There we fell a man to the minute for we were nearly surrounded."[62]

Brigadier General Carroll reinforced Frierson's analysis of the situation and added that a regiment of cavalry began a flanking movement against the left of the 15th Mississippi. In response, Carroll ordered Col. John Murray's regiment to reinforce the left of the 15th Mississippi. Shouts arose from members of Murray's command as they "led by their colonel, dashed into the thickest of the fight."[63]

Union Gen. George Thomas, now on the scene, decided to meet this "by placing a section of Kenny's battery on the left of the 4th Kentucky, which was overlapped by Carroll's line, ordered the 12th Kentucky to the left of Kenny's two guns, and Carter with the two East Tennessee regiments, and Wetmore's battery still farther to the left, in font of the Somerset road." Despite this movement, noted Colonel Kelly, "There was little opportunity for the effective use of artillery on either side."[64]

Although the effectiveness of the artillery fire may have been minimal, a member of the 4th Tennessee Cavalry, Robert Deaderick, acknowledged its impact on his emotions. The young soldier exclaimed, "the artillery commenced their fire, which with the sounds of their balls whizzing by and the whistling Minnie balls over our heads made it still more fierce." Deaderick proclaimed that he also witnessed a cannon ball "coming in my direction, striking the ground about 12 feet in front. It glanced and struck the horse on my right in the eye, knocked the horse down, throwing the rider."[65]

Capt. Arthur M. Rutledge's Tennessee Light Artillery Battery consisted of six guns and was under the command of a West Point graduate. Hailing from Davidson County, Tennessee, the battery saw action at Mill Springs as Rutledge himself served as artillery staff officer. Although, as Kelly noted, the fire of this and other batteries was of little effect, Rutledge's Battery used two guns to fire from the Mill Springs Road in support of the 15th Mississippi Regiment.[66] The sounds of the battery were undoubtedly welcome in the Confederate ranks, as the 15th Mississippi and the 20th Tennessee carried the bulk of the responsibility of the Confederate attack for more than an hour with little support.

Lt. Albert Roberts, 20th Tennessee, recalled the viciousness of the situation his regiment faced. Roberts stated,

> We were ordered to charge right in among the Yankees, and . . . went forward with a yell that made the woods resound. As we rose the first hill, the hissing of the bullets past our ears, and the dead cluck of the Minnie balls in the solid timber, seemed to exceed in shrillness the crash of the rifles that were discharged in our faces. On we went, down the slope, across the ravine and up the next hill, the leaden messengers dealing death and destruction in our ranks.[67]

A Federal soldier added, "The rebels fell like grass before the wind."[68]

Lieutenant Roberts explained the situation the members of the 20th Tennessee faced, "They reserved their fire until we had approached quite close upon their fortifications, and then they opened upon us a murderous fire, so constant, so regular and so deadly, that no troops in the world could withstand it . . . Our charge was all that saved the Mississippians . . . the enemy's bullets never came so fast as they did on this occasion. It really seemed as if one could just hold out his open hand and gather bullets by the handful!"[69]

During one of the charges upon the Federal position, the Hickory Guards of the 20th Tennessee lost eight men killed and wounded. Among this number was the temporary company commander, the "gallant and noble First Lieutenant," Balie Peyton, Jr., the son of a Tennessee Congressman who had objected to young Balie joining the Confederate army. In his late twenties, Peyton led his company in the charge and gained a position near the Federal works before being shot in the forehead. Pvt. William Wells, Company I, 2nd Minnesota, recalled that while Peyton stood "two rods from our line, firing right oblique into Company I, a bullet from his revolver had just severely wounded Lieutenant Tenbroeck Stout." Through a clearing in the smoke Lt. Calvin Uline spotted Peyton and ordered

Pvt. Adam Wickett to fire at Peyton. Wickett followed the order, striking Peyton, who then "breathed his last."[70]

Despite suffering horrendously high casualties among their ranks, the 20th Tennessee and the 15th Mississippi were able to reach the Federal line at a fence on the west side of the corn field and immediately east of the north-south running Old Road, a link to the Mill Springs Road. With the 15th Mississippi holding the southern-most position with the 20th Tennessee to its right, the two Confederate regiments occupied the area with only a fence separating them from the 4th Kentucky and, to its left, the 2nd Minnesota.[71]

The only respite from the tenacity of the struggle at the fence was the fact that the rain had temporarily ended. William Bircher, the drummer for the 2nd Minnesota Infantry, remarked that his regiment had charged up to the fence where the members engaged in a hand-to-hand struggle. Bircher's words were, "The rebels put their guns through the fence from one side and our boys from the other. The smoke hung close to the ground . . . it was impossible to see each other at times."[72]

A member of the 10th Indiana Infantry Regiment wrote an article that appeared in the March 8, 1862 issue of *Harper's Weekly* and mentioned the variety of weapons used during the struggle at the fence. The infantryman wrote, "At one time we were so close to the enemy that we bayoneted them through the fence. The Mississippians were armed with immense knives, which they intended using on us, but our bayonets outreached their knives."[73]

A Confederate's letter in the January 30, 1862 issue of the *Memphis Daily Avalanche* recorded the impression that the incidents at the fence made upon a member of Rutledge's Tennessee Battery. The artilleryman proclaimed that his battery "mowed them [Federal soldiers] down by the wholesale" while the 20th Tennessee made four charges and the 15th Mississippi a total of five. He recalled the result of the charges, "as brilliant charges as were ever made by Southern troops," was that the two Confederate regiments and the identical number of Federal units met in the deadly clash at the fence at which time the Confederates were "fighting the enemy through the fence with bayonets, or pelting the cowards over the head with the butts of their guns."[74]

The melee at the fence made lasting impressions on the men involved in the struggle. David Griffin of the 2nd Minnesota remarked that as his regiment witnessed the advancing Confederates, "the Minnesota boys came up to them with an Indian yell and such a volley as there was poured upon them for 40 minutes, was never heard . . . we were so close to each other that some of our boys pulled their guns out of their hands." Another soldier wrote, "We were so close . . . that one of the men had his beard and whiskers singed by the fire of one of the muskets . . . another caught hold of one of their muskets and jerked it through the fence. The two stood and fired at each other, their muskets crossing; both fell dead." A member of the 15th Mississippi added to the description in exclaiming, "Our entire line, putting their guns through the cracks of the fence, fired into them with ball and buckshot . . . The screams and groans, officers cursing and begging . . . to rally their men. I shall never forget the scene . . . makes my blood run cold to think of it." The situation at the fence was summed up well in the words of Minnesota infantryman Pvt. Manly Harris who stated, "It wasn't a pleasant place to be . . . it wasn't safe even a little bit . . . It was a place of carnage and death."[75]

The situation became unbearable for the Confederates when the 9th Ohio arrived and made a bayonet charge. An official report noted that the largely-German descent members "of the 9th Ohio calmly unloaded their rifles, fixed bayonets, and cheering as they advanced, made one of the few successful bayonet charges of the Civil War." The Confederate left broke into "a disorderly retreat."[76]

In what is regarded as one of the few successful bayonet charges of the Civil War, the members of the 9th Ohio had responded to Col. Robert McCook's order. McCook, in noting the "superior number of the enemy and their bravery," determined that the only means of avoiding the Confederates overrunning the Federal position was to launch a bayonet charge in hopes of reversing the tide of the battle.[77]

General Thomas described the situation in stating, "The 2nd Minnesota kept up a most galling fire in front, and the 9th Ohio charged the enemy on the right with bayonets fixed, turned their flank, and drove them from the field, the whole giving away and retreating in the utmost disorder and confusion." James Scully, a member of Thomas's staff, praised the efforts and success of the bayonet charge, calling it "the grand charge of the Gallant McCook with his Dutchman."[78]

Another Federal soldier wrote, "Our regiment then went forward to . . . 'Charge bayonets!' which was done with a will, and everything went before us."[79]

The 28th Tennessee had been on the extreme Confederate left when the collapse of the line began. The regiment was positioned in areas interspersed with grape vines and dense underbrush, when ordered to hastily retreat or be cut off. Pvt. Spencer Talley of the 28th Tennessee tried to exit the thicket when his foot became entangled in a vine. Attempts to join his comrades in the retreat were negated when Talley regularly became trampled under their feet. Talley reminisced, "I found . . . that my hat and gun were twenty feet behind me . . . I was way behind and the 'Minnie balls' flying thick and fast about me . . . we had to cross an open field, the ground was soft and wet and covered with grass which made the mud stick fast to our feet. Before I reached the woodland on the opposite side of the field my feet felt as if there was twenty pounds to each foot."[80]

Talley and his fellow Confederates found it best to comply with Gen. William Henry Carroll's order to leave the area of Logan's Crossroads. Carroll stated that he perceived the fortunes of the day were against the men in gray and that his forces could "no longer maintain the unequal contest." Thus, he made the decision to initiate the retreat toward the Confederate works at Mill Springs.[81]

During the retreat Lt. Albert Roberts of the 20th Tennessee noted, "Everybody seemed to be retreating, though nobody was running to an alarming extent." Roberts added that the occasional sound of cannon mingled with those of "the enemy shooting at stragglers in the rear." Due to the high level of fatigue he was suffering at the time, Roberts determined to "go slow and trust to luck, even at the risk of being taken prisoner."[82]

General Thomas issued additional ammunition to his Federal troops prior to their pursuit of the retreating Confederates. Effective rear guard action and a valiant effort from the 17th and 29th Tennessee and 16th Alabama slowed the pursuit of the Federal troops and enabled the Confederates to reach the safety of their works at Beech Grove. Historian Geoffrey Walden explained that after three to four hours of hard fighting, "Confederate valor and determination were simply not enough to compensate for their outdated weapons and command level confusion."[83]

The Federals closely following the Confederate retreat encountered a road frequented with materials the men in gray abandoned during the rapid retreat that had "degenerated into a panic." A Federal officer recalled, "A piece of artillery was found abandoned in a mud hole, hundred of muskets were strewn along the road and in the fields, and, most convincing proof of all, the flying foe had thrown away their haversacks filled with rations of corn pone and bacon."[84]

Under this premise, the Federal soldiers reached the outskirts of the Confederate camp at Beech Grove where, as one Federal officer observed, "As these were approached they were invested by the division deployed in the line of battle . . . During the night preparations were made for an assault . . . the following morning."[85]

Pvt. Joseph Durfee recalled joining his fellow members of the 9th Ohio Battery as they "commenced firing and continued till dark." This claim was substantiated in the words of Lt. Albert Roberts, 20th Tennessee who recorded the time of arrival at Beech Grove as approximately "five o'clock . . . and had barely set foot inside of our own breastworks before the cannon of the enemy commenced bombarding us."[86]

The Federal artillery noted in Roberts's and Durfee's recollections was deployed along high ground known as Moulden's Hill. The Federal bombardment on Beech Grove was directed from this location. A token Confederate resistance was offered as members of the 37th Tennessee "opened fire . . . which was quite briskly returned for a few minutes . . . though the bullets came in among us right lively none of us were hurt."[87]

As the Federal soldiers braced for a possible Confederate attack and prepared for the Federal advance upon the Confederate camp on the morning of January 20, the 4,000 Confederates began an evacuation across the Cumberland River. Crittenden's decision to make the move occurred near midnight when "orders came for us to retreat quietly across the river."[88]

A report of the Confederate evacuation explained, "The steamer *Noble Ellis,* with three barges attached, commenced the work of transportation, and though we abandoned baggage and wagons, horses and cannon, and everything save what we had on our backs, the whole night was consumed in getting the army over the river, which was very high at the time."[89]

In order to prevent the Federal capture of the *Noble Ellis,* General Crittenden had it burned. One Confederate officer, Capt. Victor Von Sheliha, a member of Crittenden's staff, remarked, "Fourteen pieces of artillery were placed on the boat; Gen. Crittenden ordered them spiked and the boat burned, and the guns are now at the bottom of the Cumberland." This claim is questionable, as there appears to be no proof the cannons were loaded onto the boat. Historian Geoffrey Walden has noted though that rumors abound that Confederate cannons rest on the bottom of the Cumberland River near the Mill Springs bank.[90]

Soon after daylight on January 20, the Federal soldiers entered the Confederate camp, only to find it abandoned. Though the camp lacked human occupation, the amount of goods and supplies left behind was mindboggling to the Federals. One of the invading Union soldiers recalled, "their tents having been left standing and their blankets, clothes, cooking utensils, letters, papers, etc . . . all left behind . . . all, or nearly all of their wagons, some twelve or fifteen hundred horses and mules, harness, saddles, sabers, guns . . . cannon, with caissons, are also here."[91]

Pvt. James Baker added that the captured camp included "14 pieces of artillery, a considerate amount of ammunition, 125 wagons loaded with baggage . . . hogsheads of sugar and molasses, the bags of flour and meal, piles of corn and . . . tobacco . . . some of the nicest clothing I ever saw." Expanding upon Baker's recollection, a reporter proclaimed that the Federal achievements had created "a glorious and complete victory."[92]

Sadly, the conclusion of the battle of Mill Springs created a situation that became all too familiar in the coming years of the American Civil War: caring for the wounded and burying the dead. The initial casualty reports were large for both armies as Crittenden and Thomas acknowledged the losses suffered in the bloody hours of fighting on the rain-soaked fields of Kentucky.

In his official report of the battle at Mill Springs, Brig. Gen. George Thomas listed regimental totals for officers and enlisted men. For the 10th Indiana, ten enlisted men were killed, with three officers and seventy-two men wounded. The 1st Kentucky Cavalry had one officer and two men killed and nineteen enlisted men wounded. Thomas identified eight enlisted men as killed with four officers and forty-eight enlisted members of the 4th Kentucky as casualties. For the 2nd Minnesota, twelve men were named as losing their lives at Mill Springs while two officers and thirty-one men were wounded. Lastly, among the personnel of the 9th Ohio, six enlisted men were among the killed while the numbers of four officers and twenty-four enlisted men were given for the wounded. The totals, according to this report, were 1 officer and 38 men killed with 13 officers and 194 men wounded. Preeminent Mill Springs historian Dr. Kenneth Hafendorfer conducted a thorough analysis of the company records for the units involved at Mill Springs and arrived at slightly higher totals of 44 killed, 11 mortally wounded, and 182 wounded. The driving tour pamphlet for visits counts 246 total casualties; 55 of which were killed or mortally wounded.[93]

Much higher casualty totals were given in Major General Crittenden's official report of Confederate losses at Mill Springs. He provided a total loss of 125 killed, 309 wounded, and 99 missing, and, as Thomas did, provided a regimental breakdown. For the 15th Mississippi, 44 killed, 153 wounded, and 29 missing were identified while totals for the 20th Tennessee were 33 killed, 59 wounded, and 18 missing. For the 19th Tennessee, Crittenden listed 10 killed, 22 wounded, and 2 missing. The 25th Tennessee and the 17th Tennessee totals of killed, wounded, and missing were 10, 28, 17 and 11, 25, 2 respectively. The 28th Tennessee was identified as having losses of 33 killed, 4 wounded, and 5 missing, and the 29th Tennessee had 5 killed, 12 wounded, and 10 missing. Crittenden finished his loss column with 9 killed, 5 wounded, and 12 missing from the 16th Alabama and 1 soldier wounded in Captain Saunders's cavalry. Dr. Hafendorfer, in the study acknowledged earlier, reached totals of 136 killed, 38 mortally wounded, 255 wounded, 80 captured, and 31 missing. The total provided on the official driving tour of the battlefield is 533, with 150 killed or mortally wounded.[94]

One of the most significant casualties of the action at Mill Springs was the reputation and military rank of Gen. George Crittenden. Rumors, conflicting witness accounts, newspaper articles, letters filled with accusations, and questionable actions surrounding Crittenden's sobriety prior to, during, and after the battle eventually resulted in Crittenden's tendered resignation and subsequent appointment to the rank of colonel.[95]

The highest number of battle casualties among the Confederates was in the 15th Mississippi. This unit "led the attack on Fry and fought through the whole engagement," including the struggle at the fence, and suffered an official total of 44 killed, 13 wounded, and 29 missing. The highest casualty total for a Federal unit at Mill Springs was the 10th Indiana's numbers of 10 killed and 75 wounded.[96]

Due to the haste of the Confederate retreat, large numbers of Confederate wounded were left behind with their fates largely to be determined by their foes. Sgt. Eastham Tarrant, 1st Kentucky Cavalry expressed sympathy for some of the enemy wounded who were "left on the field exhibited various dispositions . . . some spoke pitifully . . . while others were . . . stubborn and independent."[97]

Another Union soldier, a chaplain, wrote in his battle account published in the *Western Christian Advocate* that he was unable to sleep the night after the battle as the "shrieks and the groanings of the wounded and dying . . . pierced my heart." The chaplain made his way toward a blacksmith shop that had been converted to a makeshift hospital and found a mortally wounded Confederate from Paris, Tennessee. Following a brief conversation and prayer, the chaplain's heart was touched again as the dying soldier stated, "I am your enemy, but we will be friends in heaven."[98]

The sense of guilt and remorse associated with the act of abandonment is well documented in an account related to Charlie Clemenson of the 19th Tennessee. Clemenson was shot as his regiment retreated from its position near one of the fields that dotted the battlefield. A comrade of Clemenson's lamented, "Poor Charlie was dying . . . We can never forget the sad anxious expression of his face as we left him in his last sad trail of life, dying alone, deserted by all whom he thought were friends, left on the cold ground with naught but the cold rain to wash the sweat of death from his brow."[99]

Burials for the Confederate dead were performed in an inefficient manner to the level that, within two days of the battle's conclusion, local citizens were busying themselves by reburying the corpses that had become exposed in their shallow graves. The more considerate action of these citizens resulted in the mass grave known today as Zollicoffer Confederate Cemetery, located in Zollicoffer Park. The second stop on an informative and scenic battlefield tour, the cemetery is the final resting place for the vast majority of the Confederate soldiers killed at Mill Springs. Two notable exceptions are Zollicoffer and Bailie Peyton, both of whom are buried in Nashville. Located on the ground of some of the battle's most significant action, the cemetery contains a headstone for each of the approximately 150 Confederate casualties. A slab dedicated "to the brave men of Tennessee, Mississippi, and Alabama who fell" at Mill Springs is also visible at the location.[100]

Other prominent features near the cemetery include a

monument that Confederate veterans dedicated to Gen. Felix Zollicoffer in 1910. Nearby, a young lady named Dorthea Burton Hudson decorated an oak tree at the location where Zollicoffer's body was rumored to have been placed shortly after his death. Although the original "Zollie Tree," estimated to be two hundred years old and having a circumference of fifteen feet and a height of more than eighty feet, was destroyed in a June 1995 storm, a seedling from the original tree was planted the following year as a replacement for the original.[101] The new oak tree should help preserve the memory of the man who is arguably the most famous casualty of the battle at Mill Springs.

These sites are the major elements of Zollicoffer Park, established in 1931 and named for the general. The location also serves as the entry point for a heavily interpreted half-mile walking tour that enables visitors to become much more familiar with various aspects of the battle. Visitors should use caution if visiting during wet weather as the walkway can become extremely slick. In 1997 an eternal flame was added across the road from the park to serve as a lasting memorial to the battle's veterans.

In addition to the Zollie Tree and the other aforementioned sites, a tour of the Mill Springs battlefield would not be complete without entering the Visitors Center and Museum. The state-of-the-art facility was dedicated in November of 2006 and is one of the most impressive of such sites in the South. An interpretive hall, gift shop, legacy room, library, and community room combine to enrich each visitor's knowledge and appreciation of the struggle that occurred at Mill Springs. Open from 10 a.m. to 4 p.m. Monday through Saturday and 1 to 4 on Sunday, the building is located at 9020 West Highway 80 in Nancy, Kentucky. Additional information can be found on the center's Web site at millsprings.net. The museum's mailing address is P. O. Box 282, Nancy, Kentucky, 42544. By phone, interested parties can reach the visitors center at 606-636-4045, while the fax number is 606-636-4050.

Another worthwhile stop in the area is the Mill Springs National Cemetery, a location listed in the National Register of Historic

Places in 1998. The cemetery was established more than two hundred years ago and was once known as Logan's Cross Roads National Cemetery. More than seven hundred graves are present in the cemetery that is located ten miles west of Somerset on Highway 80 in Nancy.

Additional stops are included on the ten-stop driving tour. Visitors should take caution, as some of the roads are unlined, narrow, and contain numerous curves. Private residences are located near some of the stops and detract from the tour stops' viewpoints. Some locations, such as the Confederate Field Hospital Site, tour stop number four, have steep and dangerous entries. Last Stand Hill, where various Confederate units made an attempt to slow the Federal advance and allow their fellow men in gray to reach safety, contains a dangerous pull-off that necessitates crossing a highway to reach the intended destination. In an early fall tour of the battlefield's points of interest, the author noted that Timmy's Branch, tour stop number six and the location of the first action of the battle at Mill Springs, was hardly visible from the hillside that was covered with weeds. However, Timmy's Branch has recently come under the proper maintenance of an organization outside of the Mill Springs Battlefield Association and is kept mowed and more pleasing to visitors. This is a positive recent development in respect to preservation. On the same visit, the author found the Ferry Landing location, tour stop number eight, at a high level of disrepair with a steep and slick walk to the site. There was also no clear, designated parking and the area was difficult to negotiate in a typical two-wheel-drive family vehicle. This site is under the ownership of the Army Corps of Engineers, and Lake Cumberland has devastated the area due to the lake's waters rising and falling.[102]

The Civil War Sites Advisory Commission's Report on the Nation's Civil War Battlefields studied more than 4,400 acres related to the battlefield. This large amount was included in order to "more accurately reflect engagement areas and troop maneuvers" associated with the battle. The study revealed that only 400 of the 1,800 acres of potentially nationally registered lands are currently accessible to the public. Also, the U.S. Department of the Interior has designated the Mill Springs Battlefield as one of the twenty-five most endangered in the nation.[103]

Despite these minimal points of detraction and dissatisfaction, the Mill Springs Battlefield tour has numerous positives in relation to preservation. The site of the Confederate camp at Beech Grove is a beautiful stop on the tour. A short walk allows visitors to see earthen impressions of the cabins as well as gain a sense of the living conditions and terrain the soldiers of the mid-1800s faced.

The West-Metcalfe House, built in 1799, served as one of the headquarters for General Zollicoffer. After the battle the home and its grounds were used as a hospital. Several graves are also located on the property. A renovation project on the house was initiated in the first decade of the twenty-first century and should enable the structure to be preserved for numerous generations.

The Brown-Lanier House served as the headquarters for Confederate general William Carroll. It is likely that Zollicoffer used the home for the same purpose, though for an extremely short term. Union soldiers occupied the house after the battle and devoured a large portion of the food the family left behind as they fled the approaching enemy. Today the house serves as a bed and breakfast where visitors can "enjoy the peace of country living . . . Relax on one of our porches" and even "take a stroll down to the beautiful falls below the house" to see the historic Mill Springs Mill.[104]

In addition, visitors can see the damage caused when a six-pound cannonball, also able to be viewed on the premises, entered the home's interior. It is located at 9155 Highway 1275 North in Monticello, Kentucky, 42633. The Brown-Lanier House is open Tuesday through Friday from 10 to 4, Saturday from 10 to 6, and Sunday from 12 to 6. For more information, call 606-340-1656 or visit the Web site at www.millsprings.net.[105]

Annual events at Mill Springs include the Anniversary Observance in January, the Memorial Day Services in May, and a Living History Weekend in June. November witnesses the Ghostwalk, and in December the Christmas Open House takes place.[106]

The major catalyst for the positive aspects of Mill Springs Battlefield's preservation efforts is the Mill Springs Battlefield Association. Formed in 1992, the organization's purpose is to preserve, protect, maintain, and interpret the Mill Springs Battlefield. Membership dues are of various levels and range from annual amounts of $5 to $480. To join the group in its preservation efforts, contact Mill Springs Battlefield Association, P. O. Box 282, Nancy, Kentucky, 42544.

The positive preservation aspects far outweigh the negatives at the Mill Springs Battlefield. A high level of potential exists in relation to the preservation of remaining aspects of the battlefield and the resulting success of this would reflect positively upon the economy of the area. The groundwork has been laid and the wheels of preservation are in motion; only the future will reveal the realization of the goals and purpose of organizations such as the Mill Springs Battlefield Association.

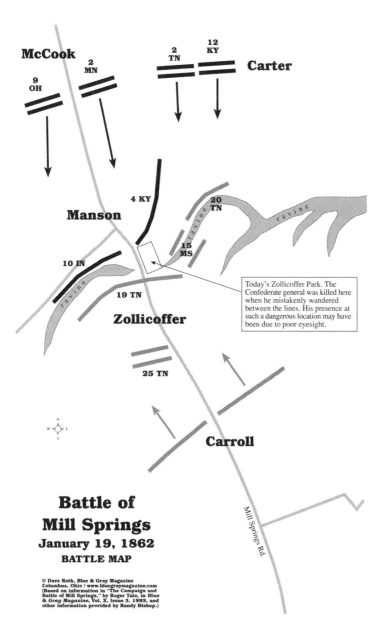

McCook

9
OH

2
MN

2
TN

12
KY

Carter

4 KY

20
TN

ravine

Manson

15
MS

10 IN

ravine

19 TN

Today's Zollicoffer Park. The Confederate general was killed here when he mistakenly wandered between the lines. His presence at such a dangerous location may have been due to poor eyesight.

Zollicoffer

25 TN

N
W · E
S

Carroll

Mill Springs Rd.

Battle of
Mill Springs
January 19, 1862
BATTLE MAP

© Dave Roth, Blue & Gray Magazine
Columbus, Ohio / www.bluegraymagazine.com
(Based on information in "The Campaign and
Battle of Mill Springs," by Roger Tate, in *Blue
& Gray Magazine*, Vol. X, Issue 3, 1993, and
other information provided by Randy Bishop.)

Confederate Gen. Felix Zollicoffer was killed in the battle of Mill Springs. (Confederate Veteran)

Federal Pvt. Austin Chasteen, 4th Kentucky Infantry, died in Somerset on February 12, 1862 from wounds received at Mill Springs. (Courtesy of Carol Sellers)

The Mill Springs Visitor Center is a state-of-the-art structure containing a wealth of information related to the battle. (Photo by author)

These markers are situated along the battlefield and Zollicoffer Park. (Photo by author)

Timmy's Branch, the site of the first shots of the battle, is privately maintained. (Photo by author)

The Brown-Lanier House served as a hospital and the post-battle headquarters for Union Gen. George H. Thomas. Today it is a bed and breakfast. (Photo by author)

The replanted Zollie Tree stands at the entrance to Zollicoffer Park. (Photo by author)

Stops on the driving tour, such as this one at Moulden's Hill, are usually clearly marked, well-interpreted, and easily accessible. (Photo by author)

CHAPTER EIGHT

RICHMOND

August 29-30, 1862

"The deadliest fire was poured into us . . . our brave troops did not falter."
—Col. Benjamin J. Hill, C.S.A.

Richmond, Kentucky holds a level of history few communities of comparable size can equal. Col. John Miller, a veteran of the American Revolution, founded the settlement in 1798 and named it after his birthplace of Richmond, Virginia. The new village soon replaced Milford as the Madison County seat and, eleven years later, was incorporated.[1]

As the mid-point of the American Civil War's first year approached, the community unwillingly became a place of significant military action and casualties. At that point of the war, Confederate Maj. Gen. Edmund Kirby Smith, envisioning an opportunity to gain control of the Cumberland Gap and establish a foothold in Central Kentucky, wrote an ambitious note to Gen. Braxton Bragg. Kirby Smith was aware of Bragg's plan to counter Union Maj. Gen. Don Carlos Buell's goal to move northward through Tennessee and Kirby Smith sent Bragg a message from his Knoxville, Tennessee, headquarters. Kirby Smith, the commander of the Department of East Tennessee, proclaimed, "There is yet time for a brilliant summer campaign with every prospect of regaining possession of Middle Tennessee and possibly Kentucky." Kirby Smith also penned the details of his proposed campaign to Confederate Pres. Jefferson Davis. In his letter to Davis, Kirby Smith remarked, "Politically, now is the time to strike Kentucky."[2]

Kirby Smith, a native Floridian and Mexican War veteran, had served as an assistant mathematics professor at West Point, but he resigned when Florida seceded. The general was no stranger to combat in the Civil War, having been wounded at First Bull Run.[3]

In the midst of the intense 1862 summer heat, Bragg and Smith met in Chattanooga "and a joint movement into Middle Tennessee was determined upon." However, a message from Col. John Hunt Morgan, regularly conducting cavalry raids into the heart of Kentucky, caused Kirby Smith to alter the plans of the Chattanooga meeting. Morgan proclaimed that, "the country outside Lexington and Frankfort . . . garrisoned chiefly with home guards . . . The whole country can be secured, and 25,000 to 30,000 men will join you at once."[4]

Bragg agreed with Kirby Smith's revised plan to march into Kentucky, but also strongly urged Kirby Smith to avoid moving too deeply into the borders of the Bluegrass State where pro-Union sentiment, despite Morgan's assertion otherwise, abounded. On August 13 Kirby Smith's force began its advance from Knoxville.[5]

Confederate Maj. Gen. Edmund Kirby Smith moved toward Kentucky. One division, numbering 9,000 men, was under Brig. Gen. Carter Stevenson. This division was ordered to keep a Federal garrison of 10,000 under the command of Brig. Gen. George Morgan, stationed at Cumberland Gap, in check. The other three divisions, each with approximately 3,000 men, comprised Kirby Smith's fighting force. Kentucky native Thomas James Churchill, a Mexican War veteran and Little Rock, Arkansas, postmaster, led one division; Irish immigrant Patrick Ronayne Cleburne, a Helena, Arkansas, druggist and lawyer, led another. Brigadier General Churchill's two brigades of the 10th, 11th, 14th, and 32nd Texas Dismounted Cavalry ; a group of Arkansas sharpshooters with the 4th, 30th, 2nd, and 1st Arkansas; and the 4th Arkansas Battalion, joined the three brigades of Brigadier General Cleburne in crossing the Cumberland Mountains through Rogers Gap. Brig. Gen. Henry Heth's division was to use Big Creek Gap as its means of entry.[6]

A soldier in Heth's division was openly critical of the route assigned to his comrades and himself. He wrote, "Why it should be called a gap it is impossible to tell. The road for miles wound round and round, always right up the steep mountainside."[7]

Likewise, a member of Cleburne's division voiced his discontent with the condition of the roads he faced. Sgt. Robert D. Smith, 2nd Tennessee Infantry Regiment, was Cleburne's divisional ordnance officer. Smith recalled, "I started my ordnance train of 25 wagons . . . this morning and at sunset did not have half my train up the first mountain . . . very steep and two miles from the base to the top."[8]

Robert M. Frierson, a self-proclaimed "boy soldier of the Confederacy" and a member of the "famous old Granite Brigade," remembered a humorous aspect of the trek through the Cumberland Mountains. Frierson remarked, "When we were making the ascent the horse of Adjutant Fowler, of the Second Tennessee, got into a bee's nest and rushed through the brigade riderless, over sleeping men, almost stampeding . . . the . . . regiments."[9]

The move across the Cumberlands of Tennessee quickly became what one historian has called "a logistical nightmare." Another has noted that the advanced position the troops held over the supply wagons necessitated a weeklong survival "off what they could find along the way." Reportedly, this was "little more than hardtack and green corn" and Kirby Smith proclaimed that the area was "almost completely drained of all kinds of supplies."[10]

From Cleburne's command, Robert Frierson reiterated these statements when he said, "We nearly starved ourselves in that sterile mountainous region."[11]

A Kentucky citizen, obviously unimpressed with the appearance of the men in gray, said that the "ragged, greasy, and dirty" Confederate troops "surrounded our wells like the locusts of Egypt . . . and they thronged our kitchen doors . . . like hungry wolves."[12]

Col. John Scott, a Louisiana planter before the war, served as a screen for Kirby Smith's infantry. Scott's brigade included the 1st

Louisiana Cavalry, a unit Scott personally raised, as well as the 4th Tennessee Cavalry, the 1st Georgia, and a small group known as the Buckner Guards from Kentucky. Kirby Smith reported Scott's brigade as numbering nine hundred men. [13]

Scott's command captured approximately forty-five Federal supply wagons on August 17 at London, Kentucky, eventually providing the severely deprived Confederate infantrymen with needed items. Scott reported that, in addition to the confiscated wagons, his men killed thirteen Union soldiers, wounded seventeen, and took more than one hundred prisoners while suffering less than a dozen total casualties.[14]

Five days later, on August 22, Scott was informed of the presence of another Federal supply train and a large number of troops near Big Hill. This prominent feature rose seven hundred feet and was located approximately seventeen miles southeast of Richmond. Big Hill has been described as making "a clear divide between the rolling Bluegrass Region and the rugged mountainous barren region through which Kirby Smith's army was advancing." Big Hill also served as "the last mountainous position where a small Federal force" held a legitimate chance of hampering Kirby Smith's movement toward Lexington.[15]

In the early afternoon of August 23, some 250 men from Colonel Scott's command reached the southwest side of Big Hill and met Federal pickets. Approximately four hundred recently recruited Federals under Col. Leonidas Metcalfe, a veteran of the Mexican War, moved forward to reinforce their pickets, but they ran into the Confederate artillery and ranks, now reinforced and out-numbering the men in blue by more than two to one. Metcalfe had raised the regiment of volunteers, known as the 7th Kentucky Cavalry, just one week earlier on August 16. The newly appointed colonel became the regiment's first commander, although his tenure as such would be short in duration.[16]

The Federal advance had failed when the inexperienced troops encountered Confederate artillery fire. A Northern-based reporter who witnessed the event wrote, "Before a dozen shells had been fired, a panic seized upon some of our men, which soon communicated to most of the column. A number of those in the rear, who had only smelled the battle from afar . . . mounted their horses and started at breakneck speed down the hill. The example was contagious. Within five minutes two-thirds of the regiment were in their saddles, leaving . . . a few of their more trusty comrades to their fate."[17]

Vicious musket volley exchanges between Scott's command and the steadily dwindling number of Federals prolonged the skirmish. One Confederate wrote, "after a sharp fight, they broke and fled toward Richmond . . . Near Big Hill we met another wagon train with its guard. They made breastworks out of the wagons and gave us a sharp fight. Some of our boys got in their rear and they surrendered . . . after supplying ourselves and horses, we burned the wagons."[18]

The number of Federal wagons that fell into Confederate hands is estimated to have been 148, with some 600 horses and mules gained as well. In addition, military supplies were captured, but the amount of materials gained proved "a burden to the advancing" Confederate cavalry.[19]

According to the official reports of the confrontation, this Confederate victory was accomplished with the loss of only twelve wounded and four killed. Federal losses were estimated to have been 120 killed and 150 captured. A pro-Union source reported that Scott captured and paroled approximately ninety-eight Federal prisoners, mostly comprised of Tennessee Unionists.[20]

Scott seized the opportunity and advanced his detachment into Richmond about dusk on August 23. Then Scott observed Federal infantry, namely the 95th Ohio as well as the 12th and 66th Indiana, all under the command of Col. William Link, advancing toward Richmond from Lexington. Scott made it clear to Link that the surrender of Richmond was desired, but Link refused. Realizing that the numerical advantage lay with the Federals at that point, Scott returned to Big Hill where he waited for reinforcements.[21]

In the ensuing days, a variety of Federal troop movements and command changes set the stage for additional combat and massive bloodshed. William "Bull" Nelson replaced Lew Wallace as Union commander in the area and summoned reinforcements from locations throughout Kentucky and Ohio. Abraham Lincoln had sent Kentucky-native Nelson, a career naval officer transferred to the Army, to Kentucky in early 1861 to observe Kentucky's leanings. While there, he established Camp Dick Robinson in the summer of 1861 as a Federal recruiting station thirty miles south of Lexington. Nelson remained in Richmond until August 28, at which time he returned to Lexington and placed brigadier generals Mahlon Manson and Charles Cruft, both from Indiana, in command of troops in and around Richmond. Nelson's exodus had been created through his false assumption that the Confederate attack at Big Hill and their subsequent withdrawal was simply "an isolated cavalry raid, and that Union forces in Richmond were safe from any immediate threat."[22]

The situation at hand could hardly have been more critical for the men in blue. The largely inexperienced troops were under the leadership of two generals with an unfortunately similar degree of military exposure. Manson, a general only since March, was a former state legislator and Crawfordsville, Indiana, druggist. However, he had seen action at Mill Springs in January 1862 as colonel of the 10th Indiana. Cruft, a former teacher and bank clerk, was a lawyer prior to his political appointment, although he had been assigned to Lew Wallace during the Fort Donelson campaign. Cruft had been seriously wounded while commanding the 31st Indiana at the "Hornet's Nest" at Shiloh in April 1862, and had been promoted to general in July.[23]

Cruft evidently believed his troops were no better prepared than he. He wrote of his men that they "knew nothing whatever of company or battalion drill" and therefore "could but indifferently execute some of the simplest movements in the manual of arms."[24]

On August 28, Confederates from Cleburne's division marched toward the summit of Big Hill. Cleburne's division consisted of the 13/15 Consolidated Arkansas Infantry, 2nd, 5th, 12th, 13th,

47th, and 48th Tennessee and 154th Sr. Tennessee Infantry, and the 1st Texas Artillery. Kirby Smith praised the conduct of these Confederates who had endured three days of marching in what one historian described as "oppressive heat."[25]

Kirby Smith remarked that his troops were "ragged, barefooted almost starved, marching day and night, exhausted [from] want of water. I have never seen such suffering, and there is not a complaint . . . Such fortitude, patriotism and self control has never been surpassed by any army that ever existed."[26]

With Cleburne's arrival at Big Hill, Scott's Confederate cavalry descended the same hill during the early hours of August 29. Union cavalry scouts of Lt. Col. Reuben Munday's 6th Kentucky Cavalry Battalion, overestimating the number of men in Scott's group, spotted movement and sent word to Manson that a large Confederate force was advancing northward. Approximately six miles from the base of Big Hill, Scott made contact with the Union cavalrymen of Munday and Col. Leonidas Metcalfe. Light Union casualties occurred during what historian Dr. Kenneth A. Hafendorfer has described as "a running engagement . . . as Metcalfe and Munday attempted to hold several positions."[27]

Manson received word that as many as 5,000 Confederates "were advancing in considerable force." Manson reportedly sent word of this to Nelson, although Manson's uncertainty of Nelson's exact whereabouts necessitated his making multiple copies and those being sent to Lexington, twenty-five miles to the north, and Lancaster, twenty-five miles to the west. Conflicting accounts on Manson's part ordered Metcalfe and Munday to either "hold the enemy in check, and ascertain if possible his strength and position" or to "fall back and carefully observe the road so that the enemy should not flank Richmond."[28]

Regardless of the content of Manson's notes to Metcalfe and Munday, the well-trained and experienced Confederate cavalrymen proved too great an obstacle for their green Union counterparts, and the latter chose "to fall back to the safety" of their infantry camps two miles south of Richmond around 2 p.m.[29]

Manson then faced the possibility of the advancing Confederates gaining control of a ridge located a mile and a half south of his camp. From that position, the Confederates would be able to gain a clear advantage over the Union camps. Manson later recalled, "The only question for me now to determine was whether I should allow the enemy to attack me in camp or whether I should advance to meet him." Noting the situation at hand, Manson said, "It did not take me a moment to decide"; he ordered his troops forward.[30]

The Confederates soon reached the vicinity of the Federal camps north of Rogersville, only to encounter cannon fire from Lt. Edwin O. Lanphere's 1st Michigan Light Artillery. That barrage caused Scott's cavalry to temporarily halt their advance. One Union defender, Capt. Thomas M. Roberson of the 71st Indiana, recalled the deployment of supporting infantry in writing, "The long roll was beaten; the companies formed and took their places in the line."[31]

Confederate cannon responded with little effect and Scott found it necessary to retreat from the area. Sensing a turn in the course of action, Manson's command closely followed that of the retreating rebels.

Despite the fact that the high temperature of well more than 90 degrees caused several of his infantrymen "to fall by the wayside," Lt. Col. John R. Mahan led the 55th Indiana forward. Mahan wrote, "One company of my command . . . found the enemy in front retreating through Rogersville, and pursued them so closely that they captured and brought back . . . one piece of the enemy's artillery."[32]

Manson's brigade, consisting of the 16th, 55th, 69th, and 71st Indiana Infantry Regiments with sections of the 1st Michigan Light Artillery, and under the orders of their over-confident commander, certain of a victory, settled into camp. Their bivouac was established at Rogersville, five miles south of Richmond. Metcalfe's cavalry was sent forward in pursuit of the Confederates.

Exhibiting military prowess and precaution that added to his military reputation, Cleburne established a picket line of his Confederates, should such a Federal action occur. After all, Cleburne's camp in Bobtown was situated just five miles south of Manson's bivouac at Rogersville. Cleburne had his men rest on their guns in line of battle with the 1st Texas Battery and various companies from the 48th Tennessee Infantry in advance.[33]

A brief passage of time occurred when panicked troopers from Scott's cavalry ran into the safety of Cleburne's newly established line. Closely behind, members of Metcalfe's cavalry followed Scott's retreating command, unaware that the darkness concealed an ambush. While shouts of "shoot down the rebels" burst from their ranks, the Federal cavalrymen unknowingly rode within twenty-five yards of Cleburne's marksmen.[34]

At that moment, the 48th Tennessee fired into Metcalfe's Federal horsemen. A brief stall in the advance preceded a return volley and an unsuccessful attempt to rally as the Union cavalry abandoned what, only moments earlier, appeared to be certain victory. Cleburne stated that the Federal cavalrymen dismounted and fired toward the Confederate campfires, located three hundred yards to the rear.[35]

A Confederate private added that any additional Federal attempts at renewing the struggle ended with the withering fire from the rebel guns, aimed blindly in the direction of the cursing and yelling voices of Federal officers. The private remarked, "They were allowed to rally, reform, march and countermarch within 200 yards of the muzzles of our cannon."[36]

The Federal retreat brought about the end of the action at Bobtown and for August 29. Confederate casualties were reported to be extremely light with only one soldier listed as wounded. Federal losses were reported as two killed and two wounded. Of additional benefit to the Confederates was the fact that they gained an estimated thirty Sharpe cavalry carbines as well as blankets and other accoutrements abandoned on the roadside.[37]

The night was spent with Confederate troop deployments and preparations for the renewal of the attack the next morning. On the Federal side, it was 11 p.m. before Metcalfe learned about the skirmish at Bobtown. Manson spent the night in Rogersville confident, according to Dr. Kenneth Hafendorfer, "that he was only facing a Confederate cavalry force." General Cruft, still in Richmond, received an order from Manson to be prepared to move southward the next morning in support of him. However, at 10 p.m. Cruft ordered his men to sleep on their arms. At 3 a.m. on August 30, Cruft's command, consisting of the 12th and 66th Indiana, 18th Kentucky, 95th Ohio and a detachment of the 7th Kentucky Infantry, along with a section of the 1st Michigan Light Artillery, were awakened and prepared for battle.[38]

On the night of August 29, the temperature cooled to 68 degrees, with a light breeze blowing toward the northeast providing the soldiers of both armies with a brief respite from the sweltering heat. Less than an inch of rain had fallen during the entire month of August as crops and grass withered and a drought "was in full effect." Dusty conditions added to the difficulties at hand as Federal and Confederate troops sought rest during the night. By 2 p.m. on the thirtieth, temperatures would reach 86 degrees and the relative humidity soared to 90 percent.[39] Much activity, death, and destruction was to take place before these horrid weather statistics grew to full force.

The communication issues that plagued the Federal forces throughout the Richmond campaign again appeared in the early morning hours of August 30. Maj. Gen. William "Bull" Nelson noted in his official report that he received Manson's dispatch at 2:30 a.m., approximately fourteen hours after the message was reportedly sent from a distance of thirty miles away. Nelson said that, much to his surprise,

> I . . . received a dispatch from General Manson, stating that the enemy was in force in his front and that he anticipated an engagement. I immediately sent couriers, with orders for him not to fight the enemy, but to retreat by way of the Lancaster road. I had ordered General Dumont to proceed from Lebanon to Danville . . . Col. Charles Anderson, with a brigade of three infantry regiments to proceed in the same direction . . . knowing that the enemy would not cross [the river] while 16,000 men were on their flank.[40]

In the Confederate ranks, Brigadier General Cleburne followed

Major General Kirby Smith's orders of the previous night that at sunrise Cleburne was to move forward with his division and two batteries toward the Federal lines. Cleburne noted his deployment and movement in writing, "At daylight I commenced the movement. The Second Brigade and the battery of Captain Douglas was in front. The First Brigade, under Acting Brig. Gen. Preston Smith, with the battery of Captain Martin, followed at the distance of a quarter of a mile. I sent the Buckner Guards in front to find the enemy."[41]

The first exchange of the day occurred approximately "half a mile north of the village of Kingston" where Cleburne reported that Confederate horse soldiers "encountered the advance guard of the enemy and soon discovered their line of battle about 500 or 600 yards in rear of their advance guard."[42]

Manson stated, "At 6 o'clock I ascertained that the enemy was advancing upon me, and sent an order to General Cruft to join me with all the forces under his command as quickly as possible." However, Cruft explained in his official report that "nothing was heard from General Manson directly" while his men ate breakfast. Cruft added that a heavy cannonade and occasional musketry were heard as early as 7:15 a.m., yet he sent forward for orders after unsuccessfully "waiting a sufficient time for a dispatch" to reach him.[43]

At the same time he allegedly sent for Cruft, Manson deployed a portion of his brigade in an effort to slow the Confederate advance. Manson reported,

I met the enemy's advance half a mile beyond Rogersville and drove them back, took possession of some woods and high ground upon the left of the road, and formed line of battle, the Fifty-fifth on the left of the road behind a fence, the Sixty-ninth Indiana on the right of the road, artillery on the left of the Fifty-fifth on high ground, the Seventy-first Indiana 300 yards in rear as a support for the battery and as a reserve. I ordered skirmishers to be thrown in front . . . those of the Fifty-fifth Indiana opening the battle in the most gallant style . . . the Sixteenth Indiana coming up, I ordered it to take position upon the left of the Fifty-fifth in the woods, which they did, gallantly maintaining their ground against a very heavy force of the enemy for more than an hour, when an attempt was made to turn their flank. I ordered the Seventy-first Regiment to go forward to their support, which in moving to the point indicated was exposed to a heavy fire from the enemy.

The 55th Indiana had some six hundred men, and the 69th Indiana contained approximately eight hundred.[44]

Positioned just south of Mt. Zion Christian Church, the 69th Indiana occupied the right flank of the Federal line. Historian B. Kevin Bennett has written that though Manson's troops were situated on a ridge that "appeared to be an excellent location from which to conduct a defense," the appearance was certainly deceiving. In addition to open fields "rolling hills and ridges could mask attacking forces . . . deep wooded ravines . . . afforded Confederate infantry a means of advancing with cover and concealment." Unfortunately for Manson and his command, the terrain could serve to hide the attacking Confederates until they were practically inside the Federal line.[45]

A creek called Hayes Fork ran west of the Irvine-Lancaster Pike and Richmond Road intersection. Approximately a mile away lay a cornfield, the northern end of which contained a ravine leading to Mt. Zion Church and the lead units of the Federal line. It has been duly noted that, "None of this was visible from Manson's position."[46]

Cleburne used his time wisely to reconnoiter the area. He said,

> I could distinctly see their first line facing us at right angles to the Richmond road, with one regiment to the right of the road, the others in the timber to the left. They had a battery masked near the Richmond road. I immediately placed Colonel Hill's brigade in line behind the crest of a low hill which ran parallel to and about 500 yards from the enemy's line. I placed Douglas' battery on the crest near my center. I ordered Smith's brigade to be formed in line within supporting distance; he accordingly formed his brigade in line behind the crest of a second hill in my rear . . . the enemy, showing only one regiment, kept up a ridiculous fire on us from a little mountain howitzer.[47]

Confederate sharpshooters were deployed for the purpose of hindering Federal troop placement. Cleburne ordered Col. Lucius Polk's combined 13th and 15th Arkansas Infantry to the right of the Confederate line in order to prevent that portion from being flanked. Cleburne wrote, "I now ordered the battery of Captain Douglas to open on what appeared to be a squad of cavalry on the Richmond road. In a moment this squad disappeared, masking a battery, which opened a rapid fire."[48]

Unfortunately, the success of the Confederate sharpshooters did not go without losses within their own ranks. Capt. James J. Newsom of Company C, 2nd Tennessee, had commanded the sharpshooters and, after locating the left end of the Federal line, sent his commander word of his discovery. Newsom fell, mortally wounded, having given his life for the sake of gaining relevant information about the enemy.[49]

In Cleburne's estimation, an artillery duel and intermittent musketry occupied the majority of the next two hours of battle. Sam Thompson, a member of Douglas's battery of Col. Benjamin Hill's brigade of Confederates, recalled four cannon being placed into action. According to historians, the four rebel artillery pieces fired slowly toward the Union lines while the returning shells were rapidly ejected, expending almost all of their ammunition.[50]

Lying near the center of the action was the brick home of Kavanaugh Armstrong. Known as Pleasant View, the house was located on a two-hundred-acre estate where a variety of crops and livestock were raised. The residence was vacant at the time of the battle as Mrs. Armstrong and her children had abandoned the home for the safety of the Palmer home, situated about ¾ of a mile to the northwest.[51]

Capt. John M. Martin, commander of the Marion Florida Light Artillery, a unit yet to be tried in combat, had a close call in response to Cleburne's order. Martin placed his battery near the Armstrong house, having misinterpreted Cleburne's order. Before Martin's battery fired a single shot, Martin was hit in the head while other members of the Marion Light Artillery were killed or wounded. Despite the serious wound, Martin was able to direct the movement of the battery to a position next to Douglas's battery.[52]

A witness to the events noted that when the batteries took their positions at Cleburne's order, Douglas's battery was "placed in a favorable position near the center of" the Confederate line. "A fire of artillery and infantry commenced, and Captain Martin, with a second battery, having arrived, it was also brought into action, and for two hours both infantry and artillery were engaged from their respective positions." The Confederate witness continued in writing that General Manson responded by pushing the Federal left forward in an attempt to turn the Confederate right.[53]

Federal General Cruft said that at approximately 7:15 a.m.,

A heavy cannonade was heard to the front. It continued for some minutes, and was evidently being actively replied to. Occasional musketry was also heard. After waiting a sufficient time for a dispatch to reach me I sent forward for orders. The cannonading now increased, and it became evident that a general engagement was imminent. I . . . wheeled the artillery and infantry into the road and took up march for the front. After proceeding 4 miles I encountered my messenger, who informed me that he had been unable to communicate with General Manson, though the fight was progressing rapidly on both sides with artillery and would doubtless soon become general. The column, already wearied with heat and thirst, was pressed rapidly up. Near Rogersvillle, a mile to the rear of the scene of the first action, a messenger from General Manson reached me, urging immediate reenforcements [sic].[54]

One Confederate officer stated that the artillery duel became less significant when, "Manson . . . in command of the Federal army . . . pushed his left forward to turn our right."[55]

General Cleburne recalled his response to Manson's bold move; the Irishman wrote,

A close fire soon commenced on the right, and became so heavy I found it necessary to sustain the right with further re-enforcement

. . . A very heavy musketry fight ensued, and learning that the enemy were still concentrating against my right . . . I ordered . . . (Acting) Brig. Gen. Preston Smith to immediately move forward the remaining three regiments of his brigade, to place them on the right of the line already engaged, and if his line overlapped that of the enemy to lap their left flank. At this time it was evident that the enemy had staked everything on driving back or turning our right flank and that they had weakened their center to effect this object. I therefore determined the moment I could hear Smith's musketry on the enemy's left flank to move Hill's brigade rapidly on the center. With this view I galloped to the right to satisfy myself Smith's brigade was getting into position.[56]

Casualties mounted for both sides as the fierce fighting erupted around Mt. Zion Church. For example, members of the 16th Indiana poured what one Confederate recipient recalled as "a galling volley of musketry" into the advancing ranks of the 154th Tennessee. From the 69th Indiana an officer remarked that after his comrades "open[ed] a broadside into" the Confederates, "they were panic stricken."[57]

Among the Confederates who fell was a former lawyer named Edward Fitzgerald. Rising to the rank of colonel, Fitzgerald was, in the account of one eyewitness, "shot through his heart" and fell from his horse. A Federal officer, mistaking Fitzgerald for a general, stated that Colonel Fitzgerald "was shot and fell from his horse but a few yards in front of me."[58]

During his aforementioned ride to view the relief upon the Confederate right flank, General Cleburne discovered his troops "moving into the position rapidly and in admirable order." Cleburne took it as his personal responsibility to oversee "the advance of Hill's brigade" and two batteries.[59]

Cleburne encountered the wounded Lucius Polk who was being moved to the rear in order to receive care for a head wound, which one Confederate remarked had made Polk "as wild as a March hare." Polk addressed Cleburne who "stopped an instant to reply." At that moment Cleburne was struck in his open mouth. Reportedly, several of the general's teeth were knocked out and the projectile exited his left cheek. The Irishman stated that the extreme pain of the wound "deprived me of the powers of speech and rendered my further presence on the field worse than useless." Cleburne maintained the presence of mind to send word of his own wounding to Colonel Hill, Major General Kirby Smith, and acting Brig. Gen. Preston Smith. The latter, at Cleburne's directive, assumed command of Cleburne's division. Fearing his left flank was about to be turned, Manson ordered most of the 69th Indiana positioned on the west side of the road, to the right, supporting Manson's left flank.[60]

At this juncture of the battle's first phase, at approximately 10 a.m., Brig. Gen. Charles Cruft's lead units arrived on the field. In addition to his artillery, Cruft moved the 95th Ohio Regiment forward near the remaining elements of the 69th Indiana, and the 18th Kentucky Regiment stood near Mt. Zion Church. The 12th and 66th Indiana Regiments were in reserve a mile to the rear. Cruft noted that soon after his troops arrived, the Confederate infantry advanced "showing not only a superior front to ours, but very large numbers at both flanks."[61]

From Cruft's brigade, the 95th Ohio Infantry, under the command of Col. William McMillen, initiated a charge and was almost immediately struck. Cruft reported that his "raw troops went to work in earnest, and for some forty minutes the rattle of musketry was terrible."[62]

The unfortunate members of the 95th began receiving fire from Maj. James Clark's men of McCray's Arkansas Sharpshooters situated to the west of the 95th. Col. Thomas McCray's brigade of four Texas regiments joined in the attack from the area southwest of the 95th Ohio and west of a barn located on the Armstrong farm. Adding insult to injury for the troops of the 95th, the 2nd Tennessee of Col. Benjamin Hill's brigade, east of the Old State Road and the 95th, sent deadly shots into the ranks of the men in blue.[63]

Cruft explained the situation in writing,

The center gave way, then the right flank. The left made still a show of resistance, and the Eighteenth Kentucky . . . was brought up to its aid. This regiment made here a gallant fight . . . and prevented the retreat at this time from becoming a rout. The men and officers of most of the regiments, however, fled in confusion to the rear through the fields. A few companies were brought off in tolerable order, but the panic was . . . universal. It was 10:30 a.m. At this juncture the whole thing was fast becoming shameful.[64]

Colonel McMillen explained that his regiment was flanked on his right and left, leaving few choices for the 95th Ohio. McMillen said of the Confederate advance, "Seeing that it would be reckless and useless to continue our assault upon the battery I ordered the regiment to halt and fall back, which they did for a time in good order, losing . . . in addition to our killed and wounded, 160 men and a large number of officers captured at this point."[65]

Lt. Col. James Armstrong, McMillen's immediate subordinate, contradicted McMillen's story. Armstrong stated that McMillen's order was for every man to save himself. Armstrong and approximately two hundred soldiers found themselves surrounded near Mt. Zion Church and surrendered to McCray's Texas troops.[66]

While the 95th Ohio and the remnants of the 69th Indiana abandoned the Federal right, the left, where the 18th Kentucky and depleted portions of the 16th and 69th Indiana Regiments stood, crumbled. Commanding the 12th Tennessee, Col. Tyree Bell held the Confederate right and was responsible for the attack upon the Federal left. Bell wrote, "In about three minutes, I don't think it could have been any longer, after I opened on them, their front line broke."[67]

The 16th and 69th Indiana Regiments began their exodus from the Federal left. Lt. Col. Melville Topping and Maj. William Conklin, both from the 71st Indiana and the two highest-ranking officers of the regiment, were killed in the retreat. Manson reported that Conklin was shot attempting to support the 16th Indiana, and Topping was "mortally wounded, while encouraging the men of his command." Eventually the situations proved overwhelming for the

18th Kentucky as well. The unit, whose heroic stand had prevented a literal rout, left their position at approximately 11:30 a.m., ending the first phase of the battle of Richmond after approximately 4½ hours of fighting.[68]

The second phase of the Battle of Richmond could legitimately owe its beginning to the 12th and 66th Indiana Regiments of Brigadier General Cruft's Second Brigade. The two regiments had not seen earlier action at Richmond and served as the foundational components upon which the Federal rally would take place.

Cruft described the situation in writing,

> No appeals availed at first to stop officers and men. The men, however, began to rally. I had the Twelfth and Sixty-sixth Indiana formed on the left of the road across the fields about 1 mile in the rear of the battlefield and in front of the retreating mass, and placed a line of cavalry still to their front. Here the greater portion of the retreating regiments . . . eventually rallied. A line of battle was established extending across the State road, and all the regiments marched in tolerable order back for a distance of 2 miles through the fields.[69]

At the Rogers House, where the Federal rally for the battle's second phase began, a field hospital was established. Here, as well at other such facilities, the patients faced treatment from medical personnel who were poorly suited and/or prepared to perform the procedures required. Dr. Bernard Irwin, medical director for the Union Army of Kentucky, wrote that the medical officers "had neither medicines, instruments, ambulances, tents, or camp equipage, to enable them to perform their duties . . . inexperienced in service and had but vague ideas as to the extent of sphere of their duties."[70]

A major issue facing the wounded and able men alike was the lack of pure drinking water. As the temperatures soared into the upper 90s, Capt. Thomas Robertson of the 71st Indiana faced a commonplace situation. Robertson said, "Seeing a large farmhouse some distance ahead of us, I thought . . . I will . . . fill my canteen . . . I was doomed to disappointment . . . the well was surrounded by a struggling mass of men . . . famishing for a drink of water."[71]

From this location the Union battle line, under Manson's orders, moved about one mile north to Castlewood, the farm home of state senator Richard White. By 1 p.m. the men in blue were standing along Duncannon Lane and the Speedwell Road, two thoroughfares that joined at the Richmond Road.[72]

Cruft's brigade was placed to the west of the Richmond Road or along Duncannon Lane with "two regiments in the woods on the extreme right and two behind the fence fronting a field of corn and to throw skirmishers forward into the corn field and woods." Manson's brigade formed to the left or east of the Richmond Road. Lanphere's artillery "was placed on the right and left, on the same ground occupied the previous afternoon."[73]

General Manson reported that after a short passage of time "the battle raged with great fierceness" along the Union line. Cruft added that the Confederates advanced through a cornfield on the Federal left and "opened a severe fire." The 95th Ohio and 69th Indiana moved forward to a fence where "a sharp conflict ensued." Cruft added, "The behavior of these regiments here was excellent, and they succeeded in driving the enemy out of the field." Likewise, Manson witnessed that, "the enemy's right soon gave way."[74]

The Confederate attack shifted to "the right in the woodland" where Manson proclaimed, "A vigorous assault was made by infantry advancing through the woods and open fields." The 18th Kentucky and the 12th Indiana of Cruft's brigade fought the attacking Confederates "in the most gallant manner" as they "held their ground for some time in a sturdy manner."[75]

Cruft ordered the 95th Ohio, 66th Indiana, the 18th Kentucky, and the 12th Indiana to advance upon the Confederates. Confederate officer Col. Thomas McCray witnessed the charge and directed the members of the 10th and 14th Texas Regiments to hold their fire. When the 66th Indiana moved within fifty yards of the Texans' position, the Confederates were ordered to open fire. A participant stated, "The effect was terrific" and, in response, "the enemy faltered and staggered."[76]

A Confederate witness to the carnage in the cornfield wrote, "The advancing columns of the enemy faltered and staggered from one end of his line to the other." In response to this situation, the same Confederate noted that his brigade of Texas regiments "was ordered to load rapidly, mount the fence and charge, which was admirably and gallantly executed."[77]

The battle's second phase, also referred to as the fight at White's Farm, had lasted less than an hour. The disintegration of the Federal line "quickly became a complete rout with units losing all organization . . . the Union army left the field tired, disorganized and demoralized."[78]

Gen. Cruft recalled the retreat in saying, "the men broke and fled down the road. The entire First Brigade had gone previously, without having opened fire . . . flying masses drifted up the road and through the fields in the direction of Richmond."[79]

As the retreating troops reached the vicinity of Richmond around 2 p.m., they encountered Maj. Gen. William "Bull" Nelson who had made the trip on horseback from Lancaster. General Cruft recalled that General Manson had ordered another rally where the Federal army had previously camped. Cruft noted that at the location an attempt was made "to collect the scattered soldiers when . . . Nelson reached the field."[80]

Nelson provided a slightly different account, noting that he arrived "3 miles south of Richmond, around 2 p.m., and found the command in a disorganized retreat or rather a rout. With great exertion I rallied about 2,200 men, moved them to a strong position, where I was confident I could hold them in check until night, and then resume the retreat."[81]

General Nelson had just more than 2,000 troops at his disposal, approximately one-third of the number of Federal soldiers present that morning. Making false promises of reinforcements, "Bull" Nelson aligned this worn-out group of soldiers along a line that ran from the Richmond Cemetery on the west to the Irvine Pike on the east. The Union line was, at that point, almost 5 miles north of the Rogers house where earlier fighting had taken place.[82]

Nelson's motivation apparently worked as one of the almost 4,000 Confederates who approached after General Kirby Smith's one-hour period of rest commend that the Federal troops formed "the prettiest line of battle I ever saw."[83]

The approaching Confederates moved within three hundred yards of the men in blue before the latter opened fire. Colonel Hill noted the irony of the action that seemed to repeat the Confederates' firing on the Union troops earlier. Hill wrote, "As we cleared a rise in the ground the deadliest fire was poured into us that occurred during the entire day, and although the bullets hailed our brave troops did not falter."[84]

Likewise, a Northern reporter and witness to the event wrote of the Union soldiers that, "Our brave fellows, raw, undrilled, and undisciplined as they were, stood their ground without flinching, pouring into the rebel ranks their leaden balls in rapid succession."[85]

Confederate casualties mounted quickly. The 2nd Tennessee lost one hundred of its three hundred men. The 48th Tennessee, standing to the right of the 2nd, suffered forty casualties from its total of approximately three hundred men.[86]

A Confederate counterattack literally saved the day for the men in gray. General Nelson wrote, "The enemy attacked in front and on both flanks simultaneously with vigor. Our troops stood about three rounds, when, struck by a panic, they fled in utter disorder. I was left with my staff almost alone."[87]

Brig. Gen. Charles Cruft backed Nelson's perception in stating, "The attack soon became general and was stoutly resisted for a few moments, when the whole line broke in wild confusion and a general stampede ensued. Both officers and men became reckless of all restraint or command, and rushed pell-mell to the rear . . . in an utter rout."[88]

General Nelson attempted to slow the Federal retreat, yet reports circulated that he did so by using extreme means. Using his sword and gun, Nelson allegedly killed two or three men attempting to flee. One reporter said,

Nelson . . . saw a number of federal soldiers who had thrown away their guns . . . He rode up to them, one after the other and with fearful oaths struck them with his saber. I will not say how many he killed in this way, but I know that I saw him strike at least half a dozen; inflicting fearful wounds. He seemed to me to be worse crazed than the poor boys whom he so brutally attacked.[89]

Another stated, "In berserker rage, hatless, his long hair streaming in the wind, his eyes glaring and bloodshot, his face red and inflamed with fury, he road wildly about the field, raging and roaring like a wounded lion, commanding his men to rally and stand firm, and beating them down with the flat of his sword when they refused."[90]

Nelson reportedly attempted to inspire his men by proclaiming, "Boys, if they can't hit me they can't hit a barn door." Col. William Link of the 12th Indiana was almost immediately struck and fell while attempting to rally the 18th Kentucky. Nearby, two lead slugs hit Nelson in the thigh. A series of volleys sent the remaining Federal troops fleeing through the streets of Richmond and toward the Lexington Road.[91]

Historian B. Kevin Bennett has explained that the fight at the cemetery, during which Nelson attempted to rally his troops and fend off the attack of the Confederates, was some of the heaviest fighting during the battle of Richmond. Bennett proclaimed, "The clash at the cemetery had been of brief duration but the casualty numbers were testament to the ferocity of the engagement." In fact, both the Federal and Confederate armies suffered their heaviest casualties during the short-lived action.[92]

Dr. Kenneth Hafendorfer reiterated Bennett's designation of the fight at the cemetery being the battle's most severe. Hafendorfer wrote that a maximum of 232 Confederates were casualties at Mt. Zion Church with some 185 casualties suffered at White's farm. Confederate losses at Richmond Cemetery were approximately 240.[93]

Meanwhile, the Confederates held several key positions in order to check the Federal retreat. A westward retreat was guarded on the Lancaster Road. Tate's Creek and Jack's Creek Pikes were covered, as was Lexington Pike. It was reported that Scott's Confederate troopers shot several Federal stragglers, leading the retreating Federals to surrender by the hundreds. One historian proclaimed, "There were so many prisoners that Scott . . . could not give . . . an accurate estimate of how many he had captured." Scott reported that the Federal prisoners amounted to "a ten acre lot full" at the Madison County Courthouse. An accurate estimate of Federal prisoners, according to some of the battle's historians, is 3,500 to 4,300.[94]

Reports list Federal casualties as 225 killed, 1,073 wounded, and 4,303 captured. Confederate losses were given as 122 killed, 478 wounded, and 3 captured. Among the Federal wounded, 140 were listed as mortally wounded; 118 Confederates were likewise designated.[95]

Among the wounded Confederates was James Nelson Rosser of Company G., 12th Tennessee Infantry Regiment. Rosser's regiment, compiled of 737 men, suffered 32 casualties at Richmond. Rosser's right arm was wounded so severely that it had to be amputated. After the war, the veteran and two of his friends formed a pact; because the three were so ashamed of the war's outcome, they would not shave for the remainder of their lives.[96]

James Lacy of the 69th Indiana was captured with the majority of his fellow regiment members. Lacy survived his term as a prisoner of war, but he died on March 24, 1864 as a result of the conditions he faced while in captivity.[97]

General Nelson noted in his official report that General Manson was to blame for the overwhelming Federal defeat at Richmond. Nelson wrote, "What the motive of General Manson was in bringing on an action under the circumstances . . . I will leave him to explain."[98]

General Manson pointed the blame for the loss in the direction of the troops under his command. Manson stated, "They were undisciplined, inexperienced, and had never been taught in the manual of arms." However, Manson praised the green troops in saying, "Taking into consideration the rawness of our troops, there has been no battle during the war where more bravery was displayed by officers and men, with a few exceptions, than there was in the first four battles near Richmond."[99]

Despite the finger pointing of the time, the Confederate victory at the battle of Richmond is tactically regarded as "one of the most complete of the entire war," yet the generally agreed upon fact is that "it was negated" in the point that the Confederates failed "to coordinate the armed forces in the campaign that ended with their retreat from Perryville."[100] Today, there is little blame to pass in relation to the preservation efforts of the Richmond battlefield. The efforts and sacrifices of the warriors of the hot day in 1862 are well documented in a series of success stories from a large number of individuals.

The Battle of Richmond Visitors Center opened in October of 2008 at the intersection of U.S. 25 and 421, south of Richmond, and is the perfect starting point for any visit to the area. The center is located just ½ mile north of Mt. Zion Church in the Rogers House, the 1811 residence that saw some of the battle's most intense action and served as a hospital for the battle's wounded. A laser-guided map provides visitors with a bird's-eye view of the battlefield where significant landmarks and troop movements can be clearly seen and studied. In addition, battlefield artifacts on a thirty-year loan from the Blue Grass Army Depot and a documentary film about the battle can be viewed. Also, an exhibit containing artifacts of Union Gen. Mahlon D. Manson is housed in the visitors center. Several pieces of Manson's furniture, his saber, footlocker, and pistol are among the items on display. Phillip Seyfrit, the historic properties director and battlefield superintendent, is a highly knowledgeable and personable individual who will gladly guide visitors in their exploration of the center and the battle's overview. The center can be contacted by calling 859-624-0013, visiting the Web site at www.battleofrichmond.org, or in mailing correspondence to 101 Battlefield Memorial Highway, Richmond, Kentucky, 40475.[101]

Pleasant View, the home of the Rogers family, also served as a hospital during and after the battle and can be viewed during a visit to the battlefield. Many of the casualties of the first phase of the battle were treated in the home where Seyfrit says, "When you're in this building, you may be standing where a soldier may have been when he took his last breath." In addition, the property surrounding the home was the location of Churchill's Confederate forces attempt to flank Federal troops located nearby. More than 350 acres of the home's property have been designated as a Civil War Battlefield Park, with two miles of walking trails and a host of interpretive signs adding to the comprehension of the battle.[102]

Phillip Seyfrit has stated that the battle of Richmond is "the only example where the Federal Army ceased to exist at the end of the battle." However, in 2001, according to Seyfrit, only three Kentucky state markers commemorated the battle. Today, the interpretation of what many historians call "the most lop-sided Confederate victory in the West if not the entire war" and "the most complete victory . . . in the entire Civil War" has grown tremendously "through the hard work of a lot of people," said Seyfrit. Their work has allowed the interpretation and preservation of the battlefield to increase through "leaps and bounds" that Seyfrit has stated he and others "want to continue."[103]

Markers in Richmond today include those denoting the Big Hill Skirmish, the Richmond-Prelude and Richmond Battle, a Civil War Field Hospital, and Civil War Action. A Kentucky Historical marker related to Cassius Marcellus Clay, U.S. Minister to Russia, is also present, located at the entrance to the Richmond Cemetery. Clay's home, Whitehall, now a Kentucky state shrine, is just north of Richmond.[104]

Securing grants for the restoration of various sites on the battlefield led Kent Clark, Madison County judge/executive to declare, "It seems like good things just keep happening for Madison County and for Richmond Battlefield Park."[105]

The Civil War Sites Advisory Commission Report on the Nation's Civil War Battlefields positively noted the large amount of preservation activities and public interpretation related to Richmond. The group's study examined more than 9,700 acres related to the battle and proclaimed that more than 1,200 acres of the land could potentially be nationally registered. With more than six hundred acres now publically accessible, the preservation of Richmond is well on the way to becoming a modern example for similar sites to follow.[106]

For example, the Texas Historical Commission worked with local Richmond groups to dedicate a Texas Monument on the Richmond battlefield on May 23, 2009. The monument became the first state monument on the battlefield and is carved from Texas Sunset Granite. The monument stands eight feet tall and overlooks a ravine where four Texas regiments of dismounted cavalry charged the Federal right flank in the early stages of the battle, which led to the collapse of the Federal position.[107]

One of the leading groups behind the success of the Richmond battlefield is the Battle of Richmond Association or BORA. Formed in early 2002 to "act as the lead organization in an effort to preserve" the Richmond battlefield, BORA helped facilitate the purchase of Pleasant View and sixty-two acres surrounding the home through funds gained from the American Battlefield Protection Program, the Civil War Trust, and other public and private sources. Joining other groups, such as the Richmond Chamber of Commerce, the Madison County Civil War Roundtable, and the Madison County Historical Society, in the impressive level of preservation and purchase of other sites to date, BORA has provided the Richmond area with "positive economic development at a very low cost." The agency's quarterly newsletter, entitled the *BORA Bulletin,* can be viewed online for recent news and exact dates of the annual reenactment of the battle, usually attended by several thousand spectators.[108] To become a member or contact this worthwhile organization, you may reach Paul Rominger at 859-248-1974 or mail Dr. Rominger at the Battlefield Park address.

BORA's Web site notes that 1,377 acres of land from phases one and two of the battle remain unpreserved to date. Six hundred and three of those acres are on the Blue Grass Army Depot, while the remainder is privately owned. The group also notes that the major threat to the battlefield exists in the form of development of "single family residences that are being constructed on both US 421 and US 25." Development along Duncannon Road, where a newly opened exit to I-75 will not only make it easier for visitors to come to the battlefield but also promote development, is also a threat as is the ever-present reality of industrial development in the area. As a result, the Civil War Preservation Trust, in 2010, placed the Richmond battlefield on its Most Endangered Battlefields List, despite the fact that "the battlefield has been well protected to date." The rationale behind the designation was "future preservation efforts will be complicated by the addition of a new highway interchange, paving the way for significant commercial growth in an area that has previously experienced little development pressure."[109]

The centerpiece of the interpretation and preservation of the Richmond battlefield is the seventeen-mile driving tour, consisting of ten tour stops and five optional stops. Markers are present at each tour station, and brochures can be obtained from the Battle of Richmond Visitors Center or Richmond Tourism, located at 345 Lancaster Avenue. The tourism group can be reached through calling 859-626-8474 or toll free at 800-866-3705. The tourism's email address is tourism@richmond.ky.us.

Included on the driving tour are stops such as the site of the August 23, 1862 cavalry engagement at Big Hill, an optional stop. The Confederate Cemetery, Mt. Zion Church, Bobtown, the Thomas Palmer House, and the three phases of the battle are among the must-see stops. In addition, the Richmond City Cemetery, where the Confederate victims of the battle are interred, is a must-see stop on the tour. As a footnote, the Federal dead were later moved to Camp Nelson National Cemetery.

The positive aspects of the Richmond, Kentucky, battlefield are numerous and certainly lay the groundwork for a bright historical and economic future for the area.

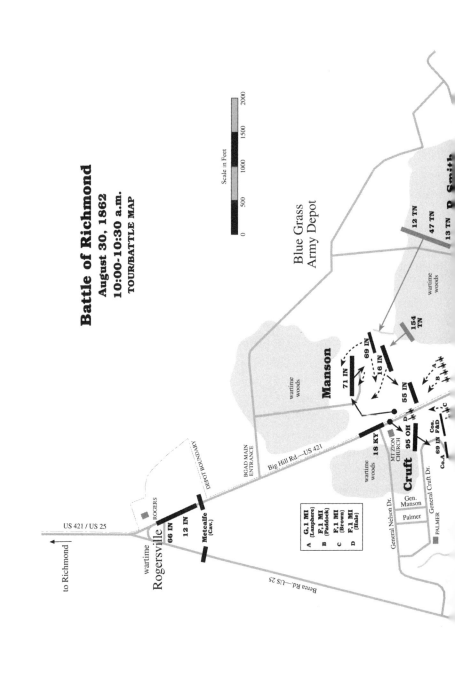

Battle of Richmond
August 30, 1862
10:00-10:30 a.m.
TOUR/BATTLE MAP

Scale in Feet

0   500   1000   1500   2000

Blue Grass
Army Depot

to Richmond

US 421 / US 25

wartime
Rogersville

66 IN

12 IN

Metcalfe
(Cav.)

ROGERS

DEPOT BOUNDARY

BGAD MAIN
ENTRANCE

Big Hill Rd.—US 421

Berea Rd.—US 25

wartime
woods

A   G, 1 MI
     (Lamphere)

B   F, 1 MI
     (Paddock)

C   F, 1 MI
     (Brown)

D   F, 1 MI
     (Hale)

wartime
woods

71 IN

69 IN

16 IN

55 IN

Manson

18 KY

MT ZION
CHURCH

Cruft

95 OH

Cos.
69 IN F&D

Co.A
69 IN

General Nelson Dr.

Gen.
Manson

Palmer

PALMER

General Cruft Dr.

154
TN

12 TN

47 TN

13 TN R. Smith

wartime
woods

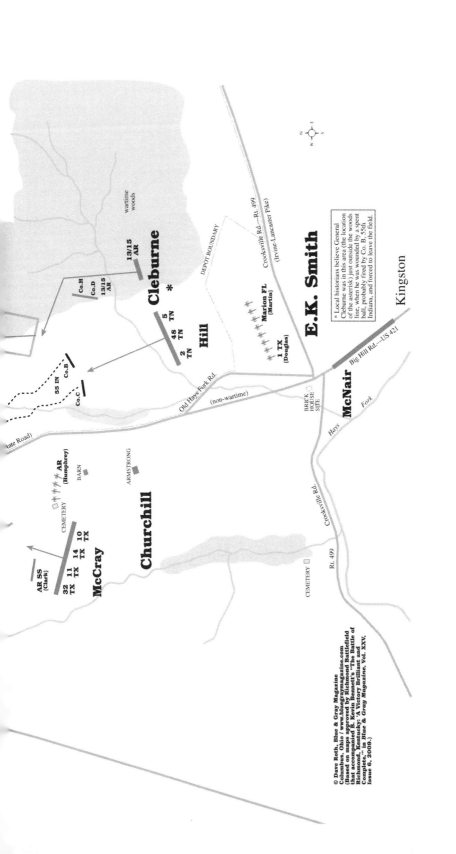

Co.H
Co.D
13/15
AR

13/15
AR

5
TN

55 IN

Co.B

Co.C

48
TN

Cleburne

*

Hill

2
TN

wartime
woods

DEPOT BOUNDARY

Marion FL
(Martin)

1 TX
(Douglas)

Crooksville Rd.—Rt. 499

Crooksville Rd.—Rt. 499
(Irvine-Lancaster Pike)

Old Hays Fork Rd.

(non-wartime)

BRICK
HOUSE
SITE

Hays

Fork

McNair

Big Hill Rd.—US 421

E.K. Smith

Kingston

* Local historians believe General
Cleburne was in this area (the location
of the asterisk) just outside the woods
line, when he was wounded by a spent
ball, probably fired by Co. B, 55th
Indiana, and forced to leave the field.

ate Road)

AR
(Humphrey)

BARN

ARMSTRONG

CEMETERY

32
TX

11
TX

14
TX

10
TX

AR SS
(Clark)

McCray

Churchill

Crooksville Rd.

Rt. 499

CEMETERY

© Dave Roth, Blue & Gray Magazine
Columbus, Ohio / www.bluegraymagazine.com
(Based on maps approved by Richmond Battlefield
that accompanied B. Kevin Bennett's "The Battle of
Richmond, Kentucky: A Victory Brilliant and
Complete," in Blue & Gray Magazine, Vol. XXV,
Issue 6, 2009.)

Nip Boren, Douglas' Texas Artillery, is buried at the base of Big Hill behind the ruins of the Merritt-Jones Tavern. (Courtesy Richmond Battlefield Park)

Col. William Hardy Link, 12th Indiana Volunteers, was wounded in the fight at Richmond Cemetery. He died at the Holloway House in late September due to complications from the amputation of his leg and is buried in Ft. Wayne, Indiana. (Courtesy Richmond Battlefield Park)

Twenty-five-year-old Color Sgt. David Setzer, 30th Arkansas, was killed at Richmond and is buried in a mass grave. (Courtesy Richmond Battlefield Park)

The Rogers House serves as Richmond's Visitor Center. (Photo by author)

Mt. Zion Church was one of the most hotly contested locations during the battle. Battle damage is still visible along the south wall. (Photo by author)

The Kavanaugh Armstrong home, known as Pleasant View, was used as a hospital following the battle. (Photo by author)

The Big Hill Welcome Center is in the Cox-Simpson House, a structure that contains some pre-war rooms. (Photo by author)

The Confederate Memorial sits atop a mass grave in Section H of the Richmond Cemetery. (Photo by author)

This portion of the battlefield sits adjacent to the Visitor Center. (Photo by author)

This sign of potential threat is located near Pleasant View. (Photo by author)

CHAPTER NINE

MUNFORDVILLE
(Green River Bridge)

September 14-17, 1862

"All at once . . . the carnage began"
—Pvt. D. A. Campbell, 10th Mississippi Infantry Regiment

September 17, 1862 holds the distinction of being the bloodiest single day in U.S. history. Along the banks of Antietam Creek near Sharpsburg, Maryland, the tragic events that transpired that day captivated Americans, and stories from that location took precedence over other news of the time. For that reason, as much as any factor, the battle of Munfordville, Kentucky, an incident that concluded on the same day as the battle at Antietam, is often overlooked, if not ignored. The incidents that transpired in the settlement of Munfordville warrant additional study and could have proven much more significant had a few situations been handled differently.

In 1819 land ceded from Hardin and Barren Counties was used to form Hart County, the sixty-first county in the state of Kentucky. Daniel Boone's family visited the area in 1775 and allegedly buried their young son near Boiling Springs. Generations earlier Native Americans resided in the area, leaving behind untold riches in artifacts. Ironically, Hart County is named for Capt. Nathaniel Gray Smith Hart, a man whom Native Americans killed during the War of 1812.[1]

Munfordville had been founded eighteen years earlier after Richard J. Munford moved from Amelia County, Virginia, and purchased 2,500 acres. Additional settlers arrived and led to Munford donating 100 acres for the settlement of a town within what became a 412 square-mile county.[2]

For decades Munfordville remained a hamlet along the Louisville and Nashville Turnpike. Travelers stopped briefly at the village's stagecoach station for their horses to be refreshed. However, the arrival of the Louisville and Nashville Railroad in the 1850s increased the number of travelers to the area as well as the prominence of Munfordville. In 1862, the town's population had increased to two hundred with the citizens divided in relation to their loyalties of the Civil War.[3]

The issue of division in loyalty was clearly reflected in the case of two of the area's most famous citizens, Confederate Gen. Simon Buckner and U.S. Gen. Thomas Wood. The two officers had been childhood friends, having played on the banks of the Green River. Buckner and Wood attended the U.S. Military Academy and served in the Mexican War.[4]

It was the Green River, or the Louisville and Nashville Railroad bridge that spanned it, that brought the opposing armies to Munfordville in 1862. The L & N Railroad was one of the major Federal supply routes through Kentucky and into the Confederacy. Prominent twentieth-century Munfordville historian Col. Hal Engerud explained that the destruction of the bridge would interrupt the flow of Federal supplies for weeks. At Munfordville, the rail line became exceptionally vulnerable to Confederate activity. Spanning the Green River at Munfordville, the railroad's five-span bridge stretched 1,000 feet in length and rose 115 feet above the river's water. Credit for the bridge's design would go to engineer Albert Fink, a German immigrant. John W. Key, an Irish stonemason, worked with his sons for two years to build the piers. The desire to control this bridge caused Munfordville residents to "grow accustomed to the rattle of musketry." The rattle became all too familiar during a multi-day struggle knows as the battle of Munfordville, the battle of Woodsonville, the battle of the Green River Bridge, or the battle of Amos's Ferry.[5]

Gen. Braxton Bragg, commander of the Army of Tennessee, felt a Confederate push into Kentucky would necessitate a Federal evacuation of most of the South and provide the Confederate Army with an opportunity to gain recruits. Bragg initially gave the impression of moving against Nashville from the east, forcing Maj. Gen. Don Carlos Buell, U.S. commander of the Army of the Ohio, to retreat from Chattanooga in order to protect his Nashville supplies.[6]

Bragg used the East Tennessee mountains to shield his movement toward Glasgow, Kentucky. If Bragg could reach the L & N Railroad, he could likely break the Federal supply line that ran from Louisville to Nashville. By the time Buell detected Bragg's move toward Kentucky, Bragg had a three-day head start. This situation gave Bragg's troops an opportunity to rest briefly at Glasgow while Buell's army was just reaching Bowling Green. As a measure of precaution, Bragg ordered Brig. Gen. James R. Chalmers to move his Mississippians to Cave City, Kentucky, to guard against Buell's approach and destroy the railroad south of Cave City.[7]

The rest that Bragg and his troops sought was well deserved and needed. The drought affecting Kentucky was several months old and fresh water was scarce. By mid-September, the temperatures still reached the mid-80s and the relative humidity on September 15 was 90 percent.[8] Such were the atmospheric conditions Bragg faced in Kentucky.

On the Federal side, Col. John Wilder left Louisville with 214 recruits on September 1, 1862. Wilder's assignment was to advance to Nashville, but a burned river bridge in Clarksville, Tennessee, and a skirmish in the same town eventually led Wilder to move his troops to Bowling Green. Wilder then received orders to "take command of the post at Munfordville, and to hold the post to the last if attacked."[9]

Informed of Bragg's intended Kentucky invasion via Glasgow and Buell's plan to intercept Bragg, Wilder took arms for his Munfordville recruits. At Munfordville, Wilder "found a bridge guard . . . of some two hundred Kentucky recruits, also the Seventy-seventh and

Eighty-ninth Regiments of Indiana Infantry of seven hundred men each."[10]

Wilder assumed command of the five-pointed-star fort at the Munfordville post known as Ft. Craig on September 8. The colonel immediately began repairing works erected the previous winter on the river's south side. The earthworks were described as consisting of "a low line of infantry breastworks encircling the south end of the bridge, and a weak stockade for fifty men at the river bank near the bridge end, and a small redoubt or star fort for two hundred men and two guns at Woodsonville, about a half mile up river, on ground commanding the bridge and the line of intrenchments near the bridge."[11]

With many of his troops being unarmed, Wilder directed the 23rd Kentucky to disperse throughout the area to scout for Confederate movements. The day after Wilder's arrival at Munfordville, John Hunt Morgan's command burned the Salt River Bridge south of Louisville, and the supplies at Munfordville soon dwindled to "one day's rations and little infantry ammunition."[12]

In response, Wilder, working his troops day and night, "repaired an old locomotive . . . with two flat cars, with the request to . . . Louisville to send . . . supplies, especially ammunition. He declined . . . I . . . soon had ten days' food for the men and animals."[13]

A participant noted that the Federal troops "quickly constructed fortifications . . . in a circle commencing with a stockade located a short distance west of the south end of the L & N bridge . . . nearly due east till they connected with a fort located in a small settlement."[14]

By the time Wilder's expansion of the Munfordville earthworks were complete, the results were impressive. The fortifications, located in front of the Anthony Woodson home, built on land that his father, Thomas Woodson, received from Thomas Jefferson as a land grant for service in the American Revolution, extended over a portion of Woodson's farm and became impregnable.[15]

Wilder's efficiency was gained through a combination of military training and business expertise. Born in 1830, the young colonel was a New York native but achieved his wealth after moving to Ohio and eventually Indiana. At the age of twenty-seven, he opened a foundry and mill right plant in Greensburg, Indiana where he had one hundred employees by 1861. The day after Ft. Sumter, Wilder enlisted as a private in an Indiana battery and was elected captain the following day. That June, he was promoted to lieutenant colonel of the 17th Indiana Volunteer Infantry. On March 2, 1862 Wilder became the unit's colonel and was then sent to Kentucky in the summer of 1862.[16]

Ft. Craig, the location of a significant strongpoint of the Federal defenses, was described as follows,

> The intrenchments within which our troops fought are situated about one mile from Woodsonville, opposite Munfordville, on the south side of the river, and are built so as to protect the Green river railroad bridge. Immediately south of the works, and three hundred yards from them, a strip of woods crosses the railroad. A portion of this had been felled, and forms an abatis in front . . . Beyond the woods is another open space . . . To the right and left of the intrenchments are extensive open fields of undulating surface, extending on the left to Woodsonville and the turnpike road.[17]

Another description said,

> On the right was a range of rifle pits sufficient to contain 3,000 men, semicircular in form, and terminating on the extreme right in a strong blockade, which stood upon the brink of the lofty bluff overlooking Green River. About 100 yards to the left of this was another rifle pit, capable of holding at least one regiment, and still further to the left and upon higher ground stood their principal work, a regular bastion earthwork.[18]

On September 12, 1862, Colonel Wilder wrote his wife and updated her on recent developments at the Federal stronghold. He said, "I now have about 2,600 men . . . we are fortifying as strong as possible . . . The rebels . . . are at Glasgow . . . in force. I think probably they will attempt to take this place. If they do, I shall give them the best fight I can."[19]

While Wilder's troops at Ft. Craig prepared for a possible attack, Confederate scouts conducted reconnaissance of the Munfordville area. Chalmers's brigade "had been sent . . . to tear up the railroad truck . . . Failing in this," Chalmers became determined to capture Wilder's command. Kirby Smith detailed Col. John A. Scott to locate Bragg, but in the process he understood that recruits occupied Ft. Craig.[20]

Scott's intelligence was more accurate than could be imagined. Wilder acknowledged, "Only five of my undrilled force had ever before been under battle fire and another 600 were made unarmed."[21]

Colonel Scott advanced his cavalry to Munfordville on the evening of September 13. Wilder recalled that Scott "demanded an immediate surrender of the place." Wilder's reply, according to a telegram sent to his superiors in Louisville, was that he "peremptorily refused" despite Scott's claim that Wilder was "cut off and surrounded." Wilder assured Maj. Gen. C. C. Gilbert, operating at the U.S. Headquarters, "I shall fight anything that comes."[22]

In turn, Scott's battery sent a few shots into the confines of Ft. Craig. Wilder stated that the Federal response was effective as the Confederates "retired out of range when we replied with shots from a twelve-pounder."[23]

Certain of an impending Confederate assault, Wilder ordered the earth embankment of the fortress to be topped with a head-log. The young colonel noted that his troops "also cuts down the timber in the pasture in front of our entrenchment, thinking that it might break the force of an attack in line." A sense of isolation must have permeated Wilder's mind as he recalled, "I sent messengers every night through the enemy's lines to Buell with all information I could secure, but he never replied."[24]

In the meantime, Scott sent word to Brig. Gen. James Chalmers, asking for assistance in an attack upon Ft. Craig. Scott's request informed Chalmers that he would attack the fort early the next morning. In response to Scott's message assuring Chalmers of the presence of only a small Federal force within Ft. Craig, Chalmers readied his troops for the fifteen-mile march from Cave City to the fort.[25]

Pvt. D. A. Campbell, 10th Mississippi, recalled, "On the 13th . . . we cooked rations and waited for the night before advancing further."[26]

Issues of insubordination and a possession of over self-confidence may have come into play for Chalmers at this time. Chalmers not only failed to seek Bragg's permission to participate in the attack upon Ft. Craig, but he also overlooked informing Bragg about the event.[27]

The opinion of various historians has been that "Chalmers saw an opportunity for an easy victory and possible promotion for himself." Another wrote, "Chalmers apparently was of the opinion that he could take the position by himself." An additional historian stated, "Chalmers was convinced that the affair would be a push-over." A captain in the 10th Mississippi remarked, "without orders from, or information first furnished his commanding officer— presumably, and as believed by all concerned, in the hope and expectancy, by coup de maitre of winning promotion, cost what it may in the loss of men."[28]

Within the Confederate ranks, the opinion of an easy victory was widespread. One infantryman wrote, "Our affairs . . . began arranging for its capture . . . the whole thing would make our brigade a good nice little breakfast and we could dispose of it before the balance of the army would come up."[29]

The men of Chalmers's brigade began their march to Munfordville around 10 p.m. and marched through the night. Chalmers arrived in the vicinity of Ft. Craig in the early morning hours of Sunday, September 14, 1862, and began to conduct a limited reconnaissance of the area.[30]

Chalmers placed Ketchum's four-gun battery and the 10th Mississippi, in support, on a rise known as the Mrs. Lewis Hill. Members of the 9th Mississippi Sharpshooters were ordered to attack the Federal pickets from the nearby woods. A reporter wrote in the September 14 issue of the *Louisville Journal*, "The pickets at the house of Mrs. Lewis . . . were first attacked, but they did not fall back until five o'clock."[31]

Mrs. Mary E. Brent, a child at the time of the battle, remarked several years after the incident, "One morning grandfather heard, at about sunup, a horse neighing . . . about that time we heard the firing of guns . . . and grandfather knew the battle was won."[32]

In conjunction with Scott's faulty estimation of the Federal strength inside Ft. Craig, Chalmers was also unable to clearly view the objective of the attack. A heavy fog hindered Chalmers from properly confirming Scott's information. In addition, Wilder's men had set the Green River Church on fire to eliminate the Confederates using it as a sharpshooters nest and the resulting smoke limited the field of vision.[33]

The limited success of Ketchum's Battery caused Chalmers to advance a portion of it to Woodson's Hill, an eminence located approximately 200 yards south of Ft. Craig. There, the detached cannon of Ketchum's artillery joined the 7th, 9th, and 29th Mississippi Infantry for an infantry assault on Ft. Craig.[34]

The 10th Mississippi stood on Mrs. Lewis's Hill with the 44th Mississippi and the remainder of Ketchum's Battery. It would be left to these two infantry regiments to attack the stockade.[35]

Col. Robert Alexander Smith, a Scottish immigrant, was given command of the 10th Mississippi at Munfordville. He was, under orders from Chalmers, to move from the river toward the stockade and storm the stronghold if the opportunity existed. Watt Strickland, a courier for Chalmers, rode to Smith at 6:30 and ordered Smith and the 10th Mississippi to move forward. Smith's reluctance about the assault, as well his duty to follow orders, became evident at this juncture.[36]

Smith said, "To charge now before the right is in place will draw upon me the concentrated fire of the enemy. Will I not be too soon? . . . The duty is mine, the responsibility belongs elsewhere."[37]

Smith's orders had been received while conferring with his captains. Smith pointed in the direction of Ft. Craig. With Smith's commands of, "Companies into line, captains to your posts. By the right of companies to the front, forward, quick time, march!" the advance of the 10th Mississippi toward Ft. Craig began.[38]

Pvt. W. L. Shaw of the 10th Mississippi recalled that after the Federal pickets were driven in, Chalmers ordered the charge upon the Federal works. Capt. E. K. Sykes of the 10th Mississippi added, "The enemy's pickets were rapidly driven in."[39]

Sykes wrote that the 10th Mississippi advanced through "an opening about half a mile in width, and under fire of the enemy's artillery and small arms from behind, what proved formidable intrenchments and earthworks."[40]

D. A. Campbell, also in the 10th Mississippi, said, "Our starting point was from one hill and the fort was on another, with a hollow intervening. Over this hollow hung a dense fog of smoke, which in a great measure obscured our way, but under cover of which, we could better make the assault. This smoke concealed the sequel to our terrible disaster. In the middle of this hollow was a ravine which had on its banks some large beech and other thick-limbed trees . . . the enemy had cut down and felled with their tops in our direction . . . unknown to us till we came immediately upon it."[41]

Private Shaw remarked that Colonel Wilder "had a most formidable blockhouse, with portholes to shoot through and with only a narrow entrance to the fort which was protected by six 12-pound cannon." Wilder reported a slight adjustment to Shaw's statement in noting that two six-pounders and two twelve-pounders were in Ft. Craig while two additional twelve-pound guns were in the stockade.[42]

The abates atop the banks of the ravine presented an unwanted surprise for the Confederates. Concealed by the smoke and fog, as Campbell noted in his earlier comments, the branches and tops of trees were "entwined to create a formidable double row" of obstacles for the advancing Confederates. [43]

Colonel Wilder wrote, "The fallen trees somewhat hindered the force of the charge."[44]

John C. Rietti, a Confederate in the 10th Mississippi, said, "The enemy was strongly entrenched, and an abatis of felled beech trees, with their thick interlacing branches, was a death trap to the assailants." Capt. E. T. Sykes estimated the abates lay "about 75 yards"[45] in front of the Federal position.

Col. Hal Engerud, the preeminent historian of the battle of Munfordville, commented on the effect the obstacles had upon the Confederate charge. Engerud explained that the felled trees, logs, and brush combined with sharp stakes to provide an effective method "to slow down and break up any attacking line."[46]

Until they reached the entanglements, the Confederates had advanced "with a yell and an unbroken line." A Federal witness vividly remembered the "loud shouts" of the charging rebels and the apparent horror these evocations caused.[47]

The effective and certain Confederate advance took a seriously negative turn at that point. The ease with which the warriors in gray had thus far moved toward the Federal position was a well-planned and activated trap.

Colonel Wilder wrote of the Confederate advance that, "The ground was of such character that [the men of the 10th Mississippi] were not exposed to the fire from the defenders of the redoubt until within two hundred and fifty yards." From the Confederate side of the attack, Pvt. W. L. Shaw recalled, "we advanced to within sixty or seventy yards" of the Federal line. [48]

Another Confederate recalled the Federal defenders, at this point, were, "raining a perfect hail storm of shot and shell into our confused and disordered ranks." The same soldier sadly noted, "all at once . . . the carnage began."[49]

A Northern journalist who witnessed the bloodshed at Munfordville wrote that the fire of the Indiana troops stifled the Confederate advance as the men in gray erupted "with demonic shouts of pain and rage."[50]

Wilder said of the conduct of the Federal troops, "Our men, entirely undrilled, stood to their works like veterans, and handsomely repulsed a most determined attack, many of the enemy . . . falling within fifty feet of our works. In all the war I never saw a more brilliant charge or more complete or resolute defense than these undrilled and half-armed men made at this point."[51]

Major Abbott, a Federal officer, jumped to the top of the fort. In one hand he held his hat while his sword occupied the other. Abbott had noticed the fort's flag had been shot down and he took it upon himself to defend it.[52]

Wilder lamented that Abbott "was instantly killed, and fell on the flag, which he honored with his life's blood; the flag had been pierced by one hundred and forty-six bullets, and the staff was struck eleven times. He fell an unnecessary sacrifice, but one of the bravest and most unselfish on record."[53]

Pvt. W. L. Shaw, 10th Mississippi, evaluated Chalmers's decision to attack Ft. Craig as "one of the great blunders of the war." Shaw most likely penned those words, not only due to the exposure he and his comrades faced from the torrid firepower from the Federals, but also for a significant and personal loss. Shaw expressed his disgust years later in writing, "Our regiment lost the gallant, brave and courageous Col. Robert A. Smith . . . and many other officers and privates."[54]

Colonel Smith had been mortally wounded in the assault. The well-respected officer was atop his horse, waving his sword over his head, in an attempt to lead his troops through the abatis when he was shot in the spine.[55]

George Fugel, color sergeant of the 10th Mississippi, joined Smith in the attempt to rally his comrades, but fell with a shot through his hip. Lieutenant Colonel Bullard and his horse were also killed when a canister round hit nearby.[56]

A witness noted the deaths of Smith and Bullard in writing,

> The spectacle before us was an awful one. Col. Smith had penetrated the timber, and was shot down . . . Col. Bullard and his noble old horse sank in a lifeless mass without a struggle, literally shot to pieces. I was near him and am satisfied that he was shot several time after being killed; the bodies of himself and horse were penetrated with some fifteen different missiles.[57]

John C. Rietti, 10th Mississippi, added that "several other

gallant officers" fell as "the Tenth Mississippi Regiment sustained the brunt of the fire and was almost decimated."[58]

A Confederate officer fortunate enough to survive "Chalmers's Great Blunder" of ordering the attack remarked, "Under a most severe and galling fire from the loopholes in the logs, with the artillery mowing us down" the men in gray sought shelter wherever it could be found. He added, "Some . . . lay down behind logs."[59]

D. A. Campbell said, "The enemy knew better than we did our position. As the smoke cleared away, their aim became more accurate, and the slaughter from then on was murderous . . . rendering it utterly out of the question for us to either go forward or retreat."[60]

Adding to the confusion of the literal death trap was the fact that Colonel Scott's Confederate cavalry had arrived and "imprudently opened fire" from cannon. Scott's attempt to "cooperate in the attack" had proven deadly to a large number of the pinned down Confederates.[61] Scott eventually recognized the error and had his artillery cease its barrage.

Prior to Scott's cessation of fire, the Confederates stayed in the ravine two hours and sought protection from the Federal fire. At 9:30 Chalmers sent a flag of truce forward, ending the devastating onslaught.

A Confederate reminisced about the events in writing,

> We were so cut up. The only reason that we were not all killed was that in charging up the hill they overshot us. Our company, what was left of it, managed to get up to within sixty or seventy yards of the stockade and we lay down behind a beech log . . . the only protection we had, and no telling what would have become of us if Chalmers had not hoisted the white flag[62]

By Wilder's estimation the battle was approaching a duration of three hours by the time of the cessation, with "the hottest portion of it not over twenty minutes." Wilder praised the valor of his troops and the Confederates in stating that the, "Mississippi regiments having shown the highest quality of courage, only equaled by the Alabama men, who fully equaled them, and fairly beaten by the brave boys in my command, who, inspired by finest patriotism, fought for their cause like the heroes they were."[63]

Using the time of truce to his most effective means, Chalmers sent a note to Wilder demanding a surrender of the Federal troops. The note said,

> You have made a gallant defense of your position, and to avoid further bloodshed I demand an unconditional surrender of your forces. I have six regiments of infantry, one battalion of sharpshooters, and have just been reinforced by a brigade of cavalry . . . with two batteries of artillery. I have two regiments on the north side of the river and you cannot escape. The railroad track is torn up . . . you can not receive reinforcements.[64]

Wilder's reply was short and strong. The Federal colonel wrote, "Your note . . . has been received. Thank you for your compliments. If you wish to avoid further bloodshed, keep out of the range of my guns . . . reinforcements . . . are now entering my works. I think I can defend my position against your entire force; at least I will try to do so."[65]

The reinforcements Wilder mentioned were under the command of Col. Cyrus L. Dunham of the 15th Indiana Volunteers. Six companies, each of some three hundred men, arrived as the battle was ending. Dunham had been able to avoid serious losses when the train transporting his troops left the track the Confederates had destroyed earlier. Dunham was also able to avoid major contact with Scott's cavalry on the north side of the river. Upon Dunham's arrival, Wilder's troops, now battle-tested and possessing a sense of victory, welcomed Dunham's command with cheers.[66]

While Federal reinforcements arrived, acts of humanity abounded under the flag of truce. General Chalmers asked Wilder's permission to approach the Federal lines to remove the wounded Confederates and bury the dead. Colonel Wilder not only agreed to grant Chalmers's requests, but he also sent out details to assist the Confederates. Federal surgeons were assigned to care of the wounded and Wilder loaded two flat cars to carry the critically wounded. A Federal officer recalled that the cars were pushed two miles by hand in order to ensure the safety of the wounded rebels.[67]

A member of the 10th Mississippi wrote, "The men of the 10th Miss promptly began the removal of its dead and wounded, carrying them to the crest of the ridge from whence we had that morning begun the advance, the relief party continuing its work until our dead and wounded . . . [and] everything of value; had been removed."[68]

That same soldier added that liquor was frequently shared at that stage of the conflict. The Confederate wrote that he shared "liquid fluid that cheers and sometimes inebriates" with a Federal officer, yet this was considered more of a "social commune" as men of both sides were given the care they needed.[69]

One of the Confederates given attention was Colonel Smith. E. T. Sykes of the 10th Mississippi recalled seeing Colonel Smith lying on the ground and suffering from his wound. Sykes wrote, "I knew him to be temperate, [but] I insisted on his taking a drink of the brandy . . . finally consenting to my request . . . I left the canteen with its contents . . .with the chivalric Colonel, who I never saw again."[70]

Smith was taken to a home where Mary E. Brent Roberts, a young girl at the time, saw the mortally wounded officer. Mrs. Lewis witnessed the officer lying on a blanket and asked, "Why did you not take him in the house and on a bed?" Smith was moved inside and reportedly said to one of the attendants, "I am mortally wounded and can't live but a few hours . . . so leave me." After Smith's death three days later, he was temporarily buried in the Lewis yard, but was reinterred in the Evergreen Cemetery in Jackson, Mississippi.[71]

In an 1884 issue of *Frank Leslie's Illustrated Newspaper,* an article and drawing featured the large crowd that gathered for the September 14, 1884 dedication of a monument to Smith and the other members of the 10th Mississippi who fell at Munfordville, twenty-two years earlier. The $4,000 monument stands some twenty feet tall, weighs thirty-five tons, and was designed in Nashville, Tennessee.[72]

As for the burials at Munfordville, a veteran of the battle recalled, "The dead are all in one long wide grave, placed according to rank . . . each wrapped in his grey blanket, with no other covering than mother earth."[73]

Sadly, the Confederates had no shovels to use for the burials of their dead. Therefore, they were dependant upon the graciousness of their Northern counterparts for the supply and use of digging implements. One historian wrote of the irony the situation held in saying, "Southern bodies . . . interred with Federal shovels in border-state ground."[74]

At 5 p.m. General Chalmers sent Colonel Wilder a message that, in his opinion, the truce was ended. Colonel Dunham, who had recently arrived with Federal reinforcements, had also assumed command of the entire Union garrison. Wilder remarked, "Dunham's commission antedated mine a few days, which entitled him to take command." In turn, Dunham requested an hour's extension of the truce, and Chalmers granted Dunham's wish.[75]

During the extra hour of the truce, General Chalmers and Colonel Scott participated in a meeting regarding the situation at hand. The two Confederate officers determined that, despite their combined forces, they lacked the ability to capture the Federal position. As a result, the Confederate forces withdrew to Cave City when the truce reached its end at 6 p.m.[76]

On September 15, Gen. Braxton Bragg, extremely agitated over Chalmers's decision to attack Ft. Craig without permission, began marching 30,000 Confederates toward Munfordville. By 9:30 that morning Bragg was at Rowlett's Station where his troops fought with forward Federal positions. The combat lasted only one hour, as the pickets and outposts were driven in. A day-long long-range fire fight ensued as a Confederate division crossed the Green River and occupied a position from which its cannon held a clear view of the Federal stockade and Ft. Craig.[77]

A Federal officer proclaimed that the Confederates' success was due to the fact that the Southern warriors "took position on ground that commanded our position."[78]

Meanwhile, Kentucky and Indiana infantrymen, as well as an Ohio battery, reached Ft. Craig. These soldiers, having departed from Lebanon Junction, increased the number of Federal troops at the Munfordville fortifications to more than 4,000.[79]

Inconsistencies and indecision within the Federal leadership at Munfordville and elsewhere led to dire situations for the occupants of Ft. Craig. Colonel Dunham arguably exhibited foresight or cowardice in his actions involving capitulation of the fortress.

Colonel Wilder recalled that late that afternoon Colonel Dunham summoned several officers, informing them of the situation. Dunham sought surrender while others in the group objected to such a decision. Meanwhile, a telegram arrived from Louisville, returning command to Wilder and placing Dunham under arrest.[80]

Subsequently, a member of Bragg's staff used another flag of truce to deliver a message from General Bragg. The note called for an immediate, unconditional surrender of the Federal troops at Munfordville. Bragg's request stated, "Surrounded by an overwhelming force, your successful resistance or escape is impossible. You are therefore offered an opportunity by capitulation of avoiding the terrible consequences of an assault."[81]

Wilder later sent a reply to Bragg, preceded by Dunham's declaration to defend the post. A short time after regaining command of the Federal forces at Munfordville, Wilder wrote, "At a consultation of officers of this command held since dark this evening, it is agreed upon that if satisfactory evidence is given them of your ability to make good your assertions of largely superior numbers, so as to make the defense of this position a useless waste of human life, we will treat as to terms of an honorable surrender."[82]

Bragg responded in a rather impatient manner in writing Wilder,

The only evidence I can give you of my ability to make good my assertion on the presence of a sufficient force to compel your surrender, beyond the statement that it now exceeds 20,000 will be the use of it. An unconditional surrender of your whole force, etc., is demanded and will be enforced. You are allowed one hour in which to make known your decision.[83]

The information Bragg provided convinced Wilder that, if the content of the message was true, the Federals were heavily outnumbered. Wilder sought advice in an interesting source, Confederate Gen. Simon Buckner. The Confederate officer was widely known as a true gentleman; therefore, Wilder felt confident in conferring with Buckner. General Buckner later stated, "I wouldn't have deceived that man under those circumstances for anything."[84]

After asking if he could take a look for himself, Wilder was led to the Confederate lines, where he was escorted through the heart of the Confederate position. Wilder was told some eighty cannon were south of the river and was convinced the Confederates had a minimal strength of 22,000. Buckner told Wilder, "It is for you to judge how long your command would live under that fire."[85]

Wilder stated to Buckner that he believed he should surrender. Buckner replied that he was largely positive of the number of troops Wilder had at his disposal, but it would be up to Wilder to determine if he could, "live under the fire that is to be opened" upon the Federal stronghold. After a time of deliberation, Wilder decided to surrender his command.[86]

With "drums beating and colors flying," Wilder's troops surrendered at 6 p.m. on September 17 at Rowlett's Station. Immediately after the surrender, 3,921 men and 155 officers were paroled. Bragg proclaimed, "The capture of this position . . . with all their artillery, arms, munitions, and stores . . . crown and completes the separate campaign of this army." Displaying compassion for his captives, Bragg made certain each Union soldier received three days' rations.[87]

Col. Philip B. Spence, a Confederate, recalled, "I shall never forget the grand sight . . . when over four thousand well dressed

Federal soldiers, with shining muskets and the beautiful stars and stripes, formed line, and at the command, 'Ground arms!' every flag and musket went down at the same moment in front of the Confederates."[88]

Today, more than two hundred acres of approximately 1,100 acres of the Munfordville battlefield is rated as protected land. The success came despite opposition from various individuals and groups. However, the determination of an equal set of interested citizens was inspired when the battlefield, which was covered with an abandoned sawmill and a junkyard at the time, was placed on the Civil War Preservation Trust's Most Endangered List. Fortunately, a driving tour, a thirteen-stop walking tour with more than two miles of trails, and wayside exhibits greet visitors to the hallowed grounds. Two of the locations able to be visited on the walking tour are the Presbyterian Church and the Munford Inn. The former served as a hospital following the action of September 1862, while the latter, a log tavern built in 1810, was General Bragg's headquarters at the time of the fight.[89]

To reach the Munfordville battlefield, visitors may take exit 65 on I-65 South and head south on Route 31W. Ft. Craig is located south of the Green River Bridge. The entrance to the site is on the Old Woodsonville Road. There is no charge and the battlefield is open daily from dusk to dawn. Various grants allowed the Battle for the Bridge Historic Preserve to set aside the land for visitation and interpretation. It is to be noted though that the trail leading to the interpretive markers is not easily traveled and is susceptible to becoming slippery in damp weather.[90]

Although the battlefield currently has no visitor's center, information can be obtained at the Hart County Historical Society Museum, located at 109 Main Street, P. O. Box 606 in Munfordville, Kentucky, 42765. Guided tours may be arranged through the museum for a minimal fee. The museum's telephone number is 207-524-0101 and its Web site is www.hartcountymuseum.org/. The museum is closed on Sunday and Monday and is easily spotted in the two-story brick building adjacent to city hall. A variety of memorabilia may be viewed, and a helpful staff can provide directions to the battlefield. Also, it will prove worthwhile to visit the Web site of the Battle for the Bridge Historic Preserve at battleforthebridge.org.[91]

The Hart County Historical Society, an agency that has worked since 1995 to preserve the battlefield, has declared that no buildings will be constructed on the preserved land. The agricultural aspect of the land is intended to be preserved while the Historical Society also desires to "provide an economic stimulus" for Hart County. A major goal of the society is "to provide an opportunity for the public to visit and learn about the history of the area." In relation to the latter, the battlefield is listed on the National Register of Historic Places.[92]

With the positive aspects of preservation far outweighing the negative, the Munfordville battlefield holds a great deal of potential. The Battle for the Bridge Historic Preserve has achieved a great deal of interpretation, preservation, and historic promise. With the groundwork firmly established, only the future will tell what additional acreage and/or battlefield sites can be saved for future generations.

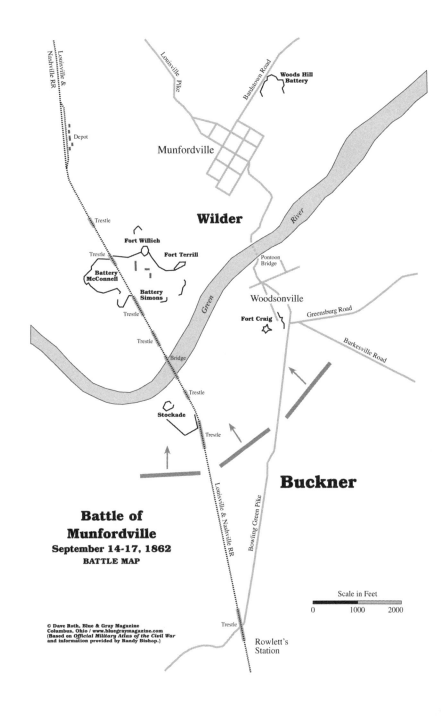

Louisville & Nashville RR

Louisville Pike

Bardstown Road

Woods Hill Battery

Depot

Munfordville

Trestle

Wilder

Green River

Fort Willich

Trestle

Fort Terrill

Battery McConnell

Pontoon Bridge

Battery Simons

Woodsonville

Trestle

Fort Craig

Greensburg Road

Trestle

Burkesville Road

Bridge

Trestle

Stockade

Trestle

Buckner

Louisville & Nashville RR

Bowling Green Pike

Battle of Munfordville
September 14-17, 1862
BATTLE MAP

Scale in Feet

0   1000   2000

© Dave Roth, Blue & Gray Magazine
Columbus, Ohio / www.bluegraymagazine.com
(Based on *Official Military Atlas of the Civil War*
and information provided by Randy Bishop.)

Trestle

Rowlett's Station

Col. John T. Wilder surrendered his Federal command after a visit to the Confederate lines. (National Archives)

Munfordville as it appeared in 1862. (Courtesy *Harper's Weekly*)

The Anthony Woodson house was located in the midst of action at Munfordville. (Photo by author)

The location of Ft. Craig is visible across the fence. (Photo by author)

The L & N Railroad Bridge was a major objective of the battle at Munfordville and is present still. (Photo by author)

Portions of the battlefield contain trails that are little more than farm roads. (Photo by author)

CHAPTER TEN

PERRYVILLE
or Chaplin Hills

October 8, 1862

"We had committed sad havoc in killing and wounding large numbers."
—Brig. Gen. Daniel S. Donelson, C.S.A.

The significance of the battle at Perryville, Kentucky, is often overlooked and hardly ever given its due credit. While the battle of Gettysburg is usually touted as the High Tide of the Confederacy, it has been suggested that Perryville, rather than Gettysburg, should receive the designation, especially in relation to the Western Theater of the American Civil War. Following the battle of Perryville, Confederate troops never again ventured into the state of Kentucky in as large numbers as they did during the Confederate offensive in the fall of 1862. This point, doubled with the fact that Perryville holds the distinction of being the largest battle of the numerous conflicts within the borders of Kentucky, is reason enough to explore the major incidents leading to and taking place during the action of early October 1862.

Confederate Maj. Gen. Edmund Kirby Smith saw the liberation of Kentucky, a state deeply divided in its loyalties, as a major catalyst for his career and prominence. Gen. Braxton Bragg, who had started the war as a major general and had been promoted on April 12, 1862, eventually postponed his own plan to regain possession of Middle Tennessee and the Volunteer State's capital of Nashville and came to view a venture with Kirby Smith as profitable for the Confederate cause. The foray into Kentucky would hopefully not only provide the incentive for badly needed recruits to come to the aid of the Richmond, Virginia-based government but would also likely hamper the Federal supply base in Louisville. Col. John Hunt Morgan's raid into Kentucky in the summer of 1862 resulted in the Confederate cavalry officer proclaiming that thousands of recruits would join the Southern cause if the Confederates would take possession of the Bluegrass State. In addition, a seemingly unlimited amount of supplies were stored at Louisville; the lure was simply too great for the Confederate generals to avoid.[1]

In response, Maj. Gen. Don Carlos Buell moved his Union army from Nashville toward Louisville in an attempt to preserve the town's supply base. Buell stated that while Nashville could be held under Maj. Gen. George H. Thomas's leadership, Kentucky had to be rescued. Following a forced march under far-from-ideal conditions, Buell's army reached Louisville on September 25.[2]

Major General Buell enjoyed the riches of recruitment, adding several thousand men to his Federal ranks while in the area. Ironically, the Confederate recruitment efforts yielded limited results. Buell sent approximately 20,000 soldiers under Brig. Gen. Joshua Sill to Frankfort with the assignment to keep Kirby Smith's Confederate forces, spread out between Frankfort and Lexington, from reinforcing Bragg. In response to reports of the Confederate movements, Buell, on October 1, ordered three corps, totaling 55,000 men, from Louisville to crush Bragg's Confederates, positioned forty miles southeast of Louisville in Bardstown.[3]

Three days later the inauguration of pro-Confederate Kentucky provisional governor Richard Hawes, replacing the Unionist James Robinson, who had moved to Louisville in order to escape the Confederate arrival, was interrupted when Sill's command began firing cannon outside Frankfort. Bragg incorrectly determined that the shots were from a mass of Buell's army and ordered Maj. Gen. Leonidas Polk from Bardstown to attack Sill. Polk found himself seriously outmanned and withdrew from Bardstown, allowing the Union army to gain possession of the town. Polk eventually positioned his troops at Harrodsburg, under Bragg's orders. Bragg also moved to Harrodsburg while Kirby Smith remained near Lexington, spreading the Confederate forces across a fifty-mile-wide area.[4]

Maj. Gen. William J. Hardee had also abandoned Bardstown and intended to join Polk and Bragg in Harrodsburg. Hardee desired that Polk join him along the route. The reunion of Polk and Hardee took place some twenty-five miles west of the Bryantsville, Kentucky, Confederate supply base, in a town called Perryville.[5]

Perryville was settled in the late 1770s under the name of Harbison's Station. Residents there constructed a fort, intended to provide a safety buffer from area natives, around a natural spring and cave on the banks of the Chaplin River. Ironically, the town's founder, James Harbison was later captured and beheaded by a group of Native Americans. In 1817 the town was renamed Perryville, after Commodore Oliver Hazard Perry, and was incorporated. The city's population had grown to almost 350 on the eve of the American Civil War and Merchant's Row, a center of trade, blossomed on the riverbanks.[6]

On October 6, 1862 Major General Hardee reached Perryville and intended to use the water supply there to quench the troops' severe thirst. The town of Perryville had grown along the Chaplin River, the body of water that had tributaries such as Doctor's Creek, Bull Run Creek, and Wilson's Creek. However, in the previous month, less than an inch of rain had fallen in the area and October 6 marked the nineteenth consecutive day with no rainfall in the area. As a result, most of the local bodies of water had dried up or contained only small pools of stagnant water.[7]

The lack of water was but one of the issues facing the Confederates who moved into Perryville. General Bragg was an extremely difficult man to work with and was and has been labeled as mentally ill, indecisive, depressed, bad tempered, sarcastic, quarrelsome, bitter, incompetent, and tactless.[8] In turn, Bragg was far from admired or respected among his subordinates or lower ranking soldiers.

The problems of a lack of suitable drinking water, as well as the absence of an abundance of admiration for the high command, also plagued General Buell's Federal troops. Considered to possibly be a traitor due to the facts that Buell married a slave owner's daughter and openly despised abolitionists, the Federal officer was labeled as aloof and cold. Buell's troops and officers had open arguments with him and held little esteem for his style of rigid discipline or his personality.[9]

In relation to failing to satisfy one of the basic needs of his troops, Buell reported the lack of water in writing, "The whole army had for three days or more suffered from a scarcity of water. The last day particularly the troops and animals suffered exceedingly for the want of it and from hot weather and dusty roads. In the bed of Doctor's Creek . . . some pools of water were discovered." Buell notified Maj. Gen. Alexander McDowell McCook, one of Buell's division commanders sent to Perryville to intercept the Confederate column, that the shortage of water throughout the area was definite.[10]

Food was an important quest for Confederates in Brig. Gen. J. Patton Anderson's Division. One member, William E. Bevens of the 1st Arkansas in Powel's brigade, recalled the adventures of a group of fellow regiment members who were camped in the main street of Perryville. The soldiers had stolen a bee-hive and were stung on their faces, causing their eyes to swell to the point of greatly inhibiting their vision. Bevens himself found the humor short-lived when he was also stung when lying down to go to sleep for what appeared to be a rather treacherous day ahead.[11]

Another Confederate, Pvt. Sam Watkins of the 1st Tennessee, Maney's brigade, Cheatham's division, had picket duty on the night of October 7. Watkins obtained food more easily than did Bevens's fellow members of the 1st Arkansas, as another man and he entered an abandoned Perryville home and procured "a bucket of honey, a pitcher of sweet milk, and three or four biscuits." Watkins stated, rather sarcastically, that it appeared the owner of the home, his family, and all Perryville citizens had, for some reason, gone visiting. Interestingly, Watkins described this incident as taking place with a Union picket. Perryville historian Kurt Holman has explained that the likelihood of a Union soldier being in Perryville that night is virtually impossible unless the Union soldier was a prisoner of war. Evidently Watkins's recollection may have been from another battlefield.[12]

In actuality, many of the residents of Perryville had fled the area with the arrival of Confederates under the command of officers such as Gen. Braxton Bragg, Maj. Gen. Leonidas K. Polk, and Maj. Gen. William J. Hardee. Others saw a similar level of threat or felt the same type of contempt for the nearby Union troops of commanders such as Maj. Gen. Don Carlos Buell, Capt. and Acting Maj. Gen. Charles C. Gilbert, Maj. Gen. Thomas L. Crittenden, and Maj. Gen. Alexander McDowell McCook.

Major General McCook commanded the First Corps of Buell's army. Initially sent toward Harrodsburg, McCook had his orders changed when Buell learned of the Confederate concentration at Perryville, some ten miles southwest of Harrodsburg. Meanwhile, Buell's Second Corps, under Maj. Gen. Thomas L. Crittenden, moved through Springfield and then went to Hayesville before turning left onto the Lebanon Road. The Third Corps, under Maj. Gen. Charles Gilbert and accompanied by Buell, moved through Springfield southward toward Perryville.[13]

Buell reported that when the Third Corps arrived at Doctor's Creek on the afternoon of October 7, "The Thirty-sixth brigade . . . from General Sheridan's division, was ordered forward to seize and hold a commanding position" overlooking the algae-laden pools of water discovered in Doctors Creek about 1½ miles from Perryville. Buell established his headquarters at the Dorsey House, approximately three miles from Perryville.[14]

Buell noted that just after midnight on October 8, "the enemy showed a determination to prevent us from gaining possession of" the pools of water located in Doctors Creek at the base of Peters' Hill. Despite this statement, the orders were carried out that night, "and a supply of bad water was secured for the troops."[15] The encounter Buell described as a "determination to prevent" the

Union troops from obtaining water served as the opening shots of the battle of Perryville.

The Federal detachment sent forward for the water was from Col. Daniel McCook's 36th Brigade of Sheridan's Eleventh Division, Gilbert's Corps. McCook was twenty-three and the younger brother of Maj. Gen. Alexander McCook, Buell's First Army Corps commander. Young McCook led the 85th Illinois, a group of new recruits, into their first action that day, facing a group of 7th Arkansas troops determined to defend Peters' Hill.[16]

The 85th Illinois was not the only relatively new group in the Federal ranks at Perryville. One-half of Major General McCook's troops had only been in the army one week prior to arriving at Perryville. Buell had commented on the lack of readiness of the men in blue in stating that the "considerable force of raw troops . . . were as yet undisciplined, unprovided with suitable artillery, and in every way unfit for active operations against a disciplined foe."[17]

Though the darkness of the early morning confrontation between the 85th Illinois and 7th Arkansas prevented the continuance of action for several hours, troop deployment occurred within the Confederate ranks. Bragg ordered Polk to attack, yet Polk recalled, "At a meeting of the general officers, held about daylight, it was resolved, in great disparity of our forces, to adopt the defensive-offensive, to await the movements of the enemy, and to be guided by events as they were developed."[18]

A Federal soldier remarked, "The day was bright and beautiful all that could be desired in that most pleasant month in the year." From the Confederate cavalry, the description of the morning of October 8 was, "The sun rose bright and clear into a cloudless sky and shone over the hottest day I ever experienced." In fact, at 7 a.m., on Wednesday, October 8, the temperature was 72 degrees Fahrenheit. The lack of clouds to interfere allowed the temperature to rise to 90 degrees by 2 p.m. that afternoon.[19]

Polk reported that the initial deployment of the Confederate line of battle placed Maj. Gen. Simon Buckner's Third Division "of the left wing, occupied the extreme right" with the Second Division under Brig. Gen. J. Patton Anderson in the center. Brig. Gen. Daniel S. Donelson, "of the right wing, under General Cheatham," held the left. Cheatham's stay on the right wing was not long, as he moved to the extreme left, arriving at that location by noon. Polk noted, "The whole of our force, including all arms, did not exceed 15,000."[20]

Although Polk wrote that the belief was held that the Federal troops far outnumbered the force Bragg had at Perryville, it is generally regarded that Bragg himself was unaware of the presence of the bulk of the Federal Army of the Ohio, an extreme situation for the Confederate troops, until late in the battle. Buell's official report of the battle stated of the Federal numbers at Perryville, "I do not think there were more than fifty thousand of the army . . . in front of Perryville." It is estimated that less than half of these would actually be engaged in the fight.[21]

Polk's hesitance in initiating the attack infuriated the temperamental General Bragg who recalled, "Having ordered the attack and that no time should be lost, I was concerned at not hearing the commencement of the engagement . . . to my surprise, however, no gun was heard, and on my arrival, about 10 a.m., I was informed that it was determined not to attack."[22]

Bragg deemed it necessary to make adjustments to the Confederate line General Polk had established and sent an order to Polk "to bring on the engagement" immediately. Becoming impatient at the delay given to this order, Bragg "dispatched a staff officer to repeat it to the general." With no reaction coming to this request, Bragg "followed in person and soon put the troops in motion."[23]

A Confederate wrote, "General Bragg returned . . . to General Polk . . . Bragg said to Polk, 'General, why are you not fighting as I instructed?' Polk replied, 'I am occupying an offensive defensive position.'" Allegedly, Bragg's comment, "Strange position to occupy" was given and Bragg proceeded to realign the men in gray.[24]

Bragg's orders sent the Confederates of Cheatham's division up the "River Road," a passageway largely consisting of the dry bed of the Chaplin River. This movement caused mass amounts of dust to fill the air, and the Federal troops incorrectly discerned that the Confederates were in retreat along the Harrodsburg road. While entire regiments of Federal troops continued to arrive at the positions of their comrades, many of the men in blue stacked their arms and enjoyed a false sense of relief that a battle had been avoided.[25]

When the Confederates reached the position Bragg desired, they initiated an artillery barrage upon the Union lines. An hour-long artillery duel ensued, in what one Confederate described in writing, "Perryville is situated in a beautiful valley being surrounded on all sides by a beautiful range of hills, one of the grandest places in the world for a cannon duel."[26]

Sam Watkins, 1st Tennessee, wrote, "Cannon on both sides were belching and blazing fire, and the air was full of bursting shells, and sulphuric smoke, and blaze of musketry was like a great forest fire among the dry leaves of autumn."[27]

A Confederate in Semples' battery estimated that his artillery crew fired about two hundred rounds that regularly caused, "quite a commotion among the enemy."[28]

During the event, one Federal recalled it as being a "fine artillery duel" in which a second stated that many Confederate shells burst over the heads of the Union soldiers, and a third acknowledged, "Rebels . . . shells occasionally dropped in among us."[29]

While the duel continued, Confederate scouts attempted to locate the end of the Federal left flank. Capt. David Stone's 1st Kentucky Battery was involved in firing at the Confederate cavalry scouts of Col. John Wharton's command. Wharton found what he believed to be the extreme left flank and reported this to his superiors. Unfortunately for the Confederate infantrymen, Wharton had seen what was the end of the Federal line at that time, but additional Union troops arrived before action would be taken, resulting in a Confederate assault upon a point farther to the Federal center.[30]

The initial Confederate attack upon McCook's Federal line came from Brig. Gen. Daniel S. Donelson's brigade at approximately 2 p.m. Donelson had Col. William L. Moore in command of the 8th Tennessee while Col. Robert C. Tyler commanded the 15th

Tennessee. The 16th, 38th, and 51st Tennessee Infantry Regiments completed Donelson's brigade and fell under the leadership of colonels John H. Savage, John C. Carter, and John Chester, respectively. However, historian Kurt Holman has noted that the attack was with only three regiments in support as the 8th and 51st were detached, supporting Carnes' Battery. The 16th was the first unit to top the bluffs and was ordered forward without waiting for the two additional regiments. This fact would contribute to the heavy casualty rate of 59 percent.[31]

The 16th Tennessee pushed back the skirmishers from the 33rd Ohio and headed toward the Union lines where units such as the 2nd Ohio stood in anticipation of their arrival. First Lieutenant George W. Landrum, a signal officer in the 2nd Ohio, remarked, "Suddenly there emerged from the wood the head of a column of men, and as they came out, their bayonets glistened in the sun."[32]

Due to the Federal deployment of the 1st Corps of the Federal left flank, a movement performed in anticipation of an attack on Perryville on October 9, Donelson's men "found themselves trapped in a vicious crossfire." Within minutes the mass amount of casualties caused Donelson to halt his advance, almost ending the Confederate attack at Perryville. The 33rd Ohio, under Lt. Col. Oscar F. Moore, and eight cannons of Lt. Charles Parsons' improvised battery, largely new recruits from the 105th Ohio, hit the assaulting Confederates in a rain of shot and shell designated as "infantry killers."[33]

A Confederate officer recalled, "We suffered terribly . . . a fellow who had become panicky and thrown himself into a ditch, three feet or more deep, where no ball direct from the front could possibly have reached him. I was shaming him for his cowardice, when a ball . . . struck him and killed him while I was talking to him."[34]

A member of Maney's brigade added, "When within fifty yards, they opened on us with musketry, and now the fight became general and looked like the whole world had been converted into blue coats, whistling balls, bursting shells and brass cannon."[35]

James D. Jordan, 9th Tennessee, lamented, "My brother, Samuel

Jordan, was killed by my side, and I was shot in the face which resulted in permanent partial deafness."[36]

Donelson's Confederates somehow managed to regroup and counterattack. Donelson wrote, "We had committed sad havoc in killing and wounding large numbers."[37]

The action captured the attention of young Mary Jane Bottom Gibson. The recently widowed lady's farm and home were in the heart of the action between Donelson's troops and the largely inexperienced Federal troops. Near her home, the Confederate attack from Donelson stopped. Fearful for the safety of her children and herself, the Widow Gibson took an axe and cut through the floor, enabling her family to hide in the joists of the house.[38]

It became apparent that a Confederate victory or defeat hinged upon the success or failure to take the Federal left flank where 2,600 green U.S. troops under Brig. Gen. William R. Terrill, a West Point graduate and professor, stood. Terrill, a Virginian who remained loyal to the Union, commanded the 33rd Brigade, a unit containing approximately 2,400 men. The 33rd Brigade was part of Brig. Gen. James S. Jackson's Tenth Division and consisted of the 80th and 123rd Illinois Infantry Regiments under the leadership of colonels Thomas G. Allen and James Monroe and the 105th Ohio of Col. Albert S. Hall. In addition, Col. Theophilus T. Garrard's detachment of 194 men from several units completed the infantry strength of Terrill's Brigade.[39]

The task of taking this position was given to the 1,900-man brigade of Brig. Gen. George Maney, an attorney before the war. Col. Hume R. Feild led the 1st Tennessee Infantry while Col. George C. Porter commanded the 6th Tennessee of Maney's brigade. The 9th and 27th Tennessee were under the command of lieutenant colonels John W. Buford and William Frierson respectively and the brigade's infantry strength was rounded out with Col. Charles A. McDaniel's leadership of the 41st Georgia.[40]

Brigadier General Terrill had been in a meeting the previous night, consulting with his friends and fellow officers Col. George Webster and Brig. Gen. James S. Jackson. Terrill and the men held a conversation that eventually evolved into a discussion of their possible deaths. Terrill, using his skills and knowledge of mathematics, assured them that the chance of all three of them meeting their deaths in a single battle was a mathematical improbability.[41] Terrill's calculations would soon prove incorrect.

At 3 p.m. Maney's Confederates were able to move through woods and advance within a short distance of a split-rail fence near the base of Open Knob, the hill that served as Terrill's position beside Parsons' battery.[42] When the Federal troops and artillerymen detected Maney's movement, they began firing into the gray ranks. Almost immediately the casualties escalated.

Lt. Col. William Frierson commanded the 27th Tennessee at Perryville. Frierson recalled the action in writing, "During the whole time of passing through the woods the battery was playing upon us with terrible effect, but as soon as the fence was reached, in full view of the battery, such a storm of shell, grape, canister, and Minie balls was turned loose upon us as no troops scarcely ever before encountered. Large boughs were torn from the trees . . . shattered as if by lighting, and the ground plowed in deep furrows."[43]

The 123rd Illinois opened fire on the Confederates as the gray-clad warriors reached the split-rail fence. A rapid exchange of gunfire erupted between the largely pinned down Confederates and the troops of Jackson and Terrill atop Open Knob. Jackson advised Maj. James Connelly of the 123rd to dismount his horse in order to avoid being shot. Ironically, two shots then hit General Jackson in the chest, killing the division commander and necessitating command of the division to fall to General Terrill.[44]

W. H. Davis, 4th Tennessee Cavalry, wrote of this phase of the battle,

Our bugler sounded "mount", and in quick succession, "Charge!"
. . . We went full speed directly against that battery, double-shotted with grape and canister. We had reached within twenty yards of the guns when the line of infantry arose and poured a volley into us, shattering our line, killing a number of our horses, and emptying numerous saddles. We retired . . . reformed, and made a second

assault, again being repulsed . . . our bugler again sounded, "Charge!" and grim determination was visible on the face of every man in that command. Away we went again . . . to do or die. The field was strewn with dead and wounded men and horses, but we continued . . . killing the gunners and Gen. J. S. Jackson.[45]

Terrill yelled for the 123rd Illinois to protect Parsons' guns. Reportedly the call was issued, "Do not let them get the guns!" An estimated 770 men of the 123rd, raw untrained troops, invoked a downhill bayonet charge toward some 1,800 well-trained Confederates. The charge proved disastrous for the 123rd as the total casualties exceeded 160 men.[46]

Federals of the 105th Ohio were able to check the Confederate attack. The arrival of the troops was in a piecemeal style, as the 123rd had arrived with Parsons' Battery. The 105th got to the location as the 123rd Ohio was running away. Lt. William Turner set up his four-gun battery two hundred yards behind Maney's line to give support to the rebel troops. Maney's soldiers pushed forward, only to be stopped within fifty feet of the Federal cannon. Regrouping again, the Confederates moved to the top of the hill and drove the previously untested Union troops from their cannons. The 80th Ohio and Garrard arrived just as the line was breaking, having gotten lost through "a misdirection of the guide." By 3:30 Open Knob was without any Federal defenders and the Confederates controlled the artillery.[47]

The incident impressed Albion Tourgee of the 105th Ohio. Tourgee wrote, "Men fell, sometime with a groan, sometime without a sound . . . line officers went back and forth encouraging, directing. We stood alone, a thin line of blue."[48]

Maney's command moved to the back of Open Knob and toward a field of corn. The cornfield lay between Open Knob and another hill where 2,200 troops of Col. John C. Starkweather's 28th Brigade were positioned. A battery of twelve cannons backed Starkweather's infantrymen of the 79th Pennsylvania, the 24th Illinois, and the 1st and 21st Wisconsin. The latter regiment had just entered service a few weeks earlier; reportedly many of the men had never before fired their guns.[49]

The deaths and wounds quickly mounted among the Confederate ranks. It was estimated that eight color bearers became casualties with the first discharge of the Federal cannon. A Confederate participant recalled, "Tom Lanier was killed some thirty feet from the battery . . . Robert was shot through the forehead . . . Jack Goodbar fell."[50]

Lt. Col. John Patterson from Maney's brigade became one of the casualties of the Confederate charge. His death was recalled in the memoirs of a veteran of the battle, "Patterson holloed to charge and take their guns, and we were soon in a hand-to-hand fight, every man for himself, using the butts of our guns and bayonets." Another participant continued, "Colonel Patterson was slightly wounded in the wrist, but he tied a handkerchief around it and continued to give orders until . . . grapeshot hit his mustache, going through his head, killing him instantly."[51]

At this point, according to an account of the battle, "A drummer boy of the 9th Tennessee quite distinguished himself. He went forward when his regiment made the charge. His drum was shattered by a fragment of a shell . . . seized a gun . . . and gallantly pressed forward . . . and . . . with the butt of his rifle crushed the skull of an artilleryman."[52]

Maney's advance toward Starkweather's position was concealed as high weeds grew thickly in the corn that was said to be as tall as twelve feet. The 21st Wisconsin was sent into the cornfield, but they soon sought shelter from the fire of the attacking Confederates. Confusion erupted as Confederate fire slammed into the ranks of the 21st Wisconsin. Adding insult to injury, Federals, "running like rabbits" from Open Knob infiltrated the 21st, creating more problems for the Wisconsin troops. General Terrill was among the panicked Federals retreating through the thick checked patterns, or tight clusters, of corn and reportedly shouted that a terrible force of rebels was advancing behind him.[53]

A member of the 38th Tennessee, Donelson's Confederate

brigade, said, "We advanced through a field where the grapeshot and shrapnel were rattling against the cornstalks, which had been cut and shocked up, also thinning our ranks . . . Colonel Carter's horse was killed and he himself wounded in the leg."[54]

Members of the 21st Wisconsin heard the rustling of corn and soon found that the source "were the remains of the 123rd Illinois fleeing in a panic." A short wait ensued before the Wisconsin troops heard "the rustling of the corn again and the banshee yells of the rebels." O. P. Clinton, chaplain of the 21st Wisconsin recalled, "The corn was so high that our men could not see the enemy until they were within thirty yards . . . rushing upon them like demons. The fire of the 21st told fearfully upon the rebels."[55]

T. A. Head of Buffalo Valley, Tennessee, recalled,

> A most remarkable wound was inflicted upon a Confederate soldier by Yankee bullets . . . Corporal H. I. Hughes, of Company F, Sixteenth Tennessee Regiment . . . was subjected to a fearful cross fire, both of infantry and artillery. In the midst of the charge, while our men were giving the old Rebel yell to perfection, this man . . . received a wound in the mouth which broke out all of his lower teeth. When taken from the field it was found that he had been hit in the mouth by two bullets at a cross fire. They had met in his mouth and each ranged with the teeth of the lower jaw, lodging one on each side of his neck. His face was not marked on the outside.[56]

An estimated two hundred men from Terrill's command rallied with the Wisconsin troops in an effort to quell the Confederate tide. To avoid killing their fellow Federal soldiers, the newly formed line of Union soldiers held their fire. This technique proved too much for the men of the 21st Wisconsin as 1,400 advancing Confederates hit their position and caused the recent inductees to flee for their lives.[57]

Brig. Gen. A. P. Stewart's five-regiment brigade of Tennessee troops entered the fray, taking a position behind Donelson and Maney. Stewart had almost 1,500 troops from the 4th, 5th, 24th, 31st, and 33rd Tennessee Infantry Regiments. The 4th and 5th were behind Maney while the 31st and 33rd were to the rear of

Donelson. Colonels Otho F. Strahl, Calvin D. Venable, Egbert E. Tansil, and Warner P. Jones commanded the 4th, 5th, 31st, and 33rd Regiments while Lt. Col. Hugh L. W. Bratton led the men of the 24th Tennessee.[58]

As Stewart's brigade moved toward Starkweather's position, the 4th and 5th Tennessee encountered the four hundred men of the 79th Pennsylvania, under the command of Capt. August Mauff. Stewart's Tennesseans pummeled the Pennsylvanians who suffered a casualty rate of more than 51 percent during the ordeal. Ramrods were fired from the guns of the Pennsylvania soldiers who were apparently too inexperienced and overwhelmed to retrieve the instruments from the barrels of their guns before firing.[59]

Starkweather was able to maintain his position and held off the assault from the remaining regiments of Stewart's brigade who were being reinforced with Maney's troops. Initially pushed to the bottom of the hill, the Confederates mounted another charge toward the summit, eventually taking the hill and shooting horses and artillerymen alike.[60]

A Confederate chaplain recalled how the scene sickened him. He noted how a cannonball struck one young artilleryman and left him "with both legs crushed" while another "had a hole through his body which would admit a man's arm." Sadly, the chaplain cited "a third, smeared with blood and brains" while the severity of other wounded soldiers ranged from some being shot "through the breast, through the lungs" while another may have lost "a big toe, another is minus a nose."[61]

Capt. Robert P. Taylor from Garrard's detachment recalled the condition of the hillside, "The ground around was slippery with blood, many a poor dark looking powder begrimed artillery man was lying stretched out upon the ground . . . torn and mutilated."[62]

Terrill attempted to push the Confederates from Starkweather's position atop the hill. An artillery round, fired from a Confederate battery a half-mile away, exploded overhead and ripped into General Terrill's left side. Maj. James A. Connolly, 123rd Illinois said,

Terrell [sic] . . . was giving me directions for rallying the men. I was the only one with him; I raised him to a sitting position and saw that nearly his entire breast was torn away by the shell. He recognized me and his first words were, "Major do you think it is fatal?" I knew it must be, but to encourage him I answered, "Oh I hope not General." He then said, "My poor wife, my poor wife."

The mortally wounded officer was carried to the nearby Wilkerson House where he died in the early morning hours of October 9.[63]

Maney's fatigued troops advanced upon another hill where Starkweather established a line consisting of a plethora of regimental representation and six guns that he managed to move before retreating from his position. Following a vicious assault, Maney pulled back to the original location of Parsons's guns, while Stewart, who had joined Maney in the attack but ran out of ammunition, also pulled back. Starkweather managed to move to a stone wall located six hundred yards from the intersection of the Mackville and Benton roads, a location known as the Dixville Crossroads.[64]

One of the Federal regiments arriving at Perryville during the Confederate dust storm was the 42nd Indiana under the command of Col. James G. Jones. The group of Hoosiers had arrived around 10 a.m. and were among those who stacked their guns on the river banks while going into the creek bed to quench their thirst and fill their canteens with the unsightly water present in Doctor's Creek.[65]

Pvt. George Morgan Kirkpatrick, 42nd Indiana, described the water from the creek near the Bottom's farm as, "a few puddles of water with green scum over it . . . in our desperate need, we skimmed the water, and put it into a pot and boiled it, making ourselves some coffee."[66]

Kirkpatrick's recollection was similar to that of William G. Putney, a bugler in Barnett's battery of Greusel's brigade in Sheridan's division. Putney recalled that while spending the night of October 7 west of Doctor's Creek, it was possible to gain a small degree of satisfaction from the body of water. Putney said, "One, with a spoon, could dip water enough into a canteen to keep down thirst yet possessing sand and mud enough to pave the throats of those who drank."[67]

With cannon fire signaling the presence of Confederate troops, the timidity of this group of Federal troops was quickly put to the test. Trapped in the creek bed and unable to climb the steep banks, many of the Hoosiers fell victim to the Confederate infantry fire. Those fortunate enough to make their escape did so along the Mackville Road, reaching a bluff on the western bank overlooking Doctor's Creek.[68]

An officer in the 42nd Indiana recalled,

It was a terrible position. In front a concealed enemy firing volley after volley; on our right a battery throwing grape . . . behind, a steep precipice, up which the men must climb, exposed to the fire of sharpshooters . . . Lt. St. John, of Lytle's staff, rode down to the edge of the bluff and waved his hand. His words I could not hear, but I supposed we were ordered to leave the ravine.

Seeing that the Confederates were "coming down the ravine" and about to flank the troops, the officer added, "We all then started up the bluff."[69]

Capt. S. F. Horrall commanded Company G, 42nd Indiana, during the battle of Perryville which, by his own admission, was his "first experience in 'grim visaged war.'" Horrall added, "I . . . in thirty minutes lost twenty two out of fifty two men, six killed outright, and I with the others received an unpleasant reminder of Confederate accurate shooting."[70]

Capt. Charles Olmstead, Company A, 42nd Indiana, was one of the Hoosiers who reached the summit of the hill near Doctor's Creek. Prophetically, Olmstead yelled to his men, "This is as good a place to die as any other." Within seconds a shot entered Olmstead's forehead killing him instantly as his brains splattered the face of a nearby soldier.[71]

Lt. Col. James M. Shanklin, 42nd Indiana, was a witness to

Olmstead's death. He wrote, "Captain Olmstead was instantly killed while bravely leading his men and cheering them on. The regiment was again met by overwhelming numbers, and fell back in perfect order, after firing every round in their cartridge boxes . . . Colonel Denby's horse was killed, and fell on him . . . he got behind, and got lost, and he did not find the regiment until late the next morning."[72]

Another Federal soldier, much younger than Olmstead, was a casualty of this phase of the battle. A Federal officer remarked,

> At the command "Fall back!" I told my company to obey . . . Water was scarce, but I had a canteen full . . . I saw the upturned face of a boy not out of his teens, head against a tree, eyes fast fixing in death, and he said, "Captain, please give me water, I am dying." . . . He was a pretty boy; no doubt some mother's darling. The canteen passed into his hands, and he drank the last drop.[73]

Pvt. William Mathews, Company E, 42nd Indiana, reached the top of the ravine and turned to fire his gun in the direction of the Confederates. A witness reported that a ball struck Mathews in the forehead and exited through the back of his head. The Hoosier soldier evidently exhibited no signs of pain as he made no sound or grimace while his lifeless form sank against a fence.[74]

Col. Thomas M. Jones led his Confederate brigade of the 27th, 30th, and 34th Mississippi through a valley toward Doctor's Creek in the east. While the valley and the creek bed served as cover for Jones and his troops, they also negated Jones from gaining an accurate view of the foe his command was moving toward. Twelve Federal cannon and 5,000 mostly raw Federal troops mixed with the remnants of the 42nd Indiana and served as the barriers of Jones's advance near the hill and a sinkhole.[75]

Jones's troops made three attempts to take the hill, but were unable to do so. Thick smoke filled the air and hampered the view of troops from both sides while canister rounds plowed into the ranks of gray-clad soldiers. The sinkhole reportedly ran red with the Confederate blood shed at the location.[76]

At 3:30 Jones retreated and Brig. John Calvin Brown led his brigade forward. Col. William F. Tucker's 41st Mississippi joined the 1st and 3rd Florida Infantry Regiments of colonels William Miller and Daniel B. Bird to compose the infantrymen of Brown's brigade. Col. Leonard Harris's 38th Indiana under command of Col. Benjamin F. Scribner and the 10th Wisconsin of Col. Alfred R. Chapin led the troops who checked Brown's assault. Although the battery of Capt. Peter Simonson, the artillery responsible for a large number of casualties upon Jones's troops, had moved farther back and no longer served as a viable obstacle, Brown had to contend with the heavy fire from more than eight hundred members of Harris's Union infantrymen. Brown's troops were persistent in their attempts to take the hill which Jones's men had been unable to gain. However, not until the Confederate left advanced into the Union right flank would Brown's diligence reap the intended results.[77]

On the Confederate left, Johnson and Adams attacked. Their position along Doctor's Creek was approximately one mile northeast of Perryville on the six-hundred-acre Henry Pierce Bottom farm.[78] The heights above the Bottom House were filled with troops of blue and gray, turning the formerly peaceful land into a literal killing zone.

The Confederate charge began with Brig. Gen. Bushrod R. Johnson's brigade of the 5th, 17th, 23rd, 25th, 37th, and 44th Tennessee Infantry Regiments, some 1,500 strong, attacking from the east of the Union right flank. Early contact occurred in the front yard of the Bottom's home place and quickly progressed toward a tandem of stone walls. Confederate batteries fired shells into the five hundred men of Col. John Beatty's 3rd Ohio from Col. William H. Lytle's 17th Brigade of Brig. Gen. Lovell H. Rousseau's 3rd Division in McCook's Corps.[79]

Pvt. W. C. Gipson, 17th Tennessee Volunteers, remarked that when the Federal soldiers retreated, "I counted thirteen of their dead in the corner of the fence, where we had seen the flag fall so often."[80]

Col. Curran Pope, 15th Kentucky, witnessed the event from a short distance away. He wrote, "As soon as the 3rd came up and occupied its ground, it was fired upon, and a desperate fire was kept up."[81]

The Union casualties mounted, as enlisted men and officers alike were shattered with minie balls and cannon fire. Thirty-eight percent of the 3rd Ohio were killed or wounded in this segment of the battle. Beatty noted the effects upon his officer ranks in writing, "Capt. H. E. Cunard . . . was one of the first to fall, shot through the head . . . Capt. Leonidas McDougal . . . waving his sword and cheering his men, fell pierced by a ball through the breast." Beatty continued, "First Lieutenant Starr . . . died like a soldier in the midst of his men."[82]

Henry Bottom's farm contained stone and rail fences on the west bank of Doctor's Creek where Bragg's left wing, under Maj. Gen. William Hardee and Maj. Gen. Alexander McCook's I Corps engaged in the most intense fighting of the battle. Bottom had attained an impressive land holding in addition to an estimated $16,000 worth of sheep and hogs. Corn, peas, potatoes, oats, rye, wheat, and beans were some of his major crops. Tending the crops were Bottom's eight slaves and two additional slaves that belonged to his sevety-seven-year-old uncle, William Bottom. Henry and his wife Margaret "Mary" Hart had two sons who also lived in the home that lay in the midst of the battlefield.[83]

Confederate cannon fire struck the log barn located on the Bottom farm and the structure quickly became engulfed with fire. Not only were oats and wheat stored in the barn, but as many as 120 wounded Union soldiers had sought refuge inside. The blaze emitted such a hot fire that nearby Federal soldiers were unable to help the wounded men trapped in the barn. The surrounding grass, dried from the drought and the intense heat of the conflagration, also blazed, as other severely wounded soldiers succumbed to the flames. A Cincinnati reporter said, "A rebel shell . . . set the barn on fire, and several of our poor wounded boys perished in the flames."[85]

The 15th Kentucky, fellow brigade members of the 3rd Ohio, replaced the hard-hit Ohioans and ceased the Confederate advance at the aforementioned fence. The struggles of the Kentuckians were similar to those the 3rd Ohio faced. A Kentucky soldier wrote, "The 15th went forward with fixed bayonets and relieved the 3rd. Shortly afterwards, Lieut. Col. Jouett was shot in the leg, and Lieut. McGrath went to his assistance. After raising him, he was himself shot dead through the head. Major Campbell was shot through the body about the same time."[85]

The 10th Ohio, almost 530 men in size and under the command of Lt. Col. Joseph Burke, held a position to the left of the 3rd Ohio and served as the point of destination for the 3rd. The 10th fired deadly rounds into Bushrod Johnson's rebels until the Southerners were able to regroup and send their own shots into the Buckeyes of Col. William H. Lytle.[86]

Sgt. W. C. Gipson, 17th Tennessee, stated that Col. A. S. Marks saw the Confederate situation as desperate and requested a charge upon the Federals located at a stone wall, some four hundred yards ahead. Gipson noted that while General Johnson felt the assault would be "too perilous . . . Marks replied, 'It can't be worse than this. We shall be killed if we stay here.'" With that comment, the Confederates were ordered forward and took the Union position after more tenacious fighting.[87]

Maj. W. T. Blakemore praised the Ohioans' fortitude, "The Tenth Ohio, whose line of battle was well defined by their dead and wounded, and their colorbearers piled five and six high around their standard, each man having been shot down as he rescued them. The last one, when shot, in his desperate extreme, stuck the staff in the ground, which, however, was shot away in a few minutes." Later wounded in the head, Lytle was captured and cared for by Johnson's surgeon.[88]

Col. John Beatty commanded the 3rd Ohio and noted, "The air was filled with hissing balls; shells were exploding continuously, and the noise of the guns was deafening." In this type of environment added Beatty, a "boyish fellow" named David C. Walker, 3rd

Ohio, saved the flag after the death of the sixth color bearer and "sprang forward . . . stepping out in front of the regiment, waved it triumphantly, and carried it to the end of the battle."[89]

At approximately the same time the Kentucky troops replaced the 3rd Ohio, Johnson's command fell back and the 2nd, 35th, and 48th Tennessee, as well as the 13th/15th Consolidated Arkansas Infantry Regiments of Brig. Gen. Patrick Cleburne's nine-hundred-man brigade from Buckner's Division took their place to attach the 10th Ohio from the front. Friendly fire struck Cleburne's ranks, as many of his men were clad in blue pants captured approximately six weeks earlier in the action at Richmond, Kentucky. A shell, likely from one of Sheridan's Federal batteries supplying an enfilading fire into Cleburne's and Adams' flanks, killed Cleburne's horse Dixie and struck the general in the ankle before word was received from Cleburne to end the barrage. By 4 p.m. Maj. John E. Austin's 150 men of the 14th Battalion, Louisiana Sharpshooters, arrived at the location and attacked the 10th Ohio from their right rear. This assault pushed the Kentuckians and three rallied companies of the 3rd Ohio from the field and toward the home and 150-acre farm of John C. Russell. The Russell residence, noted as the "White House" in numerous accounts of the battle, was serving as McCook's headquarters.[90]

The action around the Russell house was a literal bloodbath. The day after the battle a civilian witness described the home as "dotted over with hundreds of marks of musket and cannon balls. All around lay dead bodies . . . Trees no more than one foot in diameter contained from twenty to thirty musket balls and buckshot."[91]

Meanwhile, Col. George P. Webster's 3,000-member brigade of the 50th, 80th, 98th, and 121st Ohio Infantry regiments braved the attack of Brig. Gen. John Liddell's 2nd, 5th, 6th, 7th, and 8th Arkansas regiments that followed Brig. Gen. Sterling Wood's brigade of the 32nd and 45th Mississippi, the 15th Battalion of Mississippi Sharpshooters, the 33rd Alabama, the 3rd Georgia, and the 3rd Confederate Infantry. The 16th Alabama of Wood's brigade remained with Semple's Battery, therefore suffering no casualties at Perryville. Fortunately, the 3rd Confederate Infantry also escaped the fight with no casualties. The 32nd and 45th Mississippi as well as the 33rd Alabama would not be as fortunate, as these units "suffered heavily."[92]

Pvt. Wesley S. Poulson, 98th Ohio of Webster's brigade, remarked that while, "Shells, solid shot, and rifle balls were flying over" the Federal positions, he witnessed the terror of battle. Poulson recalled seeing, "Horses without riders running for life . . . hogs . . . and rabbits all running towards our line scared to insensibility almost by the advancing rebels."[93]

John H. Nichols, 16th Tennessee, saw his brother, shot through the arm and leg, fall at his side. The hair from Nichols' right temple was "furrowed with shot that burned the side" of his head and his clothes bore five distinct holes from pieces of the same projectile.[94]

Men of the 98th Ohio would "step to the top of the bank, take aim, and fire" before stepping back and reloading. Sgt. Maj. Duncan Milner stated, "Here we lost a good many of our men either killed or wounded."[95]

While Webster was mounted on his horse, overseeing the Confederate advance upon his command, he was shot and killed. A witness to the event claimed to be only twenty feet from Colonel Webster and "had fired and had turned around . . . in the act of loading, when I saw him fall. I dropped my gun, and was the first at his side. He told me he thought he was mortally wounded." Webster reportedly asked for God's mercy on his soul and said, "Tell my dear wife and children they were last in my thoughts."[96]

Webster was carried approximately a mile behind the battle lines where he received care in a home that served as a makeshift hospital. Sgt. Maj. Milner visited Webster and noted that the wound to his right hip had passed through Webster's body and lodged in his left hip. Milner recalled, "It was a dreadful place to be in, the shrieks and groans of the wounded were awful." The incident concluded with the death of Webster, Jackson, and Terrill, a fact the latter had earlier predicted would be mathematically impossible to occur.[97]

Wood's Confederates continued moving in the direction of the Benton Road and the six guns of Capt. Samuel J. Harris's 19th Battery of the Indiana Light Artillery. Using the infamous rebel yell, the men in gray advanced to within thirty yards of Harris when the cannons exploded in the faces of the assaulting force. The rebels were obliterated as cannon sent their projectiles into their ranks during a pair of charges. The saving grace for the Confederates came from the fact that four hours of fighting had almost depleted the ammunition supply of the U.S. troops and they were forced to pull back.[98]

The opening created when Harris's force pulled back allowed Wood's Confederates to move toward the junction of the Benton and Mackville Roads or the Dixville Crossroads. McCook's right and left flanks fell back to the crossroads where they were reinforced by Col. Michael Gooding's brigade of 1,400 Indiana and Illinois troops. Gooding's fresh troops were able to hold Wood's troops at bay, and Liddell moved up.[99]

During this series of events and with darkness affecting visibility, fifty-six-year-old Confederate Maj. Gen. Leonidas Polk ordered an officer to stop firing into Polk's troops, thinking friendly fire was involved. Polk, dressed in dark clothes, had the appearance of a Union soldier, yet when Col. Squire Keith of the 22nd Indiana asked for Polk to identify himself, Polk took on the role of a Union officer. Polk continued the farce, yelling for Federal troops to stop firing. When he reached the end of the Union line, Polk became determined to reach the safety of the Confederate line and began his flight toward the same as he screamed, "Every mother's son of them are Yankees." The fire that belched from the Confederate muskets killed Colonel Keith and conducted a literal slaughter on the men of the 22nd Indiana.[100]

Upon conducting the next roll call after the battle at Perryville, the remaining members of the 22nd Indiana realized the full impact of this event upon their ranks. A member of the 22nd wrote, "On calling the roll at 8 o'clock . . . to nearly every other name in the regiment there was no answer." Stuart W. Sanders, the director of the Perryville Battlefield Preservation Association, has stated, "They had Leonidas Polk to thank for the silence."[101]

Following this incident, the Federal troops moved into Perryville where, for the first time of the war, street fighting took place. Union soldiers from Maj. Daniel Gilmer's 38th Illinois and Col. John Alexander's 21st Illinois struggled with Confederates entering the town and several buildings in Perryville were burned. As darkness arrived and ended the fighting of October 8, the Federal army held the western side of Perryville while the Confederates controlled the east. The fighting in Perryville was over.[102]

Interestingly, many of the Union commanders and staff of Buell's Headquarters positioned upwind in the nearby hills and valleys south and west of Perryville were unable to hear, or correctly interpret, the sounds of the largest battle ever fought on Kentucky's soil. A phenomena known as an acoustic shadow resulted from the direction of the wind and the terrain that surrounded the battlefield. In fact, Gen. Buell, although he heard intermittent cannon fire, was unaware of the magnitude of the battle until one of McCook's aides reached him near 4 p.m. By that point, according to U.S. Maj. Gen. Charles C. Gilbert, "The cannon fire became so continuous and was so well sustained and so different from the irregular shots . . . that it was readily recognized as a battle." Gilbert stated that Buell looked at him and said, "That is something more than shelling the woods; it sounds like a fight." This fact proves interesting as some 36,000 soldiers representing 21 states and 90 cannon took part in the battle with the latter shaking windows in homes in Danville, ten miles east of the battlefield. Also, a member of Marshall's staff, located approximately twenty miles away in Bryantsville, had heard the sounds of the battle.[103]

General Bragg finally seized the full impact of the situation his Confederates had faced during the hours of fighting around and in Perryville. When he realized the number of soldiers he would have to face should the fighting resume the next day, Bragg made the decision to abandon Perryville. The *Confederate Military History* evaluated the outcome of the battle of Perryville in stating,

"Tactically it was a Confederate victory, strategically it was a defeat."[104]

Col. Thomas Claiborne, an open critic of his Confederate commander, said of Bragg, "Then he awakened to the situation . . . issued orders for the move at 1 a.m. . . . Bragg was caught with about a fourth of his effectives by Buell's army . . . Had Bragg kept his hold on the battle ground till next daylight, he would have been beaten in detail and his command slaughtered or captured." Choosing to leave his dead and many wounded behind, Bragg had his troops move to Harrodsburg, where more of his wounded would be attended to, before a Federal attack could be resumed.[105]

Perhaps Confederate Lt. Gen. Joseph Wheeler best summed up the Confederate predicament in an article written decades after the battle at Perryville. Wheeler said, "At every point of the battle the Confederates had been victorious . . . Resting quietly on the ground, the army expected, and would gladly have welcomed, a renewal of the fight on the next day, but the accumulation of Buell's forces was such as not to justify conflict in that locality . . . the troops withdrew to Perryville; and at sunrise continued the march."[106]

U.S. Maj. Gen. Charles Gilbert praised his Confederate foes in stating, "In abandoning the battleground the Confederates, although obliged to leave their wounded behind, moved without any sense of humiliation, for they had made a good fight, and appeared only to be withdrawing from the presence of a greatly superior force."[107]

Confederates J. P. Cannon from the 45th Mississippi and Luke W. Finlay of the 4th Tennessee busied themselves in gathering ammunition before Bragg's decision to withdraw was given. Cannon recalled gathering cartridge boxes from dead soldiers and exchanging his gun "for a new Enfield rifle which was lying by the side of its late owner," while Finlay likewise remarked that each soldier in his regiment "equipped themselves with Enfield rifles" before Bragg's decision was made known.[108]

Wesley S. Poulson of the 98th Ohio noted Confederate soldiers "shortly after sunset . . . running around to gather up arms, revolvers, watches, Bowie knives" and other items as he lay wounded on the field. Poulson's gun was taken and his canteen exchanged before a Confederate advised him that a wagon would pick him up before fighting would resume the next day.[109]

W. H. Davis, a member of the 4th Tennessee Cavalry, recalled his impressions of the time spent near the battlefield before moving toward Harrodsburg. Davis said, "No man ever experienced such a night of torture as we did listening to our wounded comrades, prostrate on the hot earth, crying for water."[110]

With rations low and the news of the Confederate defeat at Corinth, Mississippi circulating, Bragg held an October 12 meeting at Bryantsville with Polk, Hardee, Kirby Smith, and other general officers to determine his next move. It was decided that the abandonment of Kentucky was the best move for the safety of the Confederate troops, and on October 13 the exodus began, with Buell following the Confederates as far as Crab Orchard, Kentucky, where they ceased their pursuit on October 16. The expertise of cavalry under Joe Wheeler proved important as he provided the rear guard and kept the Federal pursuers from breaking through and capturing Bragg's retreating force.[111]

A participant in Wheeler's escapade recalled, "Our infantry abandoned the field and headed for Harrodsburg, leaving General Wheeler's command . . . to cover their retreat . . . Wheeler did not allow the infantry army to be molested."[112]

Buell's decision to abandon his pursuit cost his career dearly. Buell moved his troops toward Middle Tennessee, but in October he was relieved of his command and replaced with William Rosecrans. In 1864, while waiting for additional "orders that never came," Buell resigned. Like his counterpart, General Bragg's reputation suffered due to his decisions and conduct at Perryville. When his command, many without shoes, proper clothing, or food, reached Knoxville in November, pneumonia, dysentery, scurvy, and typhoid affected thousands. While Bragg answered Jefferson Davis's summons to Richmond and managed to satisfy the President's inquest concerning his actions, his troops would never again "follow him confidently into battle."[113]

The overwhelming task of caring for the dead and wounded took priority upon the conclusion of the battle. On the Confederate side, of the 16,800 soldiers who took part in the battle, 532 men were dead while 2,641 were reported as wounded. Additionally, 228 rebel soldiers were missing or captured. The figures from the Federal ranks of 55,261 troops were astounding. The total dead were listed as 890 with 2,993 wounded, many of whom received care at Danville, and 437 missing or captured. Including the soldiers of both sides who would later die from wounds received at Perryville, the death toll would rise to 2,377.[114]

The casualty percentages among the armies at Perryville were some of the highest of the entire Civil War. Major General McCook's I Corps had a rate of 25.3 percent for its 13,121 men who saw action at Perryville. This figure includes a 51.4 percent casualty rate for the 420 members of the 79th Pennsylvania, 49 percent rate for the 1st Wisconsin, 44.9 percent rate among the ranks of the 10th Ohio, a 40 percent rate for the 10th Wisconsin, 39.3 percent rate for the 15th Kentucky, and 39 percent rate for the 38th Ohio. The 21st Wisconsin lost one-third of its fighting force; all of the regiment's officers were wounded or killed. An almost inconceivable statistic, the 22nd Indiana lost 195 of its 300 men at Perryville, a 65.3 percent casualty rate.[115]

More than 20 percent of the Confederates who fought at Perryville became casualties. With figures being unavailable for several regiments of Bragg's Army of the Mississippi, it is reasonable to assume that this rate could be higher. The 16th Tennessee had a casualty rate of 59.2 percent for its 370-member regiment with the 27th Tennessee suffering 51.4 percent. One-half of the 4th Tennessee, 9th Tennessee, and 34th Mississippi became casualties at Perryville.[116]

Numerous soldiers remarked how a full moon accentuated the fear involved in viewing the wounded and dead soldiers on the battlefield. Federal correspondent Henry Villard recorded, "An almost full moon had arisen and lighted up the field very brightly." J. P. Cannon, of the 45th Mississippi added, "The full moon beaming down upon the pale faces of the dead made it the more ghastly and sickening"[117]

A Union soldier said, "It was a beautiful night, a clear sky and full moon . . . we came across five of the enemy lying on the hillside dead . . . faces were very pale and the light of the moon glittered on their eyes. It was fearful to behold."[118]

A Confederate chaplain assisted with the care of the wounded and dying and recalled that blood smeared his hands and clothes. The sounds of the area were proving difficult for the man to bear as he wrote of the slash of the surgeons' knife and the sound of the saw while the groans of the sufferers filled the air.[119]

It was noted that at the Methodist Church hospital in Perryville "the boys of the 10th and 3rd Ohio were crowded . . . each pew answering for a private apartment for a wounded man." Similarly, at the Bottom house, "The doctors were hard at work at a table, amputating limbs" while "The yard was full of wounded men, lying in rows, covered up with blankets, shrieking with pain, and some lying there dead."[120]

In respect to the Federal captives, Davis Biggs, a Confederate in the 38th Tennessee, stated, "Some of the prisoners we captured looked very like part of the 5,000 we had previously captured at Munfordville, and we accused them of violating their paroles."[121]

The tenacity of the action at Perryville was documented in recollections of many of the survivors of the October battle. A correspondent from the *Louisville Journal* said, "The battle of Chaplin Hills will be recorded as one of the hardest contested and bloodiest conflicts of this war." Maj. Gen. Braxton Bragg stated, "For the time engaged it was the severest and most desperately contested engagement within my knowledge." Maj. George Simonson, 80th Indiana Volunteer Infantry Regiment, proclaimed, "The fighting was said by old soldiers and Generals to be terrific, and the hardest contested battle they ever saw, this was said by both Donelson and Shiloh heroes." Another Union soldier wrote to his father, "The terrible battle which we had . . . it was terrible indeed. No pen or pencil can picture it." Another writer summarized, "The battle of Perryville, a hard-fought fight against many odds, was a favorable incident which decided nothing." Sam Watkins of *Company Aytch* fame stated, "Perryville was the hardest and most evenly contested battle that was ever fought during the war, or even any war."[122]

Military paraphernalia also suffered during the battle. The regimental flag of the 10th Wisconsin was hit forty-one times and the staff bore two bullet holes. Sadly, five color bearers from the 10th Wisconsin fell, while the sixth managed to carry the banner from the field.[123]

It has been recorded that homes, churches, and barns within a ten-mile-radius of the battlefield served as hospitals, while the lack of tents and proper medicines accentuated the problems that gangrene and starvation presented. Weeks after the battle, eleven official hospitals were established in Perryville and patients were taken to one of those. Prior to that event, area farms, such as the Bottom farm, were stripped of fences, livestock, and clothing for various uses; church pews were used to construct coffins for Federal soldiers. The Federals termed the Confederates "traitors" and detested them for having robbed the corpses of Federal soldiers. Confederate dead were initially left unburied until two pits were dug for the men who the buzzards and feral hogs had not devoured. Federal soldiers were hastily buried after the battle. By 1868 all of the Union dead were reinterred at Camp Nelson in Jessamine County, Kentucky.[124]

The Union rationale to avoid burying the Confederates may have been based upon the recollection of a private in the 42nd Indiana. The soldier recalled that he joined four of his comrades the morning after the battle with the intention of recovering Captain Olmstead's body. The soldier noted that the corpse had been stripped of everything except shoes and undergarments.[125] Such an incident would certainly have affected the view one soldier would hold for his enemy.

J. S. Newberry, secretary for the Western Department of the

Sanitary Commission, reported the deplorable facilities used for the wounded at Perryville. Newberry wrote, "The condition of the wounded in this fight was peculiarly distressing. No adequate provision had been made for their care. The stock of medicines and hospital stores in the hands of the surgeons was insignificant. They had almost no ambulances, no tents, no hospital furniture, and no proper food . . . The small village of Perryville afforded but very imperfect means for the care of the great number of wounded concentrated there."[126]

A. W. Reed, a comrade of Newberry, wrote, "We found the first hospital for the wounded" at Mackville; "this was a tavern, with sixteen rooms, containing 150 wounded and 30 sick, mostly from a Wisconsin regiment. 25 were in cots; some on straw, the others on the floor."[127]

Reed also noted the conditions that the wounded faced at Perryville. He said, "They were all very dirty, few had straw or other bedding, some were without blankets, others had no shirts, and even now, five days after the battle, some were being brought in from temporary places of shelter, whose wounds had not yet been dressed."[128]

Sgt. Edward Ferguson, 1st Wisconsin, was wounded at Perryville and remembered being "gathered up in a blanket by sympathizing comrades and friends, and transported as tenderly as possibly in an ambulance to the deserted house taken as a field hospital."[129]

Regarding the dead, an area resident, George Hughes, walked over the Perryville battlefield the day after the fight. Hughes noted, "I saw enough dead men upon the field that if they had been placed side by side would have fully covered the distance of half a mile. The sights of the field were indescribable; nobody can convey in words a true picture."[130]

Capt. Thomas H. Malone, an aide to General Maney, remarked that he felt it would be possible to walk three hundred yards upon dead bodies lining the area around Parsons Hill without touching the ground. Similarly, William L. Trask, who encountered his first battle as a member of Adams's Louisiana Brigade at Perryville, said that he saw two straight lines of dead Federals with "scarcely a man . . . out of his place in the line, and they reminded me more of a wagon road than anything else." Trask added, "Nearly all seemed to have fallen in their tracks as they had stood and fought" an indication of the bravery of his enemy—a compliment Trask passed to his deceased foes.[131]

Confederate Gen. Braxton Bragg stated of the Federals, "The ground was literally covered with his dead and wounded."[132]

Sgt. Mead Holmes, Jr., 21st Wisconsin, recalled his task of assisting in the burial of soldiers slain at Perryville. He said, "It seems hard to throw men all in together and heap earth upon them, but it is far better than to have them lie moldering in the sun. Oh! To see the dead rebels in the woods."[133]

Ironically, almost 350 of the Confederate dead were eventually reburied with the efforts of Henry Bottom, whose farm was largely destroyed during the battle. Bottom's barn and contents were burned during the fight, outbuildings were pitted with bullet holes, and the relics of war were strewn about his farm. Bottom, fellow Perryville residents, and older students from the Kentucky State School for the Deaf in nearby Danville, exhumed the bodies and placed them into a cemetery on the Bottom property a few months after the battle. Most of the soldiers were unable to be identified though several of the Mississippi troops had personal effects that allowed Bottom to properly bury the soldiers. Due to financial deficiencies, Bottom was unable to complete his plans of enclosing the cemetery with a stone wall. His dream was later completed and, on the 40th anniversary of the battle, the United Daughters of the Confederacy dedicated a beautiful twenty-eight-foot granite monument on the site.[134]

It was near the sight of the monument where the battle reached a furious level. A participant said, "Just a short distance west of where the present Confederate monument now stands, two regiments engaged . . . When orders were given to fire, it looked as if it were a solid sheet of flames."[135]

The Confederate cemetery is one of the impressive sites located within the confines of the Perryville Battlefield Historic Site, officially opened in 1954. Almost 750 acres are contained in the park and easements allow an additional 300 acres of the land to be preserved for future generations. More than 7,000 acres of land are registered as a National Historic Landmark. The Civil War Sites Advisory Commission Report on the Nation's Civil War Battlefields conducted a study of more than 16,000 acres and determined that just under 9,800 acres have the potential to be registered.[136] Thus, the preservation efforts regarding the Perryville battlefield are among the best in the nation.

Perryville's battlefield is the beneficiary of excellent interpretation through brochures, more than ten miles of ever-increasing walking trails, wayside exhibits and signs, a Web site, year round living history programs, an annual Perryville Commemoration in October, and a driving tour. In addition, the battlefield has been noted as "retaining much of its 19-century appearance." Park manager Kurt Holman was quoted in a 2010 article as saying, "This ground has remained largely unchanged . . . and, in many cases, the descendents of those who tended the land in 1862 still work their family farms today. We are always very proud to say that if a . . . soldier who fought here were to walk the battlefield today, he would say, 'I know this place; this is Perryville.'" The park's pamphlet correctly notes that other than a few modern homes sprinkled throughout the area and the presence of a few power lines, visitors can obtain an excellent idea of the battlefield's appearance in 1862.[137] Therefore, no better summary of the preservation efforts or compliment related to it can be given to Perryville than what Holman stated.

The Web site for American Byways backs Holman's statement and adds that little development can be seen for miles in the battlefield's vicinity. The Web site, with nothing to gain by stating so, adds that the Battle of Perryville State Historic Site is one of the best preserved Civil War battlefields in the United States.[138]

An avid Civil War historian complimented the preservation of Perryville in saying that it is similar to Antietam, in that it is similar in size and in a rural area but without the large number of monuments found at many Civil War battlefields. The ability to see the entire field in one day is another plus that the historian touted in his article. He concluded with, "This beautiful battlefield, with its gorgeous hills and dales and lovely views, could easily and rapidly become one of my very favorites."[139]

One of the major catalysts in preserving the Perryville battlefield has been the Perryville Battlefield Preservation Association. Founded in 1995, the group has been instrumental in raising the number of protected acres from ninety-eight to its current level. Aside from the battlefield, the association has preserved several buildings along Perryville's Merchant's Row. Dedicated to "saving Kentucky's largest battlefield," the Perryville Battlefield Preservation Association can be contacted at 859-332-1862, by mailing P.O. Box 65 in Perryville, or through visiting the Web site at battleofperryville.com.[140]

The Perryville Battlefield State Historic Site is located west of Interstate 75 at 1825 Battlefield Road, although GPS software may function better if the former address of 1825 Mackville Road is utilized. The park's post office box number is 296, and the zip code is 40468. The park can be also contacted by calling 859-332-8631.[141]

Any tour of this tremendously well-preserved battlefield should begin at the park's visitor center and museum. Clear directions to the park exist from the direction of Danville, ten miles east of Perryville. This facility was renovated in 2009 and integrates modern technology with photographs and artifacts of the past to provide visitors with a firm understanding of the battle of Perryville. A display entitled "The Faces of Perryville" contains photographs of veterans of the Perryville battle and allows visitors to read the words that many of them left as legacies. Although hours vary in the winter, the museum and bookstore, housed together, are usually open 9 to 5 Monday through Saturday and 11 to 5 on Sunday. The battlefield itself is available to be toured from dusk to dawn year round.

The series of stops within the park include the Confederate cemetery; the sites of Stewart's, Maney's, and Donelson's attacks;

Parsons' Ridge; the Cornfield; Starkweather's Hill; Simonson's Battery positions; the Widows Bottom and Gibson house sites; the Wilkerson House site; Dixville crossroads; and the Bottom House. In all, almost thirty stops are interpreted in the parks boundaries. Numerous picnic tables are present and provide ample space for refreshing yourself on a visit to the state park.

The Perryville Battlefield walking trail guide can be obtained at the visitor center. Please follow the guidelines and wear comfortable shoes and appropriate clothing. It is also recommended that water should be taken on the trails, some of which combine to take an hour and a half to complete. Following the Confederate attack will necessitate taking paths that run east-west, while Union defensive lines are viewed more easily along the north-south trails.[142]

Additional sites of significance, including downtown Perryville, a community placed on the National Register in 1976 and later designated to the Preserve America list by former First Lady Laura Bush, lie outside the park. Some of these include the site of the Russell House, a post-battle hospital burned a century after the war, and the Dorsey House site, where Buell spent his time during most of the battle. The office of Dr. Jefferson J. Polk, a Perryville physician who cared for a large number of wounded soldiers, is also outside the park's boundaries. Another building used as a hospital is the Brinton House, a structure damaged when a cannon ball crashed through the roof and an interior door. The Dye house that served as Buckner's headquarters is another interesting stop outside the Perryville Battlefield State Historic Site. Other points of interest include, but are not limited to, Bragg's headquarters at the Crawford House, the Chaplin River, and Merchant's Row, on old U.S. Highway 68.[143]

In nearby Danville, Centre College suffered from the aftermath of the battle at Perryville. Sick and wounded Union soldiers were placed into the building now known as Old Centre, where the large rooms of the two-story building were considered perfect for hospital facilities. Soldiers died so frequently at Centre College that troops were given permanent burial assignments on campus as one professor commented, "I have seen soldiers . . . taken out of there . . . for burial . . . every day or two." Caregivers and college officials also succumbed to the wide range of diseases that affected the soldiers and basically all furniture and fixtures were destroyed during the year-long occupation of the campus as a hospital. Although a small payment was all the college received for its losses, Centre College continues today as a premier institution of higher learning.[144]

The Perryville, Kentucky, battlefield is a perfect example of preservation success. A vast number of such sites across the nation could learn from the methods used to set aside this once bloodied location for the study, enjoyment, and interpretation of generations to come. In conclusion, few sites in the United States can provide visitors with the ability to step back in time and gain a complete understanding of a Civil War battlefield as Perryville's hills and valleys can.

Sgt. Jesse Forrester, left, served in the 41st Georgia at Perryville. (Courtesy Bill Forrester)

This Confederate Veteran *photograph shows the 1904 reunion of color bearer W. H. White, as well as John McConnell, J. C. Biles, and H. L. Moffitt, color guard, all members of the 16th Tenn. Regiment. All four men were wounded at Perryville.*

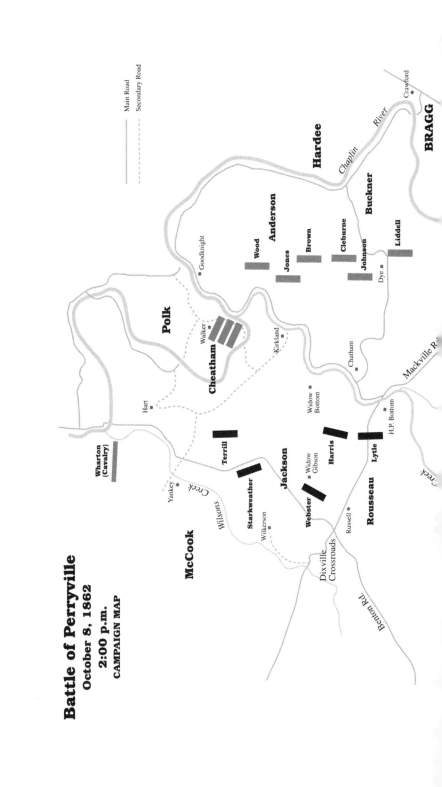

Battle of Perryville
October 8, 1862
2:00 p.m.
CAMPAIGN MAP

Main Road
Secondary Road

BRAGG

Crawford

River

Chaplin

Hardee

Buckner

Anderson

Liddell

Wood

Brown

Cleburne

Jones

Johnson

Dye

Goodknight

Polk

Mackville R

Cheatham

Walker

Kirkland

Chatham

Hart

Widow
Bottom

H.P. Bottom

Wharton
(Cavalry)

Terrill

Jackson

Widow
Gibson

Harris

Lytle

Creek

Yankey

Wilsons

Creek

Starkweather

Webster

Rousseau

Wilkerson

Russell

Dixville
Crossroads

Benton Rd.

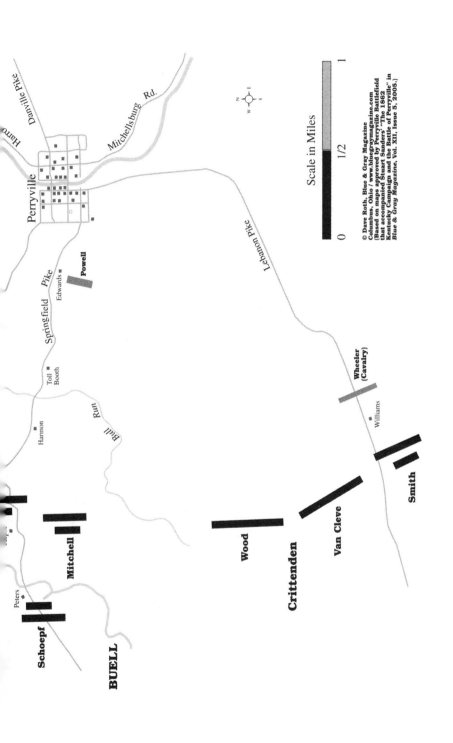

Scale in Miles

0   1/2   1

© Dave Roth, Blue & Gray Magazine
Columbus, Ohio / www.bluegraymagazine.com
[Based on maps approved by Perryville Battlefield
that accompanied Stuart Sanders' "The 1862
Kentucky Campaign and the Battle of Perryville" in
Blue & Gray Magazine, Vol. XII, Issue 5, 2005.]

Union Brig. Gen. William Rufus Terrill was killed at Perryville. (Library of Congress)

The Perryville Battlefield State Historic Site Visitor Center is an excellent location to begin your visit. (Photo by author)

This well-preserved portion of the field was the location of Donelson's attack. (Photo by author)

This is the view from Parson's Ridge, with the cornfield in the center and Starkweather's Hill in the rear. (Photo by author)

From Loomis' Heights, Union artillery participated in a duel against the Confederate position near the tree line in the rear of the photo. (Photo by author)

Doctor's Creek is in the center of this picture. The 42nd Indiana received their baptism of fire at this location. (Photo by author)

The Henry P. Bottom house survived the battle, although the farm surrounding it was ravaged by the heavy fighting. (Photo by author)

Dixville Crossroads today. (Photo by author)

The Kerrick-Parks House served as a girls school at the time of the battle. It became a hospital afterwards. (Photo by author)

Dr. Jefferson Polk cared for many of the wounded and dying in and around this building, his office. (Photo by author)

The Union Memorial is adjacent to the Confederate Cemetery. (Photo by author)

The Confederate Memorial sits in the cemetery Henry Bottom established on his farm. (Photo by author)

CHAPTER ELEVEN

MORGAN'S CHRISTMAS RAID

1862-1863

"The railroad was rendered impassable for at least two months."
—Brig. Gen. John Hunt Morgan

Kentucky resident and Confederate officer John Hunt Morgan gained a high level of notoriety for his raids into Federal-occupied regions of the South as well as for his venture into Ohio at the war's midpoint. Forays into towns such as Lebanon, Tennessee, in May of 1862 increased Morgan's reputation and elevated him to a position of fame few men experienced during or after the American Civil War. This fact holds true, despite that Morgan was less than successful in his endeavors in some instances. For example, in the aforementioned Lebanon raid, Morgan's Kentucky troops fought a largely Kentucky-based Federal force with Morgan losing as many as 150 of his horse soldiers as prisoners, while he and an estimated dozen men of his 300-man command reached safety as an organized unit.

Morgan and his Kentucky raiders regularly returned to their home state. In July of 1862, Morgan led his men into what history has simply termed Morgan's First Kentucky Raid. Morgan's Raiders surprised a Federal garrison in Tompkinsville, capturing the men in blue in action that lasted less than two hours. The raid continued as the cavalry advanced into extreme northern Kentucky before returning to the safety of Tennessee, their point of origin for the campaign.[1]

In the summer of 1863 Brigadier General Morgan's Great Raid used 2,500 men to march through the heat of Kentucky and into Indiana. During this venture Morgan's troops burned a large portion of the town of Lebanon, Kentucky, in response to the killing of Morgan's young brother at the same location.[2]

It is the Christmas Raid of 1862 that regularly gains attention in relation to Morgan and his raiders. The goal of the trip into the Bluegrass State in the winter of 1862-63 was to disrupt the supply line for Federal troops. To do so would involve eliminating the very lifeline of Union soldiers, the Louisville and Nashville Railroad.

Morgan was born in Alabama, yet his family moved to Kentucky while he was a child. Later, following an impressive tenure as a colonel, Morgan was promoted to brigadier general following a major victory at Hartsville, Tennessee. Well-loved among the men he commanded, Morgan received his promotion that many termed "a long-expected commission" as "He had been styled General by his men, and . . . habitually so addressed in official communications."[3]

One of Morgan's officers described the young general as "one of the most impressive figures of the war." He added, "Perhaps no General in either army surpassed him in the striking proportion and grace of his person, and the ease and grace of his horsemanship. Over six feet in height . . . with the air and manner of a cultivated and polished gentleman, and the bearing of a soldier, always handsomely and tastefully dressed, and elegantly mounted . . . the picture of the superb cavalry officer."[4]

In the fall of 1862 Gen. William Rosecrans replaced Gen. Don Carlos Buell and moved his Federal troops into Tennessee. Massive amounts of supplies were needed for planned actions in the state, with the Louisville and Nashville Railroad serving as the major route for transporting food and supplies to Nashville. Although the railroad was well protected, Confederate Gen. Braxton Bragg consented to Brig. Gen. John Hunt Morgan's request to obstruct the flow of supplies by striking a key point along the route.[5]

An officer in Morgan's Raiders said, "General Bragg desired

that the roads which Rosecrans had repaired in rear should again be broken, and the latter's communications with Louisville destroyed."[6]

On December 22, 1862 newlywed Brigadier General Morgan left Alexandria, Tennessee with "an effective force of 3,100 guns and seven pieces of artillery." Col. Basil Duke recalled that the force had an aggregate number of approximately 4,000, but that several hundred men "were dismounted, and totally unarmed and unequipped." Duke also noted that Morgan, at that time, "had under his command . . . the largest force he ever handled, previously or afterward."[7]

One of the raiders recalled that reveille was sounded before daybreak. The day was described as mild and beautiful and that it looked and felt like spring with a cloudless, clear sky and a bright sun soon appearing overhead. After the horses and men were fed, General Morgan took the opportunity to announce "the organization of the brigades . . . the objects of the expedition, and ordered the column to move at nine o'clock."[8]

Confederate historian John Wyeth noted, "They started with three days' cooked rations. Every man carried his own ammunition, two extra horseshoes, twelve nails, one blanket in addition to the saddle blanket, and an oil-cloth or overcoat."[9]

Morgan divided his command into two brigades. Col. A. R. Johnson had seniority over the other colonels in Morgan's command, yet he declined the responsibility of leading either brigade, instead stating his willingness to serve as a subordinate to someone with less experience than he. In response, Morgan placed Col. Basil Duke of the 2nd Kentucky Cavalry and Col. W. C. P. Breckinridge of the 9th Kentucky Cavalry each in command of one of the two brigades.[10]

The brigades were described in a manuscript written in 1915. Duke's brigade was noted as containing the 2nd Kentucky with Lieutenant Colonel Hutchinson commanding. Gano's Regiments, the 3rd Kentucky, was under the leadership of Lieutenant Colonel Huffinson as Gano was absent. The 8th Kentucky under Col. Leroy

S. Cluke and Palmer's battery of four pieces rounded out the 1st Brigade. The 2nd Brigade contained Breckenridge's regiment of the 9th Kentucky with Lieutenant Colonel Stoner commanding. The 10th Kentucky, the 11th Kentucky and the 9th Tennessee rounded out the brigade with a three-inch Parrot gun and two howitzers in support.[11]

Colonel Duke bragged on the composition and quality of the brigades. Duke said,

> The regiments had been carefully inspected . . . and every soldier and disabled horse had been taken from their regiments, and the stout men and serviceable horses only were permitted to accompany the expedition . . . with perfect confidence in their commander, and with hearts longing for the hills and valleys, the bluegrass and woods of dear old Kentucky.[12]

Duke expounded upon the quality of leadership as well in writing, "It was a magnificent body of men . . . No commander ever led a nobler corps, nor corps was ever more nobly led. It was splendidly officered by gallant, dashing, skillful men in the flush of early manhood; for of the seven Colonels who commanded those seven regiments, five became brigade commanders, the other two gave their lives to the cause."[13]

The Confederates forded the Cumberland River near dusk on December 22. Duke's brigade camped at Sand Shoals on the river's north bank. Breckinridge bivouacked between the Cumberland and Caney Fork Rivers.[14]

December 23 was spent covering thirty miles over territory that Morgan termed "very rough." Although Morgan had evidently planned to cover more miles, the roads reportedly made it "impossible to march faster than this, and keep the guns up."[15]

On Christmas Eve Morgan's Raiders advanced within six miles of Glasgow, Kentucky. Capt. W. E. Jones, an officer from Breckinridge's brigade, accompanied Colonel Duke, and moved two companies and a howitzer into Glasgow "to discover if all was clear" and then "take possession of it."[16]

As the Confederate detail reached Glasgow, they met the Federal advance guard. The lead unit of the Union horse soldiers was Lieutenant Darrow's Company C of the 2nd Michigan Cavalry. Morgan explained that darkness made the scouting companies unable to initially locate the enemy.[17]

A skirmish ensued, during which the Federals had one soldier killed, one wounded, and sixteen men captured. Captain Jones, termed "an excellent officer," was mortally wounded, as was Pvt. Will Webb. Morgan reported, "6 or 7 of my men taken prisoners," yet he also stated 22 Federal soldiers were captured.[18]

Another Confederate casualty was 1st Lt. Samuel O. Peyton, shot in the thigh and arm. It was said of his severe wounding, "He was surrounded by foes who pressed him hard, after he was wounded, to capture him. He shot one assailant, and grappling with another, brought him to the ground and cut his throat with a pocket knife."[19]

A Federal officer wrote that the darkness, combined with the fact that several of the Confederate detail's members were wearing blue uniforms, created difficulty in distinguishing friend from foe. Although Morgan's party was initially repulsed, the 2nd Michigan fell back to Cave City as the 12th Kentucky Cavalry provided the rear guard.[20]

At 5 a.m. on Christmas Day, Col. Edward H. Hobson, 13th Kentucky Infantry, ordered Colonel Shanks and the 12th Kentucky Cavalry, in addition to two battalions and two companies from both the 4th and 5th Indiana Cavalry, to advance past Cave City to Bear Wallow. Col. Isaac P. Gray, commanding the Indiana companies, moved along the Burkesville Road, south of the Green River. Orders were issued "to give battle, and, if overpowered by superior forces," skirmish during a retreat toward Woodsonville.[21]

Morgan's scouts located Gray's cavalrymen near Green's Chapel and reported to Morgan "that a battalion of cavalry was drawn up in line, awaiting our approach." Morgan detailed two companies and a section of artillery in the direction of the Federals who "after firing a few random shots, took flight and left the road clear."[22]

A Confederate participant remarked that the Confederate

advance guard "cleared the road of some Federal cavalry, which tried to contest our advance, driving it . . . rapidly, that the [Confederate] column [did not] . . . delay its march."[23]

Colonel Hobson ordered the Federal cavalry to return to camp while he dispatched troops to monitor the Confederates' movements. Hobson continuously telegraphed generals Granger, Gilbert, and Boyle about the situation at hand. General Boyle was also informed of the Federal shortage of ammunition and the fact that siege guns, received at 1 p.m. on Christmas, were lacking "proper technical fixtures" including elevating screws, sights, sponges, and rammers, these items having "been entirely neglected in shipping."[24]

Morgan and most of his command crossed the "steep and muddy banks" of the Green River and reached Hammondsville near midnight.[25] The Confederate general, known as the "Thunderbolt of the Confederacy," began his plan to mislead the Federal scouts. Morgan wrote,

I had ordered Colonel Breckinridge . . . to send two companies in that direction, with instructions to drive in the enemy's pickets, and immediately on my arrival at Hammondsville I dispatched two companies of Colonel Duke's command, with similar instructions, in the direction of Munfordville. My object was to induce the enemy to believe that I intended to attack the fortifications at Green River, and . . . to divert his attention from the combined attack which I intended to make the succeeding day on the stockades at Bacon Creek and Nolin.[26]

Preparations for the attacks upon the Federal troops were hampered as "a heavy rain" fell throughout Christmas night and into the day of December 26. The Confederate column began its march "amid the steadily pouring rain, and moved through mud that threatened to ingulf [sic] everything." Morgan reported, "it was with the utmost difficulty that the artillery and trains made any progress whatever."[27]

On the morning of December 26 Morgan was able to successfully' move the main body of his forces to Upton while another group was deployed to Bacon Creek. With the intention of attacking the stockade at Bacon Creek, Morgan deployed Duke's and R. M. Gano's regiments and a section of artillery. Lt. Col. John B. Hutcheson of the 2nd Kentucky Cavalry was given command of the artillery.[28]

At 11 a.m. Morgan heard Hutcheson's cannon open up. Morgan cut the telegraph wire at Upton and had his operator establish communication with key points such as Louisville and Cincinnati. Few messages of importance were received aside from one that informed Morgan "of the arrival of a train loaded with ammunition, small-arms, and two pieces of rifled cannon." Morgan decided to attempt to capture the train but was unable to do so.[29]

Morgan also sent Duke to the town of Nolin to attack the stockade there. Duke was able to gain the surrender of the Nolin stockade without a fight.

Colonel Duke recalled the incident at Nolin when he wrote,

> The commandant agreed to surrender if I would show him a certain number of pieces of artillery. They were shown him . . . he hesitated . . . he thought he could hold out for a while . . . He was permitted to return, but not until, in his presence, the artillery was planted close to the work, and the riflemen posted to command, as well as possible, the loop-holes. He came to us again, in a few minutes, with a surrender.[30]

In the meantime Morgan became fearful "from the duration of the firing at Bacon Bridge, that the stockade had been reinforced." General Morgan moved to Bacon Creek to assist Colonel Hutcheson.[31]

A Confederate noted the situation and surrender at Bacon Creek by saying,

> There was not more than one hundred men . . . in the stockade . . . but there was a large force at Munfordsville [sic] . . . A battalion of cavalry came out from Munfordsville [sic], but was easily driven back . . . Although severely shelled, the garrison held out stubbornly,

rejecting every demand for their surrender. Hutchinson became impatient . . . and ordered the bridge to be fired at all hazards . . . It was partially set on fire, but the rain would extinguish it unless constantly supplied with fuel. Several were wounded in the attempt . . . Some of the men got behind the abutment of the bridge, and thrust lighted pieces of wood upon it, which the men in the stockade frequently shot away . . . General Morgan arrived upon the ground . . . they surrendered.[32]

Another Confederate soldier added, "As we struck the railroad . . . we saw several Union soldiers walking along the track, each with his gun on his shoulder. Under orders, we spurred our horses rapidly forward. Captain Tom Quirk . . . shouted to them to surrender . . . firing over their heads . . . the men threw up their hands."[33]

With the surrender of Bacon Creek, Morgan gained ninety-three prisoners from the 91st Illinois Volunteers with only four casualties suffered in the Confederate ranks. Four commissioned officers were among the captured Federals. After the stockade and trestle were fired and destroyed, Morgan advanced to Nolin. When Morgan arrived there he found that three officers and seventy-three enlisted men of the 91st had surrendered. Morgan then "ordered large fires to be built all along the track for some three or four miles, in order to warp the rails, which was most effectually accomplished."[34]

That night the Confederate division camped within six miles of Elizabethtown. General Morgan learned that as many as eight companies of Union troops were stationed at Elizabethtown.[35] Plans were made to advance upon the town the next morning.

On the morning of December 27 the Confederates moved upon Elizabethtown. Lt. Col. H. S. Smith commanded some six hundred troops at Elizabethtown and was braced for a fight.[36]

As the Confederates "neared the town, a note was brought to General Morgan from Colonel Smith." The note, which Morgan referred to as a "preemptory document," was written in pencil on the back of an envelope.[37]

The note to Morgan said, "Sir, I demand an unconditional

surrender of all your forces. I have you surrounded, and will compel you to surrender."[38]

Colonel Duke stated that a Dutch corporal who spoke "very uncertain English" delivered the proposal, which he called "the most sublimely audacious" he had ever seen. General Morgan's reply was that it was actually the Union force that was surrounded. Morgan, in turn, called upon Smith to surrender. Smith boldly proclaimed that a United States officer was expected to fight rather than surrender.[39] The stage was apparently set for a military engagement.

General Morgan used the time of parley to place his troops in position. One regiment and a howitzer were left in reserve to guard the trains while Colonel Duke's troops aligned themselves to the right of the town. Colonel Breckinridge's regiment was placed to the left of Elizabethtown, and skirmishers were thrown forward to locate the position of the Union troops.[40]

Within moments of General Morgan's receipt of Colonel Smith's note, a Confederate Parrot gun, placed in the road, in addition to Capt. Baylor Palmer's four cannon to the left of the road where they "completely commanded the town," opened fire. Palmer's battery was some six hundred yards from Elizabethtown, and General Morgan "was superintending their fire."[41]

In his official report, General Morgan recognized "the excellent service" Captain Palmer and his battery performed. Morgan said that the rapid and accurate fire, with "nearly every shot striking the houses" where Union soldier were positioned greatly aided in reducing the effectiveness of the defensive position.[42]

Colonel Duke likewise stated,

> The enemy had no artillery, and ours was battering the bricks about their heads in fine style. Palmer . . . concentrated his fire upon the building where the flag floated . . . I sent for one of the howitzers . . . it was posted upon the railroad embankment . . . it played like a fire engine upon the headquarters building . . . The enemy could not well fire upon the gunners.[43]

One of the cannonballs fired into town struck a corner building, lodging under a third-story window. This was one of 107 shots fired in the first twenty minutes of the bombardment. After an estimated total of thirty minutes of "vigorous shelling," a white flag was displayed in one of the houses in Elizabethtown.[44]

Duke recalled, "there seemed to be a commotion among the garrison, and the white flag was shown from one of the houses . . . Colonel Smith was not ready to surrender, but his men did not wait on him and poured out of the houses and threw down their arms." It has been proposed that Smith, slightly wounded in the barrage, was unable to communicate with his troops, who were unable to coordinate their fire or defense while scattered among the numerous buildings in town.[45]

Morgan added, "652 prisoners, including 25 officers, fell into our hands."[46]

Another Confederate officer remarked, "the fruits of this victory were six hundred fine rifles . . . some valuable stores were also taken."[47]

The Christmas Raid continued on the morning of December 28 as the raiders moved from Elizabethtown in the direction of Bardstown. The Confederates moved along the railroad in a leisurely manner while also "destroying it thoroughly."[48]

Approximately four miles outside of Elizabethtown, General Morgan ordered Colonel Breckinridge to attack the lower stockade near Muldraugh's Hill, approximately thirty-five miles south of Louisville. Colonel Duke was given the responsibility of striking the upper stockade. Knowing the importance of the positions, General Morgan sent flags of truce forward, demanding a surrender of the trestles and stockades. A Confederate officer proclaimed the great trestle works at Muldraugh's Hill, which the stockades guarded, were the "principle objects of the expedition."[49]

The trestles were estimated to be the "largest and finest" on the entire rail line with each of them standing "some 60 feet in height and from 300 to 350 yards in length." Approximately a mile separated the trestles; their defenses were incomplete and without any artillery. General Morgan added that neither of them had previously been destroyed and that his demand for a surrender was declined. However, with less than three hours of shelling, both stockades surrendered.[50]

A participant in the capture of the positions said, "Both of the structures were destroyed and hours were required to thoroughly burn them." General Morgan added that in addition to achieving the objective of the expedition, the "railroad was rendered impassable for at least two months."[51] Thus, Rosecrans's supply line had been seriously affected.

A Confederate infantryman added, "The destruction of this immense network of timber made the most brilliant display of fireworks I have ever seen . . . every upright and crosspiece was blazing . . . when . . . they were burned through, the flaming beams began to fall, and . . . the whole structure came down . . . sparks . . . shot skyward."[52]

The Confederates reported capturing seven hundred prisoners, of whom twenty-seven were officers. In addition, "a large and valuable amount of medical, quartermaster's and commissary stores were destroyed." Uncommon for the war, "no one on either side" was killed or wounded.[53]

After spending the night of December 28 near the Rolling Fork, Morgan's 4,000 raiders began crossing the swollen waterway on the 29th. The primary ford for the group was described as "deep and difficult to approach and to emerge from," and lay "a mile or two above the point at which the road from Elizabethtown to Bardstown . . . crosses the" stream.[54]

Morgan reported that Col. R. S. Cluke took one piece of artillery to attack and burn the Rolling Fork Bridge while Col. D. W. Chenault led the 11th Kentucky Cavalry and one piece of artillery to burn the trestle and stockade at Boston. Three companies from Breckinridge's regiment moved toward New Haven.[55]

Col. John M. Harlan had led 2,900 Federal troops from Munfordville at 3 a.m. on the 28th, moving in the direction of Elizabethtown. Upon hearing of Morgan's destruction of the trestle,

Harlan moved his command of the 13th Kentucky Infantry, the Twelfth Kentucky Cavalry, and the entire Second Brigade, in Morgan's direction. Harlan discovered that Morgan was attempting to ford the river and, "A section of Southwick's battery was ordered to join the cavalry, and, in conjunction with it, to detain the rebels at the crossing until the infantry arrived."[56]

The problems encountered in fording Rolling Fork came to haunt the Confederates. A member of the 9th Tennessee recalled, "just before the 9th Tenn . . . crossed the rolling fork, a heavy force of Federal infantry and cavalry . . . attacked us and we had quite an artillery duel."[57]

Ironically, the opposing commanders, Colonel Harlan and Colonel Duke, had been friends before the war. The men had both graduated from Centre College and Transylvania Law School.[58]

Colonel Harlan reported,

> When Colonel Shanks arrived within a mile of the crossing, he discovered, in the plain below, our road from Elizabethtown was on a high ridge of Muldraugh's Hill, a body of rebel cavalry, upon whom he ordered the artillery to open . . . resulting in the rapid dispersion of the rebels . . . from a high hill I saw . . . a very large body of cavalry formed in line of battle near the river.[59]

The Federal troops formed in two lines with skirmishers from the infantry and cavalry deployed. The entire Federal front was covered as the men in blue "were ordered to advance and engage the enemy, the whole line following in close supporting distance."[60]

In response, General Morgan sent an order to Colonel Duke, located in the rear, to inform Colonel Cluke to rejoin Morgan as soon as possible. Cluke's assignment would be to "hold the enemy in check until the entire command had crossed the ford." Duke and Breckinridge moved seven companies into a line of battle and held five in reserve. Morgan said Duke, "with this force . . . several times repulsed the enemy's advance, and very nearly succeeded in capturing two pieces of the enemy's artillery."[61]

The firing reportedly became general all along the Federal right, but Harlan noted that the Confederate resistance ended as the men in gray "broke and fled precipitately in every direction." Harlan stated that several of the Confederates entered the woods while others, with their horses, swam across the chilled waters of the river.[62]

Morgan sent a courier to Duke, ordering Duke to withdraw. Duke found the order difficult to follow and recalled, "In command with quite a number of others, I devoutly wished I could. The enemy's guns, the best served of any, I think, that I ever saw in action, were playing havoc with the horses." Duke recalled that four horses were killed when shell exploded in their midst, and the bursting shells were striking "the lower ford with such frequency as to render the crossing at it by a column out of the question."[63]

Duke's claim was substantiated in Harlan's official report. The Federal colonel proclaimed that the site where he had witnessed Duke positioned contained ten dead horses within a space of an estimated 20 square feet. Southwick's battery, located on the left of the Federal line, had dealt death and havoc upon the Confederate warriors. [64]

Duke determined "a show of attack" should be made on the Federal line as the advancing Confederate line had withdrawn "as soon as it had come under" fire from the Federal lines. Colonel Duke sent Captain Pendleton, with three companies, toward the Federals to "silence a battery which was annoying us very greatly." With the distraction this action would hopefully cause, Duke planned to withdraw the remainder of the Confederate force.[65]

Seconds after these arrangements were made, a shell exploded near Duke, severely wounding the colonel in the head. The shell, which Duke said "burst in a group of us true to its aim," knocked him unconscious and killed the horse of Lieutenant Moreland, Duke's aide-de-camp.[66]

Capt. Tom Quirk took Duke to the nearby Bardstown home of Dr. Gus Cox. Duke was laid on a pallet placed in an upstairs bedroom while Dr. Thomas Allen, a surgeon in Morgan's command, attended to the wounded officer.[67]

Rev. John Cunningham witnessed Duke's treatment and wrote, "The wound was on the right side of the head . . . a piece of the skin and bone behind the ear were gone. If the direction of the flying bit of shell had been directly from the right of the victim, it would have passed through the lower part of the head and death would have been instantaneous . . . He said, 'That was a pretty close call.'" Fortunately, Duke was able to join Morgan the next day.[68]

Colonel Breckinridge assumed command of the Confederates after Duke's wounding and "energetically and skillfully" held the Federal line in check while the withdrawal was initiated. Captain Pendleton's charge accomplished "all that was expected" as several Federal artillerymen were killed and others driven from their guns. Pendleton was able to silence the Federal cannon for an estimated thirty minutes, despite the fact he was wounded when a shell fragment struck him.[69]

Morgan reported the wounding of Pendleton, Duke, and a private as the only three casualties of this affair. He estimated the Federal losses as "several officers and men killed and wounded." Likewise, Harlan stated that his casualties were far less than those of the Confederates, as he listed Lt. Henry W. Pollis of Southwick's battery as mortally wounded, as was Pvt. Louis W. Finney of the 10th Indiana Volunteers. The other two casualties Harlan reported were one soldier killed and another wounded. An unsubstantiated claim written in Harlan's report was, "Some of the citizens in the vicinity informed me that the rebel wounded were taken off and some of their dead thrown into the river."[70]

In conjunction with the action at the crossing, other Confederates whom Morgan deployed yielded varying results. Morgan reported that Colonel Chenault was able to capture and burn the Boston stockade and rejoined Morgan at Bardstown later on the 29th. However, the three-company detachment of John Hunt Morgan's 9th Kentucky Cavalry, sent to capture New Haven, "was not successful." At New Haven Capt. John K. Allen commanded approximately ninety men of the 78th Illinois Infantry Regiment and was able to drive away the Confederate attack in spite of the Confederates' two to one numerical advantage. Subsequent Confederate attempts to flank the Federal position proved unsuccessful and the 9th Kentucky withdrew, taking their casualties of two killed and ten wounded with them. The Federal defenders suffered no casualties during the attack. The men of the 9th Kentucky were unable to reach Morgan until the night of the 30th.[71]

On the morning of December 30, Morgan moved from Bardstown to Springfield, taking the entire day to travel the eighteen miles between the two towns. Morgan was informed of several facts that led him to label his position as "sufficiently hazardous." The general wrote,

> The enemy . . . had concentrated . . . at Lebanon . . . to number nearly 8,000, with several pieces of artillery . . . a column of nearly 10,000 strong was moving from Glasgow to Burkesville to intercept me . . . A superior force only a few miles in my rear . . . nearly treble my own immediately in my front, and a vastly superior force, which had only about half the distance to march that I had, moving to intercept my passage of the river.[72]

Morgan decided upon a detour to the right of Lebanon and to utilize the darkness to cover his movements to Burkesville and cross the Cumberland River. The plan was delayed as General Morgan encountered "considerable delay . . . from the difficulty in obtaining guides who were sufficiently well acquainted with the country to lead me over the route I desired to march." It was 11 p.m. before the column was on the move.[73]

Increasing the difficulties associated with the situation, cold drizzling rain changed to sleet and the road Morgan sought to traverse became frozen. Morgan knew that a march was necessary, regardless of the weather conditions. J. C. Rolling, a local hotelkeeper, was secured to lead Morgan's Raiders along the Elizabethtown Road toward the Campbellsville-Lebanon Road. Morgan exclaimed that the rough road, added to the aforementioned issues, resulted in his army advancing only eight miles from Springfield by the morning of December 31.[74]

The tension was high as many of the Confederates were aware of the attempt to avoid contacting the Federal troops in bad weather. Pvt. John Weatherred, 9th Tennessee Cavalry, recalled, "We expected to avoid a collision with a heavy force of the enemy . . . we marched and stopped and delayed all night, the most disagreeable night I think I ever experienced. Many were frost bitten."[75]

The Confederates reached Muldraugh's Hill at 1 o'clock on the afternoon of the 31st. Morgan spotted Federal skirmishers deployed in the valley below the rise. The rear guard reached the foot of the hill when "a remarkable hand-to-hand conflict took place" between the 6th Kentucky Cavalry and two Confederate companies. The most notable event of that exchange was the fact that Confederate Lt. George B. Eastin killed Federal Col. Dennis Halisy during the struggle.[76]

The Confederates were able to progress to Campbellsville, reaching the town late on the 31st. "Quite an amount of commissary stores" were in the town, a point Morgan praised, due to the fact that the Confederates "had but little for two days."[77]

The next day's march carried the Confederates to Columbia. Resting from 3 p.m. until night, the rebels resumed the march, reaching Burkesville the following morning. The Cumberland was then crossed allowing Morgan "without molestation . . . by easy stages" to reach the safety of Smithville, Tennessee, on January 5, 1863.[78]

The cost of Morgan's Christmas Raid upon his Confederate command was relatively low. He reported the losses as two killed, twenty-four missing, and sixty-four missing. The level of achievement, in only eleven days, in Morgan's words was, "The destruction of the Louisville and Nashville Railroad from Munfordville to Shepherdsville, within 18 miles of Louisville . . . capture of 1,877 prisoners, including 62 commissioned officers . . . destruction of over $2,000,000 of United States property, and . . . large loss to the enemy."[79]

On May 17, 1863, the Congress of the Confederate States of America passed a joint resolution thanking "Gen. John H. Morgan, and the officers and men of his command, for their varied, heroic, and invaluable services" during the Kentucky Christmas Raid.[80]

Kentucky has done an excellent job in preserving the memory of John Hunt Morgan's Christmas Raid by establishing the John Hunt Morgan Heritage Trail. All three of Morgan's raids are clearly mapped and detailed in a handy pamphlet available at many rest areas across the state. Additional information related to the trails can be gained through visiting the Web site 10000trails.com and clicking on John Hunt Morgan Trail. In addition, interested parties can call 270-781-6858 or write 10000 trails at P.O. Box 51153, Bowling Green, Kentucky, 42102.

A visit to Elizabethtown will enable interested students of the war to view several structures present during Morgan's Christmas Raid. These include the Eagle House, located at 112 North Main, where seven cannonballs struck and killed two soldiers; Severns Valley Baptist Church at 112 Poplar Drive, where one shell struck; the Jackie Helm House or Horace Bird's House at 210 Helm St., where shells fell in such a heavy manner that the cannonballs were collected and thrown into a well, now covered up; and the Samuel Beal Thomas House at 337 West Poplar Street is the location where Thomas, a friend of Morgan's, climbed to the rooftop and waved a white sheet to end the shelling.[81]

Sadly, the Dr. Gus Cox house, where Colonel Duke was nursed following his head wound, was destroyed in 1967. The Foerg Building, where numerous soldiers became casualties of the battle, was torn down and replaced with another structure.[82]

In Springfield, the Elias Davidson House, once located at 209 East Main, was the location of C.T. Cunningham's home, and the location where Confederate soldiers were entertained the night of December 22, 1862. Since the war, the house has been razed.[83]

In Campbellsville and Taylor County, various sites from the Morgan Raid can be seen. Redmond's Tavern, a log structure, served as Morgan's headquarters during the Christmas Raid. From Finley Ridge, atop Muldraugh's Hill, Morgan watched Federal troops deploy on December 31, 1862. The Widow Saunders House, or Clay Hill, is the location Morgan visited to determine Federal troop number at New Market and the Rolling Fork Bridge. The site of the Green River Bridge can also be seen, although the original was burned during the Christmas Raid. There is a great deal of speculation that the modern bridge was built on the abutments of the original wooden bridge.[84]

In 2004 a series of interpretive markers were developed for the purpose of providing interested visitors with the proper information regarding Morgan's Trail.[85] Such accomplishments will enable future generations to gain insight into the pivotal events in the career of Morgan and his storied command. Some of the markers include "The Cannonball" near the Hardin County Courthouse, "The Skirmish at Rolling Fork" on Boston Road near Bardstown, "Morgan's Second Raid" and "Elizabethtown Battle" in Elizabethtown, and "Make a Street Fight out of it" on Dixie Highway East in Elizabethtown.

Other interesting sites include locations in Glasgow, Bear Wallow Creek near Cave City, and the site where Morgan's Raiders destroyed the L & N Bridge at Bonnieville. Additional information can be gained by calling 270-692-0021 or by e-mailing visitlebanonky@windstream.net.[86]

The preservation and interpretation of the John Hunt Morgan Trails is a true success story for the citizens of Kentucky and all interested visitors to the state. With numerous sites that are well maintained and properly interpreted, this aspect of the American Civil War in Kentucky should continue for generations to follow.

Confederate Gen. John Hunt Morgan and his wife. (Confederate Veteran)

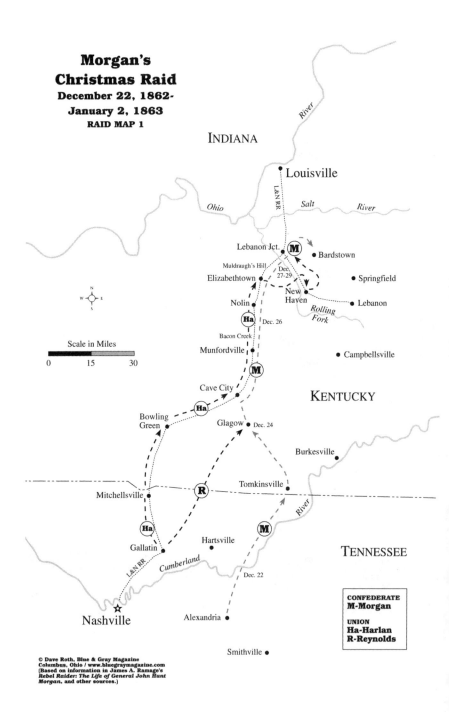

Morgan's Christmas Raid
December 22, 1862-January 2, 1863
RAID MAP 1

INDIANA

Louisville

L&N RR

Ohio

Salt

River

River

Lebanon Jct. **M**

● Bardstown

Muldraugh's Hill

Dec. 27-29

Elizabethtown ●

● Springfield

New Haven ●

Nolin ●

● Lebanon

Rolling Fork

Ha Dec. 26

Bacon Creek

Munfordville ●

● Campbellsville

M

Cave City

KENTUCKY

Ha

Bowling Green ●

Glagow ● Dec. 24

Burkesville ●

Tomkinsville ●

Mitchellsville ●

R

River

Ha

Hartsville ●

M

TENNESSEE

Gallatin ●

L&N RR

Cumberland

Dec. 22

☆ Nashville

Alexandria ●

Smithville ●

N
W ◆ E
S

Scale in Miles

0   15   30

CONFEDERATE
M-Morgan

UNION
Ha-Harlan
R-Reynolds

© Dave Roth, Blue & Gray Magazine
Columbus, Ohio / www.bluegraymagazine.com
(Based on information in James A. Ramage's
*Rebel Raider: The Life of General John Hunt
Morgan*, and other sources.)

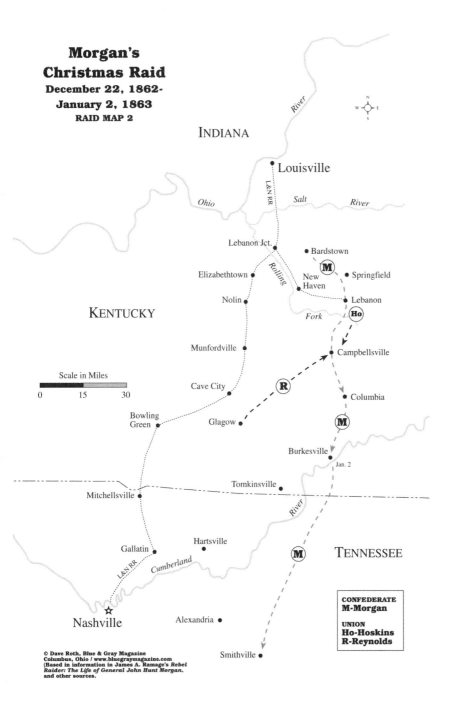

Morgan's Christmas Raid
December 22, 1862-
January 2, 1863
RAID MAP 2

INDIANA

Louisville

Ohio L&N RR *Salt* *River*

Lebanon Jct.

● Bardstown

Elizabethtown ● *Rolling* New Haven ● Ⓜ ● Springfield

Nolin ● ● Lebanon

KENTUCKY *Fork* Ⓗⓞ

Munfordville ● ● Campbellsville

Scale in Miles

Cave City ● Ⓡ ● Columbia

0   15   30

Bowling Green ● Glagow ● Ⓜ

Burkesville ●
Jan. 2

Tomkinsville ●

Mitchellsville ●

River

Gallatin ● Hartsville ● Ⓜ TENNESSEE

L&N RR *Cumberland*

Nashville ☆ Alexandria ●

CONFEDERATE
M-Morgan

UNION
Ho-Hoskins
R-Reynolds

Smithville ●

© Dave Roth, Blue & Gray Magazine
Columbus, Ohio / www.bluegraymagazine.com
(Based in information in James A. Ramage's *Rebel
Raider: The Life of General John Hunt Morgan*,
and other sources.)

CHAPTER TWELVE

PADUCAH

March 25, 1864

"The enemy opened upon us with a most terrific volley."
—Capt. H. A. Tyler, C.S.A.

The town of Paducah, Kentucky, is rumored to have gained its name from Chief Paduke, a member of Chickasaw royalty. Legend holds that he greeted the Samuel Henderson family as they ventured down the Cumberland and Ohio rivers to the mouth of Clark's River. Reported dying in 1819, Paduke, according to recorded stories, lived in a log cabin and/or a tepee and was buried somewhere along modern-day South Third Street in the city that bears his name. However, Paducah historian Hal Allen explained that a search of Bureau of Indian Affairs records revealed no Chief Paduke. Allen also found no word exists for that name in the Chickasaw language.[1] Regardless of the controversial issues facing the background of the area's namesake, there are verified aspects of the town's history that need to be mentioned.

In return for his Revolutionary War service, George Rogers Clark received a southwestern Kentucky land grant of almost 74,000 acres. The 1795 grant included 37,000 acres that comprise the modern location of Paducah. Due to his debts incurred during his five years of military service, Clark mortgaged the land. Clark died in 1818 and the ownership of the land passed to his younger brother, famed explorer William Clark.[2]

William Clark desired a town to develop at the junction of the Ohio and Tennessee rivers, so his actions led to platting lots and streets for a settlement. Clark traveled to the area from St. Louis to oversee the surveying of the lots and remained in the future town for two weeks. Twelve blocks with twelve lots each were designed with lots measuring 57½ feet by 173 feet and two-dozen smaller lots bordering the steep banks of the river. The first lot sold for $12, others for $10. Ten to twenty-five cents per acre were paid for lots in the outlying areas. In addition, Clark set aside land for public purposes such as the courthouse and the famous Market House.³

Clark evidently felt that the original area's name of Pekin was unsuited for his new settlement, and renamed the town Paducah in 1827. In an April 27, 1827 letter to his son, Clark wrote, "I expect to go to the mouth of the Tennessee River and . . . have laid out a town there and intend to sell some lots in it, the name is Paducah."⁴

In 1834 the Methodists organized the town's first church; two years later the Market House was constructed. Another major event in the town's history was the 1843 establishment of Elijah Murray's Paducah Marine Ways. It is a generally accepted statement that the river facilities of Paducah were the major catalyst to the town's early growth, as the town became a marine construction site as well as a major transportation center.⁵

The importance of the river created a high level of interest for both sides of the American Civil War. It would come to pass that troops of both armies sought control of Paducah and the citizens of the town would exhibit divided allegiances throughout the war.

The talk of the arrival of Confederates from Columbus, Kentucky, located approximately 50 miles downstream on the Mississippi, had circulated for weeks. The people of Paducah were largely pro-Confederate, though significant numbers of pro-Union and neutral residents existed. Confederate Gen. Lloyd Tilghman, a Paducah citizen, had influenced the enlistment of numerous Paducah males into the Confederate army. Talk of the arrival of gray-clad troops under Maj. Gen. Leonidas Polk excited the pro-Confederate citizenry of Paducah in early September 1861.[6] However, many of those expecting the arrival of men in gray were disillusioned when the events of September 6, 1861 transpired.

Early on the morning of September 6, Union steamboats arrived on the Illinois side of the Ohio River across the waterway from Paducah. More than one hundred barges were utilized to form a bridge that an estimated 5,000 soldiers used to cross the river into Paducah. Near the foot of Broadway, the men in blue entered and made their way through the town's streets, marching in rows of four while bands played the song "Union Forever." One Federal soldier, in particular, drew the attention of Paducah's citizens. Described as a "stocky, full-bearded man" with a "cigar stuck in the corner of his mouth," Brig. Gen. Ulysses S. Grant entered Paducah from a gunboat, as word of the Federal arrival circulated and dozens of residents attempted to flee the area.[7]

A civilian witness to the bridge stated that the Pontoon Bridge contained, "114 barges lashed together, and the army of 8,000 strong, marched four abreast" the massive structure when they entered Paducah in September of 1861.[8]

One of the first functions the Federal soldiers performed was to set up meal tents, an essential task for feeding the large number of new arrivals. Grant took over control of Paducah's telegraph office, the Marine Hospital, and the railroad depot. In addition, the Federal general found a large supply of leather military goods, and "complete rations" intended for the Confederate army.[9]

To quell the fears of the pro-Confederate citizenry and to display his intentions, Grant read a proclamation to the citizens of Paducah. Reportedly, few Paducah residents initially heard the reading of the proclamation, a fact Grant found bothersome. In an effort to make certain a maximum number of residents were aware of the proclamation, General Grant had the content published in the local paper.[10]

The proclamation stated,

I have come among you, not as an enemy, but as your friend and fellow citizen, not to injure or annoy you, but to respect the rights, and to defend and enforce the rights of all loyal citizens. An enemy, in rebellion against our common Government, has taken possession of, and planted its guns upon the soil of Kentucky and fired upon our flag. Hickman and Columbus are in his hands. He is moving upon your city. I am here to defend you against this enemy and to assert and maintain the authority and sovereignty of your Government and mine. I have nothing to do with opinions. I shall deal only with armed rebellion and its aiders and abettors. You can pursue your usual avocations without fear or hindrance. The strong arm of the Government is here to protect its friends, and to punish only its enemies. Whenever it is manifest that you are able to defend yourselves, to maintain the authority of your Government and protect the rights of all its loyal citizens, I shall withdraw the forces under my command from your city.[11]

Almost immediately preparations were made to provide as much comfort as possible to the Federal soldiers now occupying Paducah. Those 5,000 troops included members of the 12th Illinois under Col. J. McArthur, Lieutenant Millard's four-piece battery, the 8th Missouri that Col. M. L. Smith led, and the 9th Illinois, Gen. E. A. Paine's responsibility.[12]

Before returning to Cairo, Illinois, Grant placed Brig. Gen. Paine in charge of Paducah. In a written order, Grant notified Paine of his decision, stating that a portion of the troops would be stationed in the Marine Hospital. "Special care and precaution," as well as the responsibility to make sure no harm came to "inoffensive citizens" were foremost among Paine's assigned duties. Grant also stressed that Paine make certain that, "soldiers shall not enter any private dwelling, nor make any searches" unless Paine ordered such. The city, whose telegraph office, depot, and Marine Hospital were in U.S. hands, was to serve as a supply base for Federal troops intending to strike a number of Southern states. The "Federal invasion" of Paducah had begun.[13]

Paine's tenure was short-lived as he began to treat area residents more like captives than private citizens. Reports circulated that Paducah townspeople were sometimes arrested and, on occasion "executed without trial, at the order of General Paine."[14] Subsequent Federal leadership, including Gen. Charles F. Smith and future author Lew Wallace, apparently improved the image the Union commanders held in the eyes of the people of Paducah.

In an October 26, 1861 *Harper's Weekly* article, two reporters wrote about the sites they encountered in Paducah during the height of the Federal occupation. One of the men, a Mr. Travis, noted that he had ascertained from locals that the Marine Hospital was built in 1850-51 for $50,000. However, due to what Travis noted as Paducah's image as "the most healthy place in the West," the hospital had received little business. In fact, Dr. Hamilton, surgeon of the 9th Illinois Regiment, reviewed the hospitals old books, and "he never found over sixteen patients reported on any one day." [15]

In the same article, another writer stated,

> The bridge at Paducah surpasses anything of the kind ever before attempted in the United States. The river at the bridge is 3,600 feet across. It is spanned by a hundred coal barges, strongly braced together, twelve feet apart, connected by trestle-work, and planked over . . . twenty feet wide . . . constructed to carry the heaviest ordnance, at a point half a mile below the town.[16]

One statement concerning the "few inhabitants that remain[ed]" in Paducah noted that they were "entirely unmolested and secure" as Grant ordered, but that they "look guilty and sullen." Another told of a bakery located on South Third Street that was confiscated in order to supply Federal troops with badly needed bread. The proprietor would be given five barrels of flour to use in baking bread. He was paid for his services in that he was allowed to do as he wished with two of the barrels while using the other three to prepare the aforementioned foodstuffs for the Union occupants of Paducah.[17]

In early 1862, battles such as Fort Henry and Fort Donelson required most of the Federal troops stationed in Paducah to move elsewhere as needed. At times, less than 1,000 men in blue remained on duty in Paducah. However, the town became a medical center for large numbers of sick and wounded from battles in the area. Private homes, the town's female academy, the courthouse, and churches were "commandeered as shelter for the battle casualties."[18]

Mary Lucy Dosh, a nun who had been orphaned early in life and later moved to Louisville, had come to Paducah to teach music. When the occupation of Paducah began, Sister Mary, as she was then called, volunteered her services to care for Union soldiers affected by the typhoid fever outbreak. Dosh unfortunately contracted the disease herself and on December 29, 1861, at the age of twenty-two, succumbed to the disease that had claimed the lives of numerous soldiers and Paducah citizens alike.[19]

Another Paducah resident remembered a smallpox epidemic that struck Paducah. The young man would later recall that he braved the contraction of the disease while clinging to the bottom of a boat filled with victims of smallpox as the vessel departed Paducah, upon the arrival of Confederates.[20] Despite the outbreak of various deadly diseases, the Federal occupation of the town endured.

Historian E. B. Long, the chief researcher for Bruce Catton's famous three-volume work on the American Civil War, stated that the Union occupation of Paducah was of "far greater strategic importance than" the Federal victory at Shiloh. Long held that "Grant's bloodless capture of the city" eliminated a Confederate occupation of the area and "put Grant in a position to move up the Tennessee and Cumberland Rivers and send his army into the South."[21]

Defenses were eventually constructed in and around the town. A series of batteries, as many as half a dozen, contained six-foot-high palisades that crisscrossed Paducah. Abates, described as "felled trees" with "branches interlocking," were established on the city's outskirts to hamper a Confederate attack.[22]

Arguably the most significant point in the Federal defenses was a fortification built around the Marine Hospital. Known as Fort

Anderson, the structure was located on the town's northern border along the Ohio River and served as the headquarters for the Union troops in Paducah. Robert Anderson, the Union commander whose fame rose following his surrender of Fort Sumter, was the fort's namesake. Reportedly measuring some 600 feet by 160 feet, and largely surrounded by fifty-foot ditches,[23] the fort held more than 650 troops under the command of Col. Stephen B. Hicks and Lt. Comdr. James W. Shirk. It was this location that served as the focal point of the Confederate attack upon Paducah in early 1864.

As the war progressed, a large number of African Americans flocked to the "stable Union stronghold" of Paducah in order to enlist in the Federal army. The 8th U.S. Colored Heavy Artillery, the first Kentucky-formed regiment of black soldiers, was based in Paducah. Also, Company B, First Battalion, 16th Kentucky Volunteer Cavalry was organized in Paducah on March 17, 1864. A little more than a week after its formation, the 16th Kentucky would see action defending the same town in which it was raised.[24]

In early March of 1864 Gen. Nathan Bedford Forrest was in Columbus, Mississippi. While there, he finalized the organization of his command into four brigades. One brigade was under the command of Col. J. J. Neely, while Col. Robert McCulloch led a second. A third brigade was under Col. Albert P. Thompson's leadership, while Gen. Tyree Bell served as the commander of the fourth brigade. Neely and McCulloch were placed into a division under Brig. Gen. James R. Chalmers with Thompson and Bell serving in Gen. Abram Buford's division.[25]

On March 15 Forrest's troopers moved northward with Buford's division in the advance. Among the dismounted soldiers in Buford's division were several Kentucky troops "happy at the thought of having their faces turned once more to their homes." Three days later, Federal Gen. Stephen A. Hurlbut, in Memphis, reported that Forrest had reached Tupelo on the 17th headed toward West Tennessee. Hurlbut proposed, "I think he means Columbus and Paducah."[26]

J. V. Greif, a member of Forrest's command, described the

march. Greif wrote, "Our horses were all old hacks, and so weak that for many days we walked fifteen minutes of every hour to give them a rest. When we reached Tennessee, where we could get rough forage, our horses improved so rapidly that we were enabled to make longer marches and ride all of the time."[27]

While Col. W. L. Duckworth from Colonel Neely's brigade moved upon Union City, Tennessee, Forrest led a large contingent of his command toward Paducah where "a victory . . . would serve to keep the Union forces on the defensive." The goal of the move toward Paducah was reportedly not focused upon capturing the fort or taking prisoners, but instead was to gain the supplies, horses, and mules located in the Federal-occupied town. Progressing well on their march, these Confederates "camped eight miles from Mayfield" on the night of March 24.[28]

Ten Confederates from Company D of the 3rd Kentucky were detailed, "under command of Lieut. Jarrett," to serve as the advance guard during the March 25 approach upon Paducah. Colonel Hicks had sent out pickets in an effort to delay any attempt to take the Federal defenses, and these troops met the Confederate advance at Eden's Hill that afternoon. A Confederate recalled, "Nothing of importance occurred until within three miles of Paducah, when Sergt. Rosencranz . . . beckoned us from the top of a hill to come on, firing his pistol at the same time at a squad of Federal cavalry coming up the other side."[29]

J. V. Greif stated that when the Confederates reached the top of Eden's Hill, the "Federals were out of sight." It seems that Colonel Hicks had been made aware of Forrest's advance and had summoned all but his skirmishers into Fort Anderson in interest of their safety. Two gunboats, *Peosta* and *Paw Paw* were positioned near the fort to aid in its defense.[30]

Temperatures in nearby Springdale, Kentucky, reached a morning low of 38 degrees Fahrenheit and only rose to 42 degrees by 2 p.m. when the Confederates came in view of Fort Anderson. Less than one-and-a-half inches of rain had fallen so far that month, with sixteen one-hundredths falling on the night of the 24th.[31]

Thus were the conditions the warriors in blue and gray faced on the afternoon of March 25, 1864.

As the Confederates progressed into the streets of Paducah, they spotted Federal skirmishers and other men in blue moving toward Fort Anderson. A young Paducah resident witnessed the pickets running into the town and shouting that the rebels were coming.[32]

The two Union gunboats, *Paw Paw* and *Peosta,* moved toward the foot of Broadway and opened fire upon the advancing Confederates just after three o'clock. In this phase of action, as well as in the subsequent Confederate movements toward Fort Anderson, an estimated six hundred rounds were sent from the cannon on the gunboats. The *Peosta* itself fired approximately one hundred 32-pound shells, thirty grape canisters, and thirty 30-pound grape canisters. In addition, forty percussion shells, thirty 30-pound Parrott canisters, and three hundred Enfield cartridges were sent toward the soldiers attacking the Union defenses.[33]

Forrest's entire command safely gathered near 15th Street and Broadway, despite the extensive fire from *Peosta* and *Paw Paw.* It was stated that the Confederate "advance companies were followed by other detachments of Forrest's command, and . . . opened a brisk fire upon the Federals in the fort." Forrest recalled that this exchange of fire lasted approximately one hour before the Confederate general made a bold move in an attempt to end the aggression.[34]

Forrest used a flag of truce to send a message to Colonel Hicks. The content of the message was common for Forrest and has proven to provide the officer with a comparable level of both notoriety and criticism. The message was simple and straightforward, demanding the surrender of Fort Anderson.

Forrest wrote, "Colonel, Having a force amply sufficient to carry your works and reduce the place, and in order to avoid the unnecessary effusion of blood, I demand the surrender of the fort and troops, with all public property. If you surrender, you shall be treated as prisoners of war; but if I have to storm your works, you may expect no quarter." Forrest signed the note, "N. B. Forrest,

Maj.-Gen. Com. Con. Troops."[35] Colonel Hicks promptly replied that his duty was to protect the fort and he would, therefore, not surrender the position without a fight.

The truce, having lasted an estimated forty-five minutes, then came to an end. The fire from the two Union gunboats resumed, and the Confederates prepared for further action.[36] At this point, a controversial series of events ensued.

Allegations circulated that Forrest used the time of the truce to move his sharpshooters into positions that would benefit the Confederate cause. Forrest argued against the charges in writing "that these sharpshooters were advanced, while the flag of truce was up, is unfounded."[37]

Another point of argument at this juncture lies in whether or not Forrest ordered an attack upon Fort Anderson. General Buford had taken one hundred of his Confederates, under Forrest's orders, to the left of the stronghold while Forrest led his Escort to the right. When "rapid, heavy firing of small-arms" was heard in the latter, though Forrest had not given "orders looking to" attack the fort, Forrest sent his aide, Captain Anderson, "to ascertain the cause" of the action.[38]

Captain Anderson returned and reported to Forrest that the activity was the result of Col. Albert P. Thompson leading "about four hundred men of the Third and Seventy Kentucky" toward Fort Anderson at approximately 4 p.m.[39]

Thompson was a Paducah lawyer when the Civil War started and had a partnership with Joseph M. Biggers. He received a lieutenant-colonel's commission after joining the Confederacy and organized the 5th Kentucky Regiment to serve the South. The thirty-five-year-old attorney, married to the daughter of a Mayfield lawyer, was near his Paducah home and apparently sensed victory in leading an advance based upon unsubstantiated orders from Forrest.[40]

Capt. H. A. Tyler recalled the circumstances, "I had reached a point where the fort . . . was in plain view . . . About this time Colonel A. P. Thompson, moving at the head of his brigade, came up the street to where I was, and in answer to my inquiry as to what was next to be done, replied, 'I am going to take that fort.'"[41]

Tyler assumed that Thompson was acting upon Forrest's orders and joined Thompson in the advance. Tyler added, "Just as we reached the open space, he gave the command to charge, and we dashed forward in a wild rush in the direction of the fort. The enemy opened upon us with a most terrific volley."[42]

Captain Tyler lamented that at this point of the battle, "Colonel Thompson was slain and a number of the troops killed or wounded by this discharge." A second noted that Sgt. Tom Hayes, 15th Kentucky Cavalry, fired a cannon positioned inside Fort Anderson, striking Thompson and killing Capt. Al McGoodwin's horse, covering nearby Confederate soldiers with blood. Another account of the battle stated that while Thompson sat on his horse, a cannonball hit the saddle pummel, killing Thompson. The horse then, according to this account, ran approximately half a block before falling dead.[43]

Another account stated that the cannonball decapitated Colonel Thompson, yet an early twentieth century statement on the event said, "A .32 cannon ball tore his body to pieces." Still, a different recollection of the event stated that Thompson "was struck by a cannon ball that severed his body at the waist," causing the upper half to fall to the ground while the lower half remained in the saddle.[44]

A two-story brick building belonging to a Dr. Bassett was positioned at a point that allowed occupants to gain an excellent view of Fort Anderson. A Confederate participant remarked that Confederate sharpshooters were occupying the home as a sniper's nest. In turn, one of the gunboat shells "intended no doubt for the Bassett house, cut Maj. Thompson in two."[45] Thus the account of Thompson's death gains another angle.

One of the most complete accounts of Colonel Thompson's tragic death exists in an 1897 *Confederate Veteran* article. The author, J. V. Greif, stated,

Col. Thompson had halted, and his horse stood across the street, his head to the south and his front feet in the street gutter. The Colonel held his cap in his right hand above his head when he was struck by a shell, which exploded as it struck him, literally tearing him to pieces and the saddle off his horse. Col. Thompson's flesh and blood fell on the men near him. I was within ten feet of him when he was struck, and my old gray Confederate hat was covered with his blood, a large piece of flesh fell on the shoulder of my file leader, John Stockdale.[46]

Lastly, another account stated that Thompson was shot in the head during the fight while positioned near Fort Anderson. At that point, a cannonball struck him in the stomach, tearing his body to pieces. That sources stated, "His spinal column was found several feet from his mangled body."[47]

Regardless of the exact circumstances of Thompson's death, no controversy exists in respect to his bravery. An early account of the battle at Paducah proclaimed, "The was no more courageous soldier in the Confederate army, and one of the most intelligent and valuable officers in Forrest's command."[48]

Thompson's body remained at the site of the killing until the next morning. At 9 o'clock on March 26, Mayor D. A. Yeiser and John McClung recovered the "shattered body" laying a short distance from Thompson's Paducah home and placed it into a grave in Oak Grove Cemetery. Eventually the body was moved to Bowman Cemetery in Murray, Kentucky.[49]

Col. Ed Crossland replaced Thompson as the brigade's commander and immediately ordered the Confederates to fall back approximately one hundred yards behind a tobacco factory. At Tenth and Clay Streets, a rifle ball from a Confederate sharpshooter's bullet struck Crossland in the right thigh, according to one source. One of Crossland's subordinates stated that Crossland was "brave, enterprising, kind, and considerate to his men" and was idolized at times. Reportedly, Crossland, as much as any colonel in Forrest's command, "held the general's confidence" and was likely to have been promoted had the serious wound not been inflicted at Paducah. With Crossland's wounding Lieutenant

Colonel Holt assumed command and ordered the Confederates to retreat further.[50]

Prior to the Confederate retreat, Paducah citizens continued their exodus from the town, an event that started hours earlier. Crowds of people were seen on the old wharf board, awaiting passage to the safety of the Illinois side of the river. Post-war accounts also stated that George Oehlschlaeger, the baker whose services benefited the Federal army, fled Paducah, leaving behind a month's payment in silver. Though his business was later ransacked, the silver was untouched, having been hidden under a newspaper.[51]

Many Paducah citizens were unable to cross the river and "sought refuge under the bluff, out of range of shot." It was also reported that a number of citizens entered Fort Anderson and joined in the defense of the Federal structure. One man placed his family inside the fort and took part in driving away the Confederate attacks. The man was severely wounded in the arm but refused to seek aid until satisfied that his hometown was free of Forrest's troops.[52]

An unsuccessful series of charges upon Fort Anderson, during which the Confederates moved "to the very mouths of the guns" and allegedly climbed "upon the walls of the fort," left the fort under Union control; but, the Confederates controlled Paducah. With the cessation of the battle, confiscating the town's goods began.

Forrest wrote of the ensuing events that after the Federal troops were inside Fort Anderson or the gunboats, his troops "held the town for ten hours; captured many stores and horses; burned sixty bales of cotton, one steamer, and a dry-dock, bringing out fifty prisoners. My loss, as far as known, is twenty-five killed and wounded." Forrest's estimation was later revised to eleven killed and thirty-three wounded. Total casualties for the Federal troops were listed as fourteen killed and forty-six wounded.[53]

Among the wounded Confederates was Captain McKnight, an officer who had suffered an injury to his chest the previous month in the battle at Okolona, Mississippi. McKnight's wound at Paducah occurred when a Federal shell hit a chimney, causing it to fall on the soldiers nearby and striking McKnight in the head. McKnight recovered from his wound and was able to participate in one of Forrest's greatest victories, the battle of Brice's Crossroads, in June. McKnight was not as fortunate the next month at Harrisburg or Tupelo where his left leg was shattered between the ankle and knee, ending his military service.[54]

The Confederates withdrew and moved "some four miles southward," where they established their camp for the night. The fifty prisoners were in tow, with the four hundred horses and mules, "and a very large supply of clothing and quartermaster's subsistence and military supplies including saddles and other horse equipment," the latter elements being the primary purpose "of which . . . the expedition had been mainly made." Jordan and Pryor, in their extensive exploration of Forrest's campaigns, noted that another object of the Paducah raid was "to confuse, distract, and defensively occupy the Federal forces that, for some time previously, had been used to harass and despoil the people of West Tennessee and North Mississippi."[55]

Sadly, the citizens of Paducah suffered following Forrest's attack on Paducah. Forrest had destroyed the New Orleans and Ohio depot located between Fourth and Fifth Streets; buildings located at the foot of Broadway were also burned, as was the aforementioned steamboat designated *Dacotah*. These structures had contained whiskey, quartermaster supplies, and commissary supplies and had provided Forrest's troops with the bulk of their prisoners. Homes that had been used to benefit Union troops were also burned.[56]

Federal soldiers under Maj. George Barnes, 16th Kentucky Cavalry, followed orders from Colonel Hicks to "burn all the houses in musket range of the fort from which the sharpshooters of the enemy fired upon us." This action has been deemed as "needless" due to the fact the Confederates had left the town and showed no indication of renewing the attack.[57] Approximately sixty houses were destroyed, as civilians bore the brunt of loss in the event intended to have military goals.

After the war, the owners of the sixty homes petitioned Congress for compensation for their losses. Congress approved the bill and determined that the full amount of restitution should be paid to the victims of the incident. However, President Grant vetoed the bill, citing that the homes were burned as a necessary act of war.[58]

Ed Moss, Company D, 3rd Kentucky, had been killed during the Confederate advance and his body had been placed in a Paducah home to await burial. One of his comrades recalled, "His remains were burned in the building . . . when the Federals burned that end of town."[59]

Meanwhile, Forrest's Confederates, upon arriving at Mayfield, were allowed to disband for a few days. This decision allowed many of the troopers to visit family members they had not seen in months. In addition, recruits were gained during the disbandment, while returning cavalrymen, for the most part, "procured good mounts and comfortable clothing."[60]

The news of the battle at Paducah made headlines as far away as London. *The Illustrated London News* edition of April 16, 1864 contained an article that said, "Forrest . . . on the 25th occupied Paducah . . . from which he removed many valuable spoils. He also attacked the fort, but . . . was compelled to desist. Two Federal gunboats . . . opened fire to dislodge his forces, during which a large portion of the city was destroyed."[61]

Col. Stephen Hicks stated after the battle that while Forrest had failed to capture Fort Anderson, Forrest had also overlooked approximately one hundred horses and mules while the Confederates were confiscating animals in Paducah. Hicks was bold enough to tell a reporter that the animals were housed in a foundry outside Paducah. When Forrest read the statement carried in one of several newspapers, he sent Gen. Abraham Buford back to Paducah to take the animals for the Confederate cause. It has been duly noted that while Buford successfully carried out this assignment, which came to be known as the Skirmish of Paducah, it is unknown whether Hicks conducted subsequent interviews.[62]

A modern visit to Paducah will result in a mixed exposure to sites related to the battle that took place in 1864. A Civil War Sites

Advisory Commission Report conducted a study of more than 3,000 acres and disclosed that none of the acreage is currently considered as protected.[63] Aside from wayside exhibits, signs, and a walking tour, little has been done in respect to preserving the history of the Civil War aspect of Paducah's rich history.

The Paducah/McCracken County Convention and Visitors Bureau, located at 128 Broadway, should serve as the point of origin for any interested party's visit to the area. Stopping by the bureau will enable visitors to obtain a guide to Paducah's downtown Civil War walking tour. The bureau can be contacted at 502-443-8783 or 1-800-paducah. Paducah's zip code is 42001.

Several of the significant sites related to the battle of Paducah can be visited on the walking tour. These include the site of Fort Anderson, the important base built in 1861 and once home to 5,000 Federal soldiers. Other sites include the location of Col. Albert Thompson's death, Hummel's Gunsmith shop, and Hick's Headquarters. Civil War enthusiasts can also visit the spot where General Grant read his proclamation on September 6, 1861, announcing his intent on entering Paducah. Grace Episcopal Church, a Federal hospital during the war, still stands at 820 Broadway. The home of Confederate general Lloyd Tilghman, a victim of the battle of Champion Hill, Mississippi, is also available for tours and stands at 7th and Kentucky Avenue. The Tilghman House and Civil War Museum is open Wednesday through Saturday from noon until 4 and can be reached at 270-575-5477 or by mailing correspondence to 631 Kentucky Avenue.[64]

The William Clark Market House Museum is located at 121 South 2nd Street and is open from noon to 4, Monday through Saturday. Visitors can view pieces of Grant's furniture as well as a quilt Robert E. Lee's wife made. Additional information can be obtained by contacting 270-443-7759. Also, a series of murals are present on the floodwall located on the riverfront at 1st and Broadway. One of the murals is Civil War themed and depicts Fort Anderson, Grant's entry into Paducah, the recruitment of African American troops, and other incidents of Paducah's rich Civil War history.

Other noteworthy locations in Paducah include the Katterjohn Building, a structure that now occupies the site where Nathan Bedford Forrest had his headquarters in a grove of trees during the battle of Paducah. Campsites of various Federal units, including the 40th Illinois Volunteer Regiment, the 11th Indiana, and the 8th Illinois can be seen on the walking tour.

Paducah is a city with unlimited potential related to preservation of its Civil War sites. Although many of the sites are currently the locations of empty lots or abandoned structures, the lack of a group centered on the purpose of setting aside the locations for future generations may result in the loss of these sites and the inability of Paducah to capitalize on the economic opportunities that exist in preserving them.

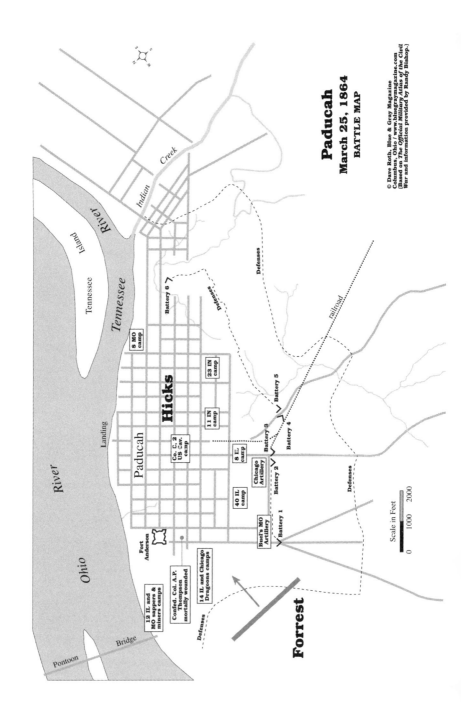

Paducah
March 25, 1864
BATTLE MAP

© Dave Roth, Blue & Gray Magazine
Columbus, Ohio / www.bluegraymagazine.com
(Based on *The Official Military Atlas of the Civil War* and information provided by Randy Bishop.)

Ohio River

Tennessee River

Tennessee Island

Tennessee

Indian Creek

Landing

Paducah

Hicks

Fort Anderson

Pontoon Bridge

12 IL and MO sappers & miners camps

Confed. Col. A.P. Thompson mortally wounded

14 IL and Chicago Dragoons camps

8 MO camp

23 IN camp

11 IN camp

Co. C, 2 US Cav. camp

8 IL camp

40 IL camp

Chicago Artillery

Buel's MO Artillery

Battery 6

Battery 5

Battery 4

Battery 3

Battery 2

Battery 1

Defenses

railroad

Forrest

Scale in Feet
0   1000   2000

The Katterjohn Building occupies the location where a grove of trees once stood. Here, Forrest had his headquarters. (Photo by author)

Confederate Col. Albert Thompson of Paducah was killed at this location. (Photo by author)

Grace Episcopal Church served as a Union hospital after the battle. (Photo by author)

This building now occupies the site where Ft. Anderson stood. (Photo by author)

CHAPTER THIRTEEN

CYNTHIANA

June 11-12, 1864

"No pen can capture that awful scene."
—*Cynthiana Democrat,* June 1896

Cynthiana, Kentucky, is the location of the last significant Civil War battle in the Bluegrass State. Today's population of more than 6,000 people far outdistances the 1,200 residents present at the time of the battle. In addition, manufacturing facilities and agricultural production are major sources of income and provide a more diverse economic base than existed in 1864. The town's official Web site gladly proclaims that it is an excellent example of "small town America" within the "golden triangle" of Cincinnati, Ohio, and Lexington and Louisville, Kentucky.[1] The town has another claim to fame: it is the sight of not one, but two, battles during the American Civil War. Although the July 17, 1862 battle is noteworthy, this chapter will primarily focus on various aspects of the second battle, a struggle that lasted two days in June 1864.

The town of Cynthiana owes its existence to the family of Robert Harrison. In 1793 Harrison established the town and provided the name based upon those of his two daughters, Cynthia and Anna. Although Cynthiana is located in Harrison County, the county's name came from another settler in the area. By the time of the Civil War battles in Cynthiana, the town was viewed as strongly Confederate in its sentiment. Ironically, Federal troops occupied the town and found it necessary to invoke martial law due to the acts of arson, riots, and executions that took place within the city limits.[2] It was this situation that elevated the interest of the town in the mind and strategy of John Hunt Morgan and his Confederate raiders.

With the Confederate high command's approval, Morgan conducted a raid upon the town on July 17, 1862. Morgan and approximately 875 men used two cannon to defeat less than 350 Federal soldiers under Lt. Col. John Landram, capturing approximately 250 of Landram's men. Landram's casualties, not including those captured, were listed as seventeen killed and thirty-five wounded. Morgan reported just eight killed and twenty-nine wounded in the raid.[3]

It has been duly noted that the first raid differed greatly from the second, in that the June 1864 raid was epitomized by pillage, insubordination, and dissipation as Morgan's command appears to have become "fatally flawed." This fact seems rather ironic when it is taken into account that Cynthiana had exhibited strong Confederate sympathies up to that time, especially during the previous raid. The 2005 study prepared by Gray and Pape, Incorporated of Cincinnati for the Cynthiana-Harrison County Chamber of Commerce stated that this was due largely to the fact that a majority of Morgan's men from the July 1862 raid had either been captured or killed by the time of the June 1864 event. "Replaced by thugs," Morgan's command was filled with men who were then under the leadership of a man "acting without orders,"[4] and tended to tarnish the career and reputation of a Confederate officer otherwise touted as one of the premier cavalry leaders of either side during the war.

Basil Duke, a member of Morgan's staff, recalled that Morgan's Raiders began a difficult march across mountainous terrain, entering Kentucky on June 2, 1864. Three brigades made up Morgan's force at that time, with a division of the troops taking place five days later. The intent of this division was to confuse the

Federal troops in Kentucky and hopefully disperse the defensive capacity of those men into a wider area, freeing Morgan for a more successful campaign.[5]

A Kentucky doctor wrote that when the rebels entered Winchester in Clark County the crops were suffering heavily and gardens were drying up due to a severe drought. By June 11, morning temperatures were 56 degrees Fahrenheit. A cool 70 degrees would be the high for the day, but the dry conditions continued through the area.[6]

Raids in various towns, such as Mount Sterling, had made Kentucky residents aware of Morgan's presence and gave the citizens the advantage of time to hide livestock from the possible captors. G. D. Ewing, a member of the 4th Kentucky Cavalry, recalled that while the garrison at Mount Sterling "put up a good fight, their capture was soon effected." The town of Mount Sterling had gained a reputation as "being the home of numerous bushwhackers," and the deaths of two Confederate captains were reported to be from this lot who fired at the raiders "from their homes." Ewing continued, "After our long march through the mountains, not having feasted before we started, all commissary and other supplies captured were liberally used immediately, without much thankfulness to those furnishing them."[7]

Ewing continued his recollections in stating, "Morgan had learned that there were as many as five hundred soldiers at Cynthiana and the usual good supplies . . . It had been arranged . . . to move from Cynthiana to Augusta, then to Maysville, and on to Big Sandy River, and into Virginia. But we had a fight on hand first at Cynthiana."[8]

At approximately 3:30 on the morning of June 11, Morgan arrived at the outskirts of Cynthiana and divided his troops. Morgan took Col. H. L. Giltner's Kentucky troops and advanced on the Leesburg Pike, a direct route into town. The two remaining brigades under colonels Robert Martin and D. Howard Smith moved eastward to take an approach on New Lair Road toward Magee Hill.[9]

The Union troops on Magee Hill retreated toward the depot and took refuge in some of the nearby houses. The retreat appeared to be rather quick as other Union soldiers found shelter in the depot itself. Confederate Lt. John Headly stated that Morgan watched the events from a location "just beyond a brick residence to the right" and some 200 yards from Magee Hill. The fight, known as the Battle Grove portion of the fight at Cynthiana, lasted some thirty minutes before the Union troops surrendered.[10]

Morgan moved into the Cynthiana downtown area and fought a group of Union soldiers positioned on Raven Creek Pike. The Federal soldiers, whose breakfast was interrupted, were standing behind a stone fence near a covered bridge. Here, some fifty Union soldiers were captured.[11]

Alleged acts of cruelty abounded as General Burbridge, the commander of the Federal soldiers at Cynthiana, stated that one of his officers, Colonel Berry, was shot while attempting to surrender. Berry's son, Confederate Capt. Robert Berry, was given permission to go to his father's side. Colonel Berry, with his son in attendance, passed away six days later.[12]

Additional Federals retreated toward the courthouse while others sought refuge in a hotel that belonged to a Mr. Rankin. It was said, "The Confederates . . . charged into these several places, causing the utmost consternation among the inhabitants." Federal Adjutant Edmund Wood was one of at least two soldiers who hid in the clock tower of the courthouse while the fighting continued below. While trying to surrender at the hotel, U.S. Colonel Garis was shot in the shoulder. A stable beside the hotel burst into flames, yet the proprietor was able to negotiate the salvation of the hotel itself. The cost to Mr. Rankin was substantial, as he had to serve his entire stock of liquor to the Confederate warriors in return for the hotel escaping destruction.[13]

Colonel Duke recalled, "After a short fight the garrison . . . was captured . . . a large quantity of stores were captured and destroyed at Cynthiana."[14]

Later that morning G. D. Ewing made the following observation from his post on the railroad. Ewing said,

I had been at my point . . . only a short time when, some miles north, I saw black smoke arising as though from two trains running close together . . . There were two trains, the one in front coming in less than three hundred yards of where I was concealed, the rear train running up close to the first. As best I could I counted the coaches, and soon the men in blue began dismounting, almost as thick as bees from a hive at swarming time.[15]

Ewing estimated as many as 1,500 men had arrived to assist in the Federal effort. The Confederate scout also felt that the troops were "mostly ninety day men, hastily gotten together by General Hobson to meet this special emergency."[16]

The Confederates rapidly advanced upon these Federal troops near Keller's Bridge. A participant wrote, "the wild rebel yell of our men was very different from the peaceful pursuits of their pastoral lives at home . . . our men steadily pressed them back into the bend of the river. With all chances of exit cut off . . . there was nothing for him [to do] but surrender." Official numbers state that some six hundred of Gen. Edward Hobson's men were captured in the action of the Keller's Bridge phase of the battle of Cynthiana.[17]

Keller's Bridge had been burned a few days prior to this engagement as the Confederates had attempted "to cut off communication between Cynthiana and Cincinnati."[18]

The fires raged in the town of Cynthiana while Morgan refused to allow the deployment of the town's fire engine. As this indifferent approach of Morgan's was unfolding, his men looted the stores in the path of the fire. Eventually, Morgan consented to the use of the fire engine, although it proved too late for some thirty-seven of the businesses. The storeowners subsequently petitioned the Congressional Committee on War Claims, seeking compensation for the loss of their buildings. Unfortunately, the $231,500 claim total failed to pass.[19]

A story written three decades after the battle stated,

No pen can picture that awful scene. Stores whose cellars were filled with whiskey and other inflammable liquids, had fragments of their contents sent like rockets far into the air on blue and yellow flames that reached to heaven. The rattle of musketry, men bearing the dead and dying . . . all combined to make a horrible picture never to be forgotten.[20]

A witness to the battle wrote of the concluding action of June 11, "The fight continued about five hours . . . Gen. Hobson was finally compelled to accept . . . Morgan's conditions of surrender . . . the private property of the troops should be respected, and the officers retain their side arms."[21] More allegations surfaced that Morgan's men took possession of a large amount of property from the surrendered men, creating more negative press for the Confederate raiders.

As for the surrender, it was said, "The Federal forces were drawn up along the pike, their arms stacked and burned, and they were marched through Cynthiana, a mile east, to a grove, where they found the other Federal forces" who had been taken prisoner during the action at Battle Grove, "prisoners like themselves."[22]

One of Morgan's men relished what appeared to be a complete victory. He wrote, "Our first day at Cynthiana . . . had been an eventful one, as well as a successful one on our part . . . but the ammunition that we captured would not fit our guns. By some mistake the captured guns and ammunition were burned, and our almost constant fighting had well-nigh exhausted the ammunition for our Enfield rifles."[23]

The Confederates, by their own admission, "were almost worn out." This, doubled with the shortage of ammunition, would prove to be "quite disastrous in the next twenty-four hours."[24]

That night, Morgan's men camped in line of battle, expecting an attack from Gen. Stephen Burbridge's Federal troops. Morgan aligned his troops one mile east of Cynthiana, formed in a line that extended from Claysville Pike toward Poplar Hall, the home of John W. Kimbrough, and toward Battle Grove and to Magee Hill.[25] The Confederates held these positions as they awaited the attack to come. The wait would not be long, nor would the results prove as positive for Morgan's men as the fighting on Saturday, June 11 had.

Burbridge and 2,400 Federal soldiers arrived at Cynthiana early on the morning of Sunday, June 12, 1864. A reporter stated that, "in place of the sound of church bells calling the repentant to prayer, the rattle of musketry and all the noise of deadly conflict were to be heard."[26]

Allegedly, Morgan, while eating breakfast, was informed of Burbridge's arrival. With his command deployed "all over the town," Morgan chose to send orders to the soldiers guarding the prisoners at Battle Grove to march those men northward where they would be paroled. The "prisoners were taken to Claysville and Morgan's orders respecting them put into execution."[27]

One Confederate recalled, "Burbridge made a rapid assault upon our lines." A Federal reporter stated, "The fighting began at Battle Grove. Soon the women who had watched from windows and half opened doors saw their husbands, brothers, and sons go by with only a glance as a farewell, and to some it was a last parting."[28]

The Confederates, "their number diminished by many brave soldiers who had fallen in the two previous battles" and who were "depleted by hard fighting the day before," attempted to make a stand. A participant recalled that the Federals were "met with firmness, and thrown back" despite the fact that the men in blue held a three-to-one advantage.[29]

Burbridge's men were able to flank the Confederates, forcing the men in gray to soon give way. Many of the Confederates had only one round to meet the advancing Federal troops whose second advance made the flanking movement possible. A Confederate said, "It was soon apparent to the enemy that our men were now helpless. Giltner ordered them to fall back slowly so as to maintain formation . . . there was so much confusion as they were falling back through the town."[30]

The goal of the Confederates was to reach the bridge, but by the time they reached the bridge, Burbridge's men held it. It was said that the Confederates began "fording the river some distance below the bridge, but in easy range, and many of the men and horses were killed or wounded in the water."[31]

One source said the Confederates "one by one . . . fell back through the town, crossed the river, and followed the Raven Creek Pike." Another added, "Soon the retreat of Morgan's men became a rout. The men fell back in squads and singly, and on every face was written a determination not to be taken alive."[32]

A Confederate who managed to escape wrote,

> I reached the river, and . . . I went nearer to the bridge . . . I had gotten a fine, spirited horse . . . and spurred him into the water, which was deep there. We both went under, but soon rose and swam to the opposite shore. As the horse climbed the steep bank, the girth of my saddle broke and I was thrown violently down the bank, knocking the breath out of me . . . I unsnapped my carbine rifle and threw it as far as I could . . . intending to surrender . . . Frank Miller . . . came out of the water on a fine horse and insisted that I get up behind him. The Federals were . . . cursing us as rebels and demanding our surrender, but Miller pointed his empty pistol in their direction . . . I was watching for a good mount among the horses of our men lost in the river, and soon obtained a good one . . . Miller's pistol and my gun sling looked formidable. We both had good racers and soon outdistanced our new acquaintances. We made our escape, but our command had suffered a serious and useless loss . . . in both cases caused by excessive optimism taking the reins from cool and calculating military judgment.[33]

Morgan and several hundred of his men used the Claysville Pike as their route of escape, reaching the safety of Virginia on June 20. Dozens of other Confederates were killed, wounded, or captured at Licking Creek. Although Morgan did not report his losses for the battle, Union estimates of Confederate losses were 400 captured, 300 killed, and 300 wounded. Morgan did, however, report his losses for the entire Kentucky Raid of 1864 as 450 captured, 125 wounded, and 80 killed. Federal losses were given as 280 missing, 17 wounded, and 280 killed.[34]

One of the wounded Confederates was Capt. William Johnston Stone. During the retreat, Stone was shot in his right leg just below the hip joint. Initially considered to have received a mortal wound, Stone was nursed back to health, although his leg was amputated. Stone later married Cornelia Woodyard, the young lady from Cynthiana who served as his nurse, and was elected to serve several terms in the Kentucky State Legislature and served five terms in Congress.[35]

Others were not as fortunate as Captain Stone. Ira Allen, a member of the 13th Kentucky Cavalry, was listed as missing and presumed dead following the action of June 11, 1864. It is generally regarded that Allen is one of the Confederates buried in the mass grave at Cynthiana. Second Sgt. David May, a merchant and State Representative before the war, declared his allegiance to the Confederacy and was expelled from office due to his stance. May drowned in the days after or during the battle of Cynthiana, and his wife was denied the receipt of benefits as he "was not killed by bullet or saber."[36]

The graves of Allen and others are preserved in Battle Grove Cemetery, the site generally regarded to be the location of some of the strongest fighting during the second battle of Cynthiana. The cemetery, opened in 1868, is one of fourteen stops on the driving tour for the battle at Cynthiana and contains the oldest Confederate Memorial in the state of Kentucky. The cemetery is located at 531 East Pike Street and is open daily, with hours varying throughout the year. During the winter months, Battle Grove Cemetery's hours are 7:30 a.m. to 5:30 p.m. Additional information and updated hours for the cemetery can be obtained by calling 859-234-5323.[37]

The Cynthiana-Harrison County Chamber of Commerce, located at 203 W. Pike Street in Cynthiana, 41031, can be contacted at 859-234-5236 or via e-mail at cynchamber@setel. com. The chamber of commerce, open from 9:00 a.m. to 4:00 p.m., is a wonderful place to start a visit to the Cynthiana battlefield and is the most productive site at which to begin the driving tour. Other stops include the covered bridge site, the depot site, the Rankin

House, the courthouse, and Keller's Bridge. Poplar Hill, Magee Hill, and the Episcopal Church are additional stops of locations that prominently figured into the battles at Cynthiana. Artifacts from the two Cynthiana raids can be seen at another tour stop, the Cynthiana-Harrison County Museum at 124 S. Walnut Street. The museum is open from 10:00 a.m. to 5:00 p.m. Friday and Saturday and may be contacted at 859-234-7179.[38]

The Civil War Sites Advisory Commission's Report on the Nation's Civil War Battlefields noted that although 830 acres of land are associated with the battles of Cynthiana, none are actually categorized as protected. Three state markers, "The Battle of Cynthiana," "The Confederates Here," and "Morgan's Last Raid" are located nearby, giving some amount of interpretation to the battles that occurred in Cynthiana. Additionally, an annual reenactment is held in July, allowing additional insight into the event.[39]

A reasonable effort has been given to the preservation of Cynthiana's Civil War sites, but much remains to be done. The residents of Cynthiana would benefit economically from the tourism dollars that a proposed visitors center and additional interpretation would bring to the area. The need exists for an advocacy group to undertake the project and only the future will determine if that will be done.

Morgan's Last Kentucky Raid

May 29-June 20, 1864 (including the Battle of Cynthiana, June 11-12)

RAID MAP

CONFEDERATE
M-Morgan

UNION
B-Burbridge H-Hobson

Dates on the Map denote the Confederates' arrival at that place.

After the disaster at Cynthiana, Morgan makes his way back to Abingdon (on June 20) by way of Flemingsburg, West Liberty, Paintsville, and Pikeville. Part of Morgan's command under Colonel Giltner is cut-off during the battle and travels through Georgetown and Nicholasville, then "the severest trip I ever experienced" (Giltner's words), to Pennington Gap and Abingdon. In late August, Morgan is relieved of command pending the outcome of a court of inquiry into the raid. Ignoring orders, he takes the remnant of his command into East Tennessee to confront a Union force rumored to be at Greeneville. He is killed at Greeneville on September 4, 1864.

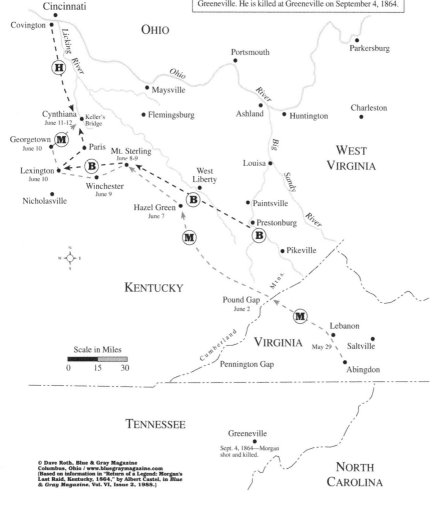

Confederate 2d Sgt. David May was a pre-war merchant and served as a Kentucky State Representative in the early months of the war. He drowned when Union soldiers blasted a millpond and his grave is marked in Battle Grove Cemetery. (Courtesy of Fred May)

Prior to surrendering, Union soldiers fired from the second floor of the courthouse. (Photo by author)

The depot was located at this site. (Photo by author)

The Confederate Monument in Battle Grove Cemetery is the oldest Confederate Memorial in Kentucky. (Photo by author)

NOTES

Abbreviations
B & L: Battles and Leaders of the Civil War
BORA: Battle of Richmond Association
C.V.:   Confederate Veteran
HCHS: Hart County Historical Society
MCPL: McCracken County (Kentucky) Public Library
PKPL: Paducah Kentucky Public Library
TSL&A: Tennessee State Library and Archives

Introduction
1. "The History of the Orphan Brigade," C.V. 6, no. 7 (July 1898): 317; R. M. Kelly, "Holding Kentucky for the Union." B & L. (1884; reprint, New York: Castle Books, 1956), 374-75.
2. Robert Collins Suhr, "Kentucky Neutrality Threatened," America's Civil War 5, no. 2 (July, 1992): 24-25.
3. Robert Kennedy, "Governor Magoffin's Neutrality." Harpweek.com (accessed November 7, 2011); www.civilwar-pictures.com (accessed November 7, 2011).
4. Alice Hamilton Cromie, A Tour Guide to the Civil War (Chicago: Quadrangle Books, 1956), 102-3.
5. Ibid., 103.
6. Bruce Catton, Terrible Swift Sword (Garden City, NY: Doubleday and Co. Inc., 1963), 35-36.

Chapter One
1. Joseph E. Brent, "Barbourville Civil War Interpretive Park," The Knox Countian19, no. 3 (Fall 2007): 54.
2. Charles Reed Mitchell; http://www.cityofbarbourvillekentucky.org/index. html; http://www.uky.edu/KentuckyAtlas/ky-barbourville.html.
3. Ibid.
4. Capt. J. H. Putnam, A Journalistic History of the Thirty-First Regiment (Louisville, KY: John P. Morton & Co., 1862), 42; Kenneth A. Hafendorfer, The Battle of Wildcat Mountain, (Louisville, KY: KH Press, 2003), 48.

5. "The Story of Camp Dick Robinson." *Courier Journal.* 1895. Accessed via http://kentuckyexplorer.com/nonmembers/3-camps.html.

6. Ibid.

7. *New York Times*, November 1, 1861.

8. Roy P. Basler, ed. *Abraham Lincoln: Speeches and Writings. 1861-1865.* (Library of America), 265-66.

9. Phillip Seyfrit, "Nelson only naval officer to become major general." http://www.thekentuckycivilwarbugle.com/bullnelson.html (accessed November 7, 2011).

10. Ibid.

11. Hafendorfer, *Wildcat*, 20; Samuel P. Carter, *A Biographical Sketch.* (Washington, D.C.: Library of Congress, n.d.).

12. Hafendorfer, *Wildcat*, 25-27.

13. Brent, "Barbourville," 53.

14. Winfred Partin, "Contesting Cumberland Gap." *America's Civil War* 20, no. 2, 28.

15. Hafendorfer, *Wildcat*, 29; W. J. Worsham, *The Old Nineteenth Tennessee Regiment, C.S.A.* (Knoxville, 1902), 11; W. J. McMurray, *History of the Twentieth Tennessee Regiment Volunteer Infantry.* (Nashville, 1904) 118.

16. Worsham, *The Old,* 16; *Kentucky Counties,* (Lexington, KY: Kentucky Images), 10; James R. Binford, *Recollections of the Fifteenth Regiment of Mississippi Infantry, C. S. A.,* vol. 5 of *Henry (Patrick) Papers.* (Mississippi Department of Archives and History).

17. Hafendorfer, *Wildcat*, 32-34.

18. Ibid; Adkins, *Battle of Barboursville, Kentucky,* 2nd ed., (n.d.), 87; *Louisville Daily Democrat*, September 25, 1861; Worsham, *The Old,* 14; Brent, "Barbourville," 53; Richard Hancock, *Hancock's Diary.* (Nashville, TN: 1887), 44; U.S. War Department, *The War of the Rebellion: A Compilation of the Official Records of the Union and Confederate Armies,* 129 vols. (Washington, D.C.: 1880-1901). 1, 4, 1, 199. Hereafter referred to as *OR. OR* citations are given by series number, volume number, part number if applicable, and page numbers.

19. Hafendorfer, *Wildcat,* 34; *OR,* 1, 4, 1, 199; Sergeant E. Tarrant, *The Wild Riders of the First Kentucky Cavalry.* (Louisville, KY: 1894), 36.

20. Hafendorfer, *Wildcat,* 36; *OR,* 1, 14, 1, 199; *Louisville Daily Democrat,* September 25, 1861.

21. *Louisville Daily Democrat,* September 25, 1861; Inslee Deaderick, Letter of September 20, 1861, to "Dear Father," *The Knox Countian,* (Barborville: Spring 2007) 23.

22. *Louisville Daily Democrat,* September 25, 1861; "The Fight at Barboursville," *Knox Countian,* (Barbourville, KY: Spring 2007), 22.

23. *Louisville Daily Democrat,* September 25, 1861; Deaderick letter.

24. Hafendorfer, *Wildcat,* 38-39; Adkins, *Battle,* 40; www.aotn.homestead. com/richoob.html.

25. Adkins, *Battle,* 41; *Daily Dispatch*, October 2, 1861; http://kyclim.wku. edu/factsheets/thebattleofBarbourville.html (accessed November 8, 2011).

26. *Daily Dispatch*, October 2, 1861.
27. Adkins, *Battle*, 41; "Fight at Barborville," 22.
28. *Louisville Daily Democrat,* October 2, 1861.
29. J. P. Coffin, *C.V.* 8, no. 8 (August 1900), 122.
30. Ibid.
31. http://tennessee-scv.org/Camp1817/ (accessed December 15, 2011); www. battleofbarbourville.com.
32. Coffin, 122; Hafendorfer, *Wildcat*, 42; "Fight at Barborville", 22; McMurray, 192.
33. *Daily Dispatch*. October 2, 1861.
34. Deaderick letter.
35. "The Fight . . .", 22.
36. *Henry Melvil Doak Memoirs*. (Nashville, TN: Tennessee State Library and Archives, n.d.)
37. "The Fight . . .", 22.
38. Ibid; *OR*, 14, 1, 199.
39. U. S. Department of the Interior, National Park Service, American Battlefield Protection Program, *Update to the Civil War Sites Advisory Commission Report on the Nation's Civil War Battlefields*. October 2008. 19.
40. Mitchell.
41. Brent, 1.
42. *The Knox Countian*, 19, no. 3 (Fall 2007); Samantha Swindler, http://www. thetimestribune.com/features/local_story_255085107.html.

Chapter Two
1. *OR*, 1, 4, 1, 418-19, 425.
2. Thomas D. Clark, *A History of Laurel County,* (London, KY: The Laurel County Historical Society, 1989), 202; www.wildcatbattlefield.org (accessed November 8, 2011).
3. Tarrant, 37; *Toledo Daily Herald & Times*, October 26, 1861; *Daily Toledo Blade*, October 29, 1861; "Schoepf Turns back Zollicoffer's Rebel at Camp Wildcat!" *The Southern Star,* Laurel County, October 21, 1861. http://aotn. homestead.com/wildcat.html.
4. "The Campaign in Kentucky," *New York Times*, November 1, 1861.
5. *OR*, 1, 4, 439.
6. *OR*, 1, 4, 203; *Louisville Daily Journal*, October 7, 1861.
7. Hancock, *Diary*, 57.
8. *OR*, 1, 4, 309; Garry D. Nation, "Alvis Duncan Hicks in the Civil War," http://pages.suddenlink.net/gnation/A._D._Hicks.html (accessed November 8, 2011).
9. O. P. Cutter, *Our Battery,* (Cleveland: Nevins' Book & Job Printing Establishment, 1864), 8-9; *Diary of David Fately*, (Indianapolis, IN: Indiana State Library, n.d.); *Louisville Daily Journal,* October 29, 1861.
10. Tarrant, 41-42; *Indianapolis Daily Journal*, October 26, 1861.
11. *Nashville Banner*. October 30, 1861.
12. Ibid.

13. *Daily Toledo Blade*, October 29, 1861; "Schoepf Turns . . ."

14. *Indianapolis Daily Journal*, October 25, 1861; *National Tribune*, July 5, 1883.

15. *Toledo Daily Herald & Times*, October 26, 1861.

16. Hafendorfer, *Wildcat*, 120-121.

17. William H. Isom, *Reminiscences of the 17th Tennessee Volunteers*, n.d.

18. *Nashville Banner*, October 30, 1861.

19. Tarrant, 42-43.

20. John A. Chase, *History of the Fourteenth Ohio.* (Toledo, Ohio, 1881), 16-17; *The Western Star*, November 7, 1861; James Cooper, Memoirs, TSL&A.

21. *OR*, 1, 4, 309.

22. Hafendorfer, *Wildcat*, 144.

23. Ibid, 147; *Nashville Banner*, October 30, 1861.

24. Hafendorfer, 152-153; *Nashville Banner*, October 30, 1861.

25. *National Tribune*, July 5, 1883; www.wildcatbattlefield.org (accessed November 8, 2011); *Louisville Daily Democrat*, October 24, 1861.

26. *OR*, 1, 4, 208; www.wildcatbattlefield.org (accessed November 8, 2011).

27. *OR*, 1, 4, 208; *National Tribune*, October 5, 1889.

28. *OR*, 1, 4, 208; *Louisville Daily Journal*, October 29, 1861.

29. *OR*, 1, 4, 213.

30. *New Albany Daily Ledger*, October 24, 1861.

31. Lt. Castillo Barfield, *Letter*. Abraham Lincoln Museum, Lincoln Memorial University in Harrogate, TN.

32. *New Albany Daily Ledger*, October 24, 1861; William E. DeMoss Letter, October 30, 1861. TSL&A., Nashville, TN.

33. *Louisville Daily Journal*, October 24, 1861; *Louisville Daily Journal*, October 29, 1861; "Schoepf Turns . . . ".

34. Barfield letter; *OR*, 1, 4, 208.

35. *OR*, 1, 4, 208; "Schoepf Turns . . . ".

36. *Nashville Banner*, October 30, 1861.

37. Ibid; *OR*, 1, 4, 207; Barfield letter; Hafendorfer, *Wildcat*, 243; *Indianapolis Daily Journal*, November 5, 1861.

38. Nation; www.breckinridgegreys.org (accessed November 8, 2011).

39. *Daily Toledo Blade*, October 29, 1861.

40. *Indianapolis Daily Journal*, November 5, 1861; *The Weekly Lancaster Gazette*, November 7, 1861.

41. Nation.

42. *Nashville Banner*, October 30, 1861.

43. *OR*, 1, 4, 207, 210, 213; Hafendorfer, *Wildcat*, 239, 275-278.

44. Ibid; www.thssite.tripod.com/sstone/wild.html (accessed September 22, 2009).

45. *National Tribune*, October 5, 1889.

46. www.wildcatreenactment.org (accessed November 8, 2011).

47. Ibid; U.S. Department of the Interior, National Park Service, American Battlefield Protection Program, *Update to the Civil War Sites Advisory*

Commission Report on the Nation's Civil War Battlefields. October 2008.
48. Battle of Camp Wildcat pamphlet; *Update.*

Chapter Three
1. http://mayhouse.org/perry/oldhouse5.html; Faron Sparkman, "5th Kentucky Voluntary Infantry (Original) Brief History," http://www.bencaudill.com/documents_msc/5th.html.
2. Ibid.
3. Rev. Edward O. Guerrant, "Marshall and Garfield in Eastern Kentucky." *B & L,* 393; *OR,* 1, 4, 225; Capt. Thos Speed, *The Union Regiments of Kentucky,* http://www.mt.net/ mtsysdev/civilwar/ history.htm.
4. *OR,* 1, 4, 225.
5. Ibid.
6. Ibid; Guerrant, 394; Ivy Mountain Interpretive sign.
7. Ivy Mountain obelisk.
8. http://kccserv1.estb.wku.edu/factsheets/civilwar/ivymountain.html (accessed November 8, 2011).
9. *OR,* 1, 4, 226.
10. Ibid, 225.
11. Ibid, 226; http://civilwar.morganco.freeservers.com/ajmay.htm. (accessed November 8, 2011).
12. *OR,* 1, 4, 226.
13. http://breckinridgegreys.org/history.html.
14. *OR,* 1, 4, 226.
15. Ibid.
16. Ibid.
17. Ibid.
18. Ibid, 227.
19. Ibid, 226.
20. Ibid, 226-27.
21. Ibid.
22. Ibid.
23. Guerrant, 394-95.
24. *Update,* 12, 13, 15.
25. www.prestonsburgky.org/history_culture.html; civilwardiscoverytrail.org/location_detail.php?SiteID=500; prestonsburgky.org/visit_info_details.php?id=121; embers.tripod.com?cornelius_carroll?id33.htm; civilwar.morganco.freeservers.com/ajmay.htm. All sites accessed November, 2011.

Chapter Four
1. James Barnett, "German's hollow square repelled Texas Rangers in Kentucky fight," *Mill Creek Valley News,* Lockland, Ohio. December 21, 1961; James Barnett, "Munfordville in the Civil War," *The Register of the Kentucky Historical Society* (October 1971): 339.

2. Barnett, "Munfordville," 340; Dr. Fred Whittaker, "The Battle of Rowlett's Station," Hart County Historical Society (n.d.), 8.

3. *Harper's Weekly*, February 25, 1860.

4. Whittaker, "Battle," 1; Barnett, "German's," 1; Dr. Fred Whittaker, *America's Civil War*, 13, no. 5 (November 2000): 8, 60.

5. Ibid.

6. Whittaker, "Battle," 6; Whittaker, *America's*, 60; Barnett, "Munfordville," 341.

7. Barnett, "Munfordville," 341-42.

8. Charles D. Stewart, "A Bachelor General." *Wisconsin Magazine of History* 12 HCHS (1933),143-44.

9. Filbeck manuscript, Lilly Library, Indiana University Bloomington, HCHS; "32nd Indiana Infantry (1st German)." http://www.geocities.ws/ind32ndinfantry/monument.html.

10. Barnett, "Munfordville," 342; Whittaker, "Battle," 6.

11. *OR*, 1, 7, 19.

12. "A soldier's 1861 Letter from Munfordville," *Hart County News,* February 15, 1974.

13. Capt. C. W. Carroll, Letter to his wife. December 19, 1861. Courtesy HCHS; "Battle of Rowlett's Station," http://kyclim.wku.edu/factsheets/thebattleofrowlett.html

14. *OR*, 1, 7, 19.

15. James K. P. Blackburn, "Reminiscences of the Texas Rangers," *Southwest Historical Quarterly* 22, (1918-19): 48; *New Birmingham Times*, undated clipping, 1891.

16. Blackburn, "Reminiscences," 51.

17. *OR*, 1, 7, 19-20; Barnett, "Munfordville," 343.

18. *OR*, 1, 7, 20.

19. Ibid.; Whittaker, "Battle," 7.

20. *OR*, 1, 7, 16; Whittaker, "Battle," 7; Carroll letter; Mikel Peake, "Baptism of fire at Rowlett's Station, Kentucky," geocities.com/ind32infantry/bfrs.html; *Daily Ledger*, December 18, 1861.

21. Peake, "Baptism"; *OR,* 1, 7, 21.

22. *OR,* 1, 7, 17.

23. *New Birmingham Times*, undated clipping, 1891.

24. *OR*, 1, 7, 17; Barnett, "German's" 1; Frank Moore, *Civil War in Song and Story*. (P. F. Collier, 1889); "Report of Capt. Schwarz," n.d. Courtesy HCHS.

25. *OR*, 1, 17, 18.

26. "32nd Indiana Casualties," www.lib.iupui.edu/kade/peake/p31.html; *Indianapolis Daily Journal*, December 19, 1861; L. B. Giles, *Terry's Texas Rangers*, (Austin, TX: Von Boeckman-Jones Co., 1911); Andreas Mehr, Letter to the *Louisville Anzeiger*. October 13, 1862; http://www.terrystexasrangers.org/histories/giles_lb/chapter2.htm (accessed November 30, 2011).

27. *OR*, 1, 17, 20; Barnett, "Munfordville," 345; Whittaker, "Battle," 9.

28. Mark L. Evans, Letter to wife. December 19, 1861. Printed in *C.V.* 12, no. 2 (February 1905): 61.

29. Ibid.

30. "Exciting new from Kentucky: A skirmish at Green River:—Brilliant Exploits of the Texas Rangers—Death of Col. Terry," *Nashville Union and American*, December 19, 1861, http://terrystexasrangers.org/newsclippings/nashville_union_and_american/1861_12_19.html.

31. "Funeral Obsequtem of the Intrepid Patriot, Col. B. F. Terry." *Nashville Union and American*. Dec. 19, 1861. terrystexasrangers.org/newsclippings/nashville_union_ and_american; Steele, A. L. *C. V.* 2, no.10 (October 1895): 315.

32. *Daily Dispatch*, December 25, 1861, Richmond, VA.

33. Ibid.; Barnett, "Munfordville," 345.

34. Ibid; Barnett, "German's," 5; Whittaker, "Battle," 10; Moore, *Civil*; Frank Moore, *Rebellion Record,* (New York: G. P. Putnam,1864), 2.

35. Moore, *Rebellion*, 2; Barnett, "German's," 4.

36. "Old Letter Describes Battle of Rowlett's Station," *Hart County News*, October 17, 1974. HCHS.

37. "Rowlett's Station," Unpublished article, n.d., HCHS.

38. Barnett, "Munfordville," 347-48.

39. *OR*, 1, 7, 18.

40. Barnett, "German's," 7.

41. *OR*, 1, 7, 20.

42. Funeral Obsequies.

43. "32nd Indiana," lib.iupui.edu

44. "32nd Indiana Monument," http://maxkade.iupui.edu/peake/p31.html; "32nd Indiana," geocities; www.cem.va.gov/cems/nchp/cavehill.asp (accessed November 30, 2011).

45. Ibid.

46. "Preservation of oldest Civil War Memorial: Bloedner Monument moved from Cave Hill National Cemetery," www.cem.va.gov/hist/BloednerMon.asp (accessed November 9, 2011); Diane Comer, "Public meeting about Bloedner Monument, the oldest Civil War monument in the U.S., will be September 23 in Louisville," August 28, 2009. http://www.heritage.ky.gov/news/bloednermonmtg.htm; "Face-lift for the Bloedner Marker," *Civil War Times,* (December 2009): 14.

47. http://www.usafuneralhomesonline.com (accessed November 30, 2011).

48. Mikel Peake, "1st German, 32nd Indiana News Update," Pamphlet, n.d. HCHS; *Update*, 64.

49. "Texas Monument is Dedicated at 1862 Battlefield in Richmond, Ky," August 2009. http://www.civilwarnews.com/archive/articles/09/august/richmond_080905.html (accessed November 30, 2011).

Chapter Five

1. Gen. Thomas Jordan, and J. P. Pryor, *The Campaigns of Lieut.-Gen. N. B. Forrest, and of Forrest's Cavalry,* (Dayton, OH: Press of Morningside Bookshop,

1977), 49; Brig. Gen. Adam R. Johnson, *The Partisan Rangers of the Confederate Army,* (Louisville: 1904), 147.

2. John K. Ward, "Forrest's First Fight," *America's Civil War* 6, no. 1 (March 1993): 50-57; Calhoun Driving Tour pamphlet, Courtesy of McLean County (KY) Historical and Genealogy Museum, n.d.; Battle of Sacramento Driving Tour pamphlet, McLean County (KY) Historical Society.

3. Jordan and Pryor, 50; *OR,* 1, 7, 64; John A. Wyeth, *Life of General Nathan Bedford Forrest,* (Dayton, OH: Press of Morningside Bookshop, 1975), 30.

4. *OR,* 1, 7, 65.

5. Ibid.

6. Calhoun Driving Tour; Don Wilson, "The Boys from Calhoun," February 2008, McLean County Historical Society, 3.

7. Wilson, "The Boys," 3; Don Wilson, "The Boys that never left Calhoun," n.d. McLean County Historical Society.

8. Ken Ward, "The 31st Indiana Infantry: Drilling and Disease," *McLean County News,* May 4, 2000.

9. Battle of Sacramento Driving Tour pamphlet; www.battleofsac.com/History. htm (accessed November 10, 2011).

10. www.battleofsac.com/sacramento.htm.

11. Jordan & Pryor, 50.

12. Ibid.

13. Ibid; *OR,* 1, 7, 65

14. *OR,* 1, 7, 65; Edna Shewcraft Macon, "A ride into history," McLean County Historical Society; Glen Hodges, "Kentucky Belle warned rebels of nearing troops," *Messenger-Inquirer,* n.d. McLean County Historical Society.

15. Jordan and Pryor, 50-51.

16. Ibid., 51; Wyeth, 30.

17. Wyeth, 30-31; Jordan and Pryor, 51.

18. Wyeth, 28, 30-31; Jordan and Pryor, 51.

19. Ibid; *OR,* 1, 7, 65; Capt. J. C. Blanton, "Forrest's old regiment," *C. V.* 3, no. 2 (February 1895): 41; "Proposed statue to General Forrest," *C. V.* 4, no. 2 (February 1896): 41.

20. *OR,* 1, 7, 65; Wyeth, 31.

21. Wyeth, 31.

22. Ibid.

23. Ibid., 31-32; Jordan and Pryor, 51-52; Blanton, 41; William J. Stier,. "Fury takes the field," *Civil War Times,* (December 1999): 45.

24. *OR,* 1, 7, 66; Jordan and Pryor, 52; Wyeth, 32.

25. *OR,* 1, 7, 65.

26. Ibid.

27. Ibid.

28. Ibid.; Jordan and Pryor, 53; Glenn Hodges, "Confederate general used legendary tactic for 1st time in McLean," *Messenger-Inquirer,* April 20, 1992. McLean County Historical Society; Ward, "Forrest's."

29. Ibid; B. L. Ridley, "Chat with Col. W. S. McLemore," *C. V.* 8, no. 6 (June 1900), 262.

30. Wyeth, 32; *OR*, 1, 7, 65-66.

31. Ibid.

32. Wyeth, 33.

33. *OR*, 1, 7, 66; Wyeth, 32; Jordan and Pryor, 52.

34. Ibid.

35. Wyeth, 32.

36. Ibid.

37. *OR*, 1, 7, 66; Blanton, 41.

38. Ibid.

39. *OR*, 1, 7, 66.

40. Ibid.

41. Charles W. Button, "Early engagements with Forrest," *C. V.* 5, no. 9 (September 1897): 479.

42. *OR*, 1, 7, 66.

43. Ibid, 63, 67.

44. Ken Ward, "The Battle of Sacramento," Historical Commentary, July 11, 1991, HCHS.

45. Ward, "Forrest's first," 56.

46. Ward, "Meandering."

47. *Louisville Daily Democrat*, January 3, 1863.

48. Button, 479.

49. *OR*, 1, 7, 65.

50. Blanton, 41.

51. Ibid.

52. Macon, "A ride…".

53. Mint Julep and the Old General, "Forrest fights his first battle," *The Civil War Courier*, 25, no. 3 (July 2010), 17-19; "City, county now own battle site," *McLean County (KY) News*, April 18, 2002.

Chapter Six

1. Rev. Edward O. Guerrant, "Marshall and Garfield in Eastern Kentucky., *B & L.*, 394.

2. Ibid.

3. Ibid.

4. Ibid.

5. Ibid.

6. Ibid.

7. Ibid., 394-95.

8. Ibid., 395.

9. Ibid.

10. Ibid.

11. Ibid.; Middle Creek Driving Tour pamphlet.

12. Ibid.

13. Guerrant, 395; *OR*, 1, 7, 46-50; www.middlecreek.org/history.htm (accessed November 30, 2011); www.geocities.com/rlperry/geo/DesperateFight.html.

14. Ibid.

15. Middle Creek Driving Tour pamphlet; Guerrant, 396.

16. Ibid.; *OR*, 1, 7, 29.

17. Ibid.

18. *OR*, 1, 7, 46-50; Guerrant, 396.

19. Middle Creek Driving Tour pamphlet.

20. Guerrant, 396.

21. www.middlecreek.org/history.htm.

22. Middle Creek Driving Tour pamphlet; *OR*, 1, 7, 46-50; http:// www.geocities. com/rlperry/geo/DesperateFight.html; http://www.geocities.com/rlperry/geo/Union Assault.html.

23. Middle Creek Driving Tour pamphlet; Guerrant, 396; www.middlecreek. org/history.htm (accessed November 10, 2011).

24. Ibid.

25. Ibid.

26. *OR*, 1, 7, 29; Middle Creek Driving Tour pamphlet.

27. *OR*, 1, 7, 56; Middle Creek Driving Tour pamphlet.

28. www.middlecreek.org/history.htm (accessed November 10, 2011).

29. *Update*, 13, 15, 17, 29; Kathryn Jorgensen, "Middle Creek Battlefield in Kentucky Open in July," *Civil War News* 32, no. 6 (October 2008); www. civilwartraveler.com/WEST/KY/east-KY.html (accessed November 10, 2011).

30. *Update*, 13, 15, 17, 29; Jorgensen, "Middle"; www.middlecreek.org/history. htm (accessed November 10, 2011).

31. Ibid.

32. Ibid.

33. http://www.friendsofmiddlecreek.org (accessed November 10, 2011).

34. Middle Creek Driving Tour pamphlet.

Chapter Seven

1. www.cem.va.gov/cems/nchp/millsprings.asp (accessed November 30, 2011); Geoffrey R. Walden, "What's in a name?" http://reocities.com/Pentagon/ Quarters/1864/name.htm (accessed November 30, 2011); Kenneth A. Hafendorfer, *Mill Springs: Campaign and Battle of Mill Springs, Kentucky.* (Louisville: KH Press, 2001), 17.

2. Hafendorfer, *Mill Springs,* 67; waymarking.com/waymarkets/WMPKE (accessed November 30, 2011).

3. Hafendorfer, *Mill Springs,* 67; Mill Springs Driving Tour pamphlet, n.d.

4. Hafendorfer, *Mill Springs,* 73, 75, 598; *OR*, 1, 7, 7 & 10.

5. Ibid.

6. Ibid.

7. *OR*, 1, 7, 11.

8. Ibid.

9. Ibid.

10. *OR*, 1, 7, 10 & 11; Hafendorfer, *Mill Springs*, 81.

11. Ibid.

12. *OR*, 1, 7, 797; Mill Springs Driving Tour pamphlet, n.d.

13. *OR*, 1, 7, 715; Mill Springs Driving Tour pamphlet, n.d.

14. Ibid.

15. Mill Springs Driving Tour pamphlet, n.d; Hafendorfer, *Mill Springs*, 100; Faw, Walter Wagner Letters, TSL&A, Nashville, TN.

16. Henry M. Cist, *The Army of the Cumberland*. (New York: Charles Scribner's Sons, 1882), 58; "The Battle of Mill Springs, and other interesting tidbits." http://serene-musings.blogshot.com/2007/01/battle-of-mill-springs-and-other.html.

17. Morgan Parker, Letter to wife. *Daily Tribune*, Detroit. February 4, 1862, 1.

18. *Indianapolis Daily Journal*, February 6, 1862, 2.

19. Jefferson Davis, *The Rise and Fall of the Confederate Government, Volume II* (New York: D. Appleton and Company, 1881), 20.

20. John Hapley [happy], "Battle of Fishing Creek." *Memphis Daily Avalanche*, January 31, 1862, 2.

21. Mill Springs Driving Tour pamphlet, n.d.; "The Diary or Register of David Anderson Deaderick, Esq." David Anderson Deaderick Papers, Library of Congress, Manuscript Division.; John B. Lindsley, *Military Annals of Tennessee—Confederate*, (Nashville: J. M. Lindsley & Co., 1886, reprinted by Broadfoot Publishing Company, Wilmington, NC, 1995), 349.

22. Ibid.

23. Hapley.

24. George W. Ewing, "General Bragg's Kentucky Campaign," *C.V.* 34, no. 6 (June 1926), 214.

25. James Baker, Letter to his father, January 21, 1862, *History of Newaygo County Michigan Civil War Veterans*, (1894).

26. Diana Flynn, June 14, 1997. http://files.usgwarchives.org/ky/ky-footsteps/1997/vo01-112.txt.

27. Joseph G. Durfee, *Jeffersonian (Ohio) Democrat*, February 2, 1862.

28. Lt. Oliver Eckels, Letter of January 1, 1861 from camp near Somerset, KY. www.geocities.com/Pentagon/Quarters/1864.name.htm?200919.

29. *Memphis Daily Avalanche*, January 31, 1862.

30. Ibid.

31. Spencer B. Talley, "The Battle of Fishing Creek." Geocities.com/Pentagon/Quarters/1864.name.htm?200919.

32. Mill Springs Driving Tour pamphlet; Hafendorfer, *Mill Springs*, 181.

33. Mill Springs Driving Tour pamphlet

34. Ibid.

35. *OR*, 1, 7, 106.

36. Ibid.

37. Hafendorfer, *Mill Springs*, 187, 190.

38. *Louisville Courier Journal*, September 29, 1933.

39. R. M. Kelly, "Holding Kentucky for the Union." *B & L*. (New York: Castle Books, 1956), 388.

40. "Battle of Mill Springs," *Harper's Weekly*, March 8, 1862.

41. Kelly, "Holding," 388.

42. Ibid.

43. James L. Cooper, *C.V.* 33, no. 16; *Cincinnati Enquirer*, February 12, 1862.

44. Ibid.

45. Hapley.

46. Kelly, "Holding," 388.

47. Hafendorfer, *Mill Springs*, 288; William Preston Johnston, *The Life of Albert Sidney Johnston*, (New York: D. Appleton and Company, 1879), 402.

48. Mrs. Anna McKinney, "F. K. Zollicoffer First and Last Battle," *C.V.* 17, no. 4 (April 1910): 163.

49. J. H. Battle, W. H. Perrin, and G. C. Kniffin, *Kentucky, A History of the State*, (Louisville, KY: F. A. Bailey Publishing Company, 1885), 393.

50. Hafendorfer, *Mill Springs*, 288-90; Richard B. Lewis, "Felix Zollicoffer and the Zollie Tree," (n.d.); Cist; Kelly, "Holding," 389; "Battle of Mill Springs," *Harper's Weekly*, March 8, 1862; Gilbert Wilson, e-mail to Randy Bishop July 27, 2011; *Memphis Daily Avalanche*, January 28, 1862.

51. Ibid.

52. Ibid; Hafendorfer, *Mill Springs*, 570-75.

53. Thomas C. Potter, Letter to his sister, January 24, 1862.

54. Lemuel F. Drake, Letter to editor, *New Lexington (Ohio) Perry County Weekly*, January 29, 1862.

55. Hafendorfer, *Mill Springs*, 570-75.

56. Tarrant, *Wild*, 65.

57. Octavia Zollicoffer Bond, *C.V.* (February 1902): 100.

58. Gen. Bennett Young, "Address." *C. V.* 18, no. 12 (December 1910): 568.

59. Margaret Boyles, "Gen. F. K. Zollicoffer." *C. V.* 15, no. 1 (January 1907): 28.

60. W. J. Worsham, *The Old Nineteenth Tennessee Regiment. C. S. A.* (Knoxville: Press of Paragom printing company, 1902), 182; *OR*, 1, 7, 107; Kelly, "Holding," 389; Hafendorfer, *Mill Springs*, 301.

61. *OR*, 1, 7, 107.

62. http://www.geocities.com/Pentagon/Quarters/1964/frierson_letter_htm.

63. *OR*, 1, 7, 107.

64. Kelley, "Holding," 389.

65. Deaderick diary.

66. Mill Springs Driving Tour pamphlet.

67. Hapley.

68. Baker letter.

69. Hapley.

70. Mill Springs Driving Tour pamphlet; Ibid.

71. Hafendorfer, *Mill Springs*, 327, 330.

72. William Bircher, *A Drummer Boy's Diary: Comprising Four years of Service with the Second Regiment Minnesota Veterans Volunteers, 1861-1865.* (St. Paul Book & Stationery Company, 1889) 13.

73. "The Battle," *Harper's Weekly*, March 8, 1862.

74. "Fishing Creek Battle," *Memphis Daily Avalanche*, January 30, 1862.

75. Mill Springs Driving Tour pamphlet; *National Tribune*, December 3, 1903.

76. Kelly, "Holding," 389; *OR*, 1, 7, 95.

77. Mill Springs Driving Tour pamphlet.

78. Ibid.

79. "The Battle," *Harper's Weekly*, March 8, 1862.

80. Talley.

81. Mill Springs Driving Tour pamphlet.

82. Hapley.

83. Geoffrey R. Walden, "Disaster on the Cumberland: The Battle of Fishing Creek, Mill Springs, Kentucky." *C.V.* 4, (1998): 39.

84. Kelly, "Holding," 390.

85. Cist.

86. Hapley.

87. *Chatfield (Minnesota) Democrat,* n.d.

88. Hapley.

89. Ibid.

90. "Fishing Creek Battle," *Memphis Daily Avalanche*, January 28, 1862.

91. "Report from the 1st Michigan Engineers and Mechanics," *Marshall (Mich.) Statesman*, January 29, 1862.

92. Baker letter.

93. Hafendorfer,*Mill Springs*, 591; Battle of Mill Springs Driving Tour pamphlet; Jerry McFarland, William Neikirk, David Gilbert, and the Mill Springs Battlefield Association. Publication. Somerset, KY, 1999. 53.

94. Ibid., Hafendorfer, 588.

95. Hafendorfer, *Mill Springs*, 530-58.

96. Kelly, "Holding," 389.

97. Battle of Mill Springs Driving Tour pamphlet.

98. *Western Christian Advocate,* n.d.

99. Worsham, 93-94.

100. Battle of Mill Springs Driving Tour pamphlet; *The Somerset Times,* 4, no. 37 (October 28, 1910).

101. Battle of Mill Springs Driving Tour pamphlet; Lewis.

102. Wilson, e-mail.

103. McFarland; *Update.*

104. The Historic Brown-Lanier House Bed and Breakfast pamphlet, n.d.

105. Ibid.

106. McFarland.

Chapter Eight

1. Richmond, Kentucky pamphlet, Richmond Tourism and Main St. Dept. Richmond, KY, n.d.

2. OR, 1, 16, 752-53; Phillip Seyfrit, E-mail to author, July 22, 2011.

3. Confederate Maj. Gen. Edmund Kirby Smith pamphlet, Battle of Richmond Association.

4. R. M. Kelly, "Holding Kentucky for the Union." B & L. (New York: Castle Books, 1956), 4.

5. Ibid.

6. Seyfrit e-mail; B. Kevin Bennett, "The Battle of Richmond, Kentucky." Blue and Gray, 25, no.6, (2009): 8; D. Warren Lambert, The Decisive Battle of Richmond, Kentucky, (Richmond, KY: BORA,, n.d), 16; Confederate Brig. Gen. Patrick R. Cleburne, BORA; Confederate Brig. Gen. Thomas James Churchill, BORA.

7. Lexington Kentucky Statesman, September 17, 1862.

8. Seyfrit e-mail; Jill K. Garrett, transciber, Confederate Diary of Robert D. Smith. (Columbia, TN: Captain James Madison Sparkman Chapter, United Daughters of the Confederacy, 1975).

9. Robert M. Frierson, "Gen. E. Kirby Smith's Campaign in Kentucky." C.V. 3, no. 10, 295.

10. Bennett, 8; D. H. DeBerry, "Kirby Smith's Bluegrass Invasion," America's Civil War 10, no. 10 (March 1997): 57.

11. Frierson, 295.

12. Deberry, 57.

13. Bennett, 8; Kenneth A. Hafendorfer, Battle of Richmond, Kentucky. (Louisville, KY: KH Press, 2006), 14.

14. Jon P. Harrison, "Tenth Texas Cavalry," Military History of Texas and the Southwest. 22. (n.d.): 179.

15. Bennett, 8; Hafendorfer, Richmond, 46.

16. Bennett, 8; Hafendorfer, Richmond, 48; Seyfrit e-mail; Robert C. Moody, "The Battle of Big Hill," 2008.

17. Cincinnati Enquirer, August 29, 1862.

18. Byron Smith, "Battle of Richmond, Kentucky." C.V. 30, no. 8 (August 1922): 298.

19. Ibid.

20. OR, 1, 16, 886; Cincinnati Enquirer, August 29, 1862.

21. Lambert, 110-112; Seyfrit e-mail.

22. Lambert, 114; Seyfrit e-mail; Bennett, 21; Hafendorfer, Richmond, 65.

23. Seyfrit e-mail; Federal Brig. Gen. Charles Cruft, BORA; Federal Brig. Gen. Mahlon Manson, BORA; Roy Morris, "Battle in the Bluegrass," Civil War Times Illustrated, 27, no. 8 (December 1988): 20.

24. OR, 1, 16, 918.

25. Lambert, 114; Bennett, 22.

26. Kirby Smith, Letter to Cassie Smith, August 29, 1862, Kirby Smith Papers, Southern Historical Collection, University of North Carolina Library.

27. Hafendorfer, *Richmond,* 82-84.
28. Seyfrit e-mail; *OR,* 1, 16, 911; L. D. Manson, Letter to State Sen. R. J. White of Kentucky, *Louisville Courier-Journal,* April 6, 1878.
29. Hafendorfer, *Richmond,* 84; Seyfrit e-mail.
30. *OR,* 1, 16, 911; Manson letter.
31. *Washington National Tribune,* May 10, 1894.
32. Ibid.
33. Morris, 21; Bennett, 22; Seyfrit e-mail.
34. *OR,* 1, 16, 944 & 949.
35. Ibid.
36. Hafendorfer, *Richmond,* 102; Douglas.
37. *OR,* 1, 16, 949.
38. Ibid., 919; Hafendorfer, *Richmond*, 102; Lambert, 117; Morris, 21; Seyfrit e-mail.
39. http://kyclim.wku.edu/factsheets/thebattlerrichmond.html (accessed December 1, 2011).
40. *OR,* 1, 16, 908.
41. *OR,* 1, 16, 945.
42. Ibid.
43. Ibid., 912, 914.
44. Ibid.
45. Bennett, 23.
46. Lambert, 120.
47. *OR,* 1, 16, 945.
48. Ibid.; Lambert, 120.
49. The Civil War Battle of Richmond, Kentucky driving tour pamphlet.
50. Bennett, 24; Lucia R. Douglas, ed., *Douglas's Texas Battery, C.S.A.* (Tyler, TX: Smith County Historical Society, 1966), 197-98.
51. Seyfrit e-mail; A History of the Pleasant View House and Farm pamphlet, BORA.
52. A. C. Quisenberry, "The Battle of Richmond, Kentucky," *Register of Kentucky Historical Society*, (September 1918).
53. Kelly, 4-5.
54. *OR,* 1, 16, 920.
55. Kelly, 5.
56. *OR,* 1, 16, 946.
57. *Washington National Tribune,* March 8, 1894; "J.G. Law Diary." 12, 538.
58. *Washington National Tribune,* March 8, 1894.
59. *OR,* 1, 16, 946.
60. Ibid.; Seyfrit e-mail.
61. *OR,* 1, 16, 920.
62. Ibid.
63. Hafendorfer, *Richmond,* 137.
64. *OR,* 1, 16, 919-20.

65. Ibid., 929.

66. Ibid., 252-253.

67. Seyfrit e-mail; Nathaniel C. Hughes, with Connie W. Moretti and James M. Browne, *Brigadier General Tyree H. Bell C.S.A.* (Knoxville: University Press of Tennessee, 2004), 163.

68. *OR*, 1, 16, 35, 912; Bennett, 43.

69. *OR*, 1, 16, 920.

70. The Civil War Battle of Richmond, Kentucky driving tour pamphlet.

71. *Washington National Tribune*, May 10, 1894.

72. Hafendorfer, *Richmond*, 203.

73. *OR*, 1, 16, 912, 920.

74. Ibid.

75. Ibid.

76. Seyfrit e-mail; Hafendorfer, *Richmond*, 215-16; *Washington National Tribune*, April 19, 1894; *OR*, 1, 16, 940, 942.

77. *OR*, 1, 16, 942.

78. Bennett, 45.

79. *OR*, 1, 16, 920.

80. Ibid.

81. Ibid, 908.

82. Lambert, 125; The Civil War Battle of Richmond, Kentucky driving tour pamphlet.

83. The Civil War Battle of Richmond, Kentucky driving tour pamphlet; Boggs, William. *Military Reminiscences of General William R. Boggs, C.S.A.* The Seeman Printery, Durham, N.C. 1913.38

84. *OR*, 1, 16, 951.

85. *Daily Ohio Statesman*, September 7, 1862.

86. *OR*, 1, 16, 936, 952.

87. Ibid., 908.

88. Ibid., 921.

89. J. B. McCullaugh, Letter to Sen. R. J. White, March 10, 1878, *Lexington Herald-Ledger*, August 30, 1957.

90. Quisenberry, 12-13.

91. Seyfrit e-mail; Lambert, 128; The Civil War Battle of Richmond, Kentucky driving tour pamphlet.

92. Bennett, 48.

93. Hafendorfer, *Richmond,* 275.

94. Bennett, 48-50; Lambert, 128; *OR*, 1, 16, 939.

95. Bennett, 50.

96. E. W. Rosser, E-mail to author, December 15, 2009.

97. "James C. Lacy." http://suvcw.org/past/jclacy.htm (accessed December 1, 2011).

98. *OR*, 1, 16, 908.

99. Ibid, 914.

100. Richmond, Kentucky pamphlet.

101. "A History of the Rogers House," (BORA, n.d.); Kathryn Jorgensen, "Richmond, Ky. battlefield will soon open a visitors and heritage center," *Civil War News,* 32, no. 9 (October 2008): 5; http://visitorcenter.madisoncountyky.us/ (accessed December 1, 2011).

102. "A History of the Pleasant View House and Farm," (BORA, n.d.).

103. Jorgensen, Richmond; Seyfrit e-mail; Justine Barati, "Former Army property becomes a Civil War Interpretive Center," October 2, 2008, Blue Grass Army Depot. Richmond, Kentucky; www.americanbyways.com/index. php?catid=359 (accessed December 1, 2011).

104. Seyfrit e-mail; www.trailsrus.com/civilwar/region4/richmond.html (accessed December 1, 2011).

105. "Richmond, Ky., battlefield to receive grant," *The Civil War Courier,* 20, no. 7 (September 2009): 10.

106. *Update,* 43.

107. "Texas Monument is Dedicated at 1862 Battlefield in Richmond, Ky," August 2009, http://www.civilwarnews.com/archive/articles/09/august/ richmond_080905.html (accessed December 2, 2011); "Texas 'silent Sentinel' dedicated at Battle of Richmond," *The Civil War Courier* 24, no. 4 (July 2009): 1.

108. Craig L. Barry, "Richmond, Kentucky," *Civil War Courier* 12, no. 10 (October 2008): 5; Seyfrit e-mail; http://battleofrichmond.org/?page_id=94 (accessed December 2, 2011); http://battleofrichmond.org/?page_id=20 (accessed December 2, 2011).

109. www.battleofrichmond.org; Seyfrit e-mail.

Chapter Nine

1. "Hart County Facts."http://www.n2genealogy.com/kentucky/ky-county-hart.html (accessed December 2, 2011); http://hartcountychamber.com/index. php?option=com_content&task=v (accessed December 2, 2011).

2. Ibid.

3. Bob Hill, "Hart County's fields bear witness to war," *Courier Journal,* July 3, 1978, HCHS; Stuart W. Sanders, "Honor and Ego at Munfordville," *Civil War,* 63: 19.

4. Tammy Hensley, "Battle of Munfordville on National Register of Historic Places," n.d.; Dan Kidd, "Grant Awarded to Munfordville group," n.d.

5. Hill; Sanders, Honor, 19; Col. Engerud, "Remarks," Presented at the Munfordville Civil War Centennial Observance, September 15, 1962, HCHS, 5; "The Battle for the Bridge," July 16, 1994, HCHS.

6. Robert L. Becker, "The Battle of Munfordville," n.d., HCHS, 3; Robert J. Cull, "Battle of Munfordville called highly significant Civil War event," *The Kentucky Explorer,* January 1996,HCHS, 82.

7. Becker, 3.

8. "The Battle of Munfordville," http://kyclim.wku.edu/factsheets/thebattle munfordville.html (accessed December 2, 2011) .

9. Gen. John T. Wilder, "The Siege of Munfordville: A Paper read before the Ohio Commandery, M.O. L. Legion in 1902," HCHS, 56.

10. Ibid., 57.

11. Ibid.

12. Ibid.

13. Ibid.

14. W. H. Davidson, Letter to Mr. George Seymour, June 9, 1932, HCHS.

15. Ibid.

16. Samuel C. Williams, *General John T. Wilder*, (Bloomington, IN: 1936), 1-7.

17. *Louisville Daily Journal*, September 16, 1862.

18. "The Battle for the Bridge," July 16, 1994, HCHS.

19. J. T. Wilder, Letter to My Dear Pet, September 12, 1862, HCHS.

20. Stuart Sanders, "Surrender at bridge based on foe's word." http://www.washingtontimes.com/news/2003/sep/05/20030905-082356-2243r/print/ (accessed December 2, 2011); W. L. Shaw, "Hard fighting –Franklin-Munfordville," *C.V.* (n.d.) 221-22.

21. Wilder, Siege, 60; Becker, 5; Sanders, Honor, 22.

22. Wilder, Siege, 58; *OR*, 2, 16, 518.

23. Wilder, Siege, 58.

24. Ibid.

25. Sanders, Honor, 22.

26. D. A. Campbell, "The Battle of Munfordville," *Jackson (MS) Clarion*, n.d.

27. Cull, 82.

28. Ibid.; Becker, 6; Engerud, Remarks, 5; E. T. Sykes, "An Incident of the Battle of Munfordville, KY," n.d., HCHS.

29. Campbell, The Battle, 2.

30. Becker, 6; Engerud, Remarks, 5.

31. Ibid.; Sanders, Honor, 22; *Louisville Journal*, September 14, 1862.

32. Myra J. Logsdon, "The Battle of Munfordville as remembered by a young girl," *Filson Clubs History Quarterly* 14, no. 3 (July 1940)HCHS.

33. Cull, 82; Becker, 6.

34. Becker, 6; Sanders, Honor, 22.

35. Ibid.

36. Cull, 82.

37. Ibid., 82-83.

38. Ibid, 83.

39. Sykes, Incident, 537; Shaw, Hard, 221.

40. Sykes, Incident, 538.

41. Campbell, 3.

42. Shaw, Hard, 221; Wilder, Siege, 58-59.

43. Cull, 83.

44. Wilder, Siege, 58.

45. John Rietti, "The Robert A. Smith Monument," *C.V.* 4, no. 8 (August 1896): 279; Sykes, 538.

46. Engerud, Remarks, 6.
47. Campbell, 3; *Louisville Journal*, September 16, 1862.
48. Wilder, Siege, 59.
49. Campbell, 3.
50. *Louisville Journal*, September 16, 1862.
51. Wilder, Siege, 58-59.
52. Ibid., 59.
53. Ibid.
54. Shaw, 222.
55. Cull, 83.
56. Ibid.
57. Campbell, 4.
58. Rietti, 279.
59. "Chalmers Great Blunder at Munfordville," *C.V.* 17, no. 5 (May 1909): 222.
60. Campbell, 4.
61. Sykes, 538.
62. "Chalmers Great," 222.
63. Wilder, Siege, 60.
64. Ibid., 60-61.
65. Ibid., 61.
66. Ibid.; Sanders, Honor, 22.
67. Wilder, Siege, 61.
68. Sykes, 539.
69. Ibid.
70. Ibid., 540.
71. Logsdon.
72. Rietti, 279; Bill Thomas, "Old Forts, Monuments at Munfordville Reminders of Bloody Civil War Fighting in Battle of Bridge," *The Park City (KY) Daily News,* June 23, 1957, HCHS.
73. Campbell, 2.
74. Sanders, Honor, 23.
75. Becker, 8; Wilder, 61.
76. Engerud, Remarks, 10.
77. Becker, 8.
78. Wilder, Siege, 61.
79. Becker, 8.
80. Wilder, Siege, 62.
81. *OR*, 1, 16, 968-69.
82. *OR*, 1, 16, 970.
83. Ibid., 971.
84. "Battle of Munfordville." *C.V.* 17, no.2: 85.
85. Ibid.
86. Ibid.
87. *OR*, 1, 16, 841-42, 978.

88. Col. Philip B. Spence, "Campaigning in Kentucky," *C.V.* 9, no. 1 (January 1901): 22.

89. *Update*, 35; http://www.trailsrus.com/civilwar/region3/munfordv.html (accessed December 2, 2011).

90. http://civilwardiscoverytrail.org/location_detail.php?siteID=512 (accessed December 2, 2011).

91. http://civilwardiscoverytrail.org/location_detail.php?siteID=511 (accessed December 2, 2011).

92. Gina Kinslow, *Glasgow Daily Times*, n.d.; "Kentucky battlefield named to national 'Most Endangered' list," *Daily Times*, March 24, 2004, HCHS.

Chapter Ten

1. Wide Awake Films. *The Battle of Perryville: The Invasion of Kentucky*. 2007; Stuart W. Sanders, "The 1862 Kentucky Campaign and the Battle of Perryville." *Blue and Gray Magazine* 22, no.5, (Holiday 2005): 7; Kurt Holman, E-mail to author, August 2, 2011.

2. Sanders, "1862," 8; *OR*, 1, 16, 960-61; Stephen D. Engle, "Success, Failure, and the Guillotine: Don Carlos Buell and the Campaign for the Bluegrass State" *The Register of the Kentucky Historical Society,* 96 (Autumn 1998): 320-21.

3. *OR*, 1, 16, 1023-1024; Engle, 303-4; Kenneth W. Noe, *Perryville: This Grand Havoc of Battle*, (Lexington, KY: The University Press of Kentucky, 2001), 95-96, 98; Larry J. Daniel, *Days of Glory: The Army of the Cumberland, 1861-1865*, (Baton Rouge: Louisiana State University Press, 2004), 141.

4. *OR*, 2, 16, 900-902; Thomas Lawrence Connelly, *Army of the Heartland* (Baton Rouge: Louisiana State University Press, 1967), 235; Sanders, 1862, 9; Frank Van Der Linden, "General Bragg's Impossible Dream: Take Kentucky," http://www.civilwar.org/battlefields/perryville/perryville-history-articles/general-braggs-impossible.html (accessed December 2, 2011)

5. Sanders, 1862, 10; Connelly, *Army,* 235; *OR*, 1, 16, 1093, 1098, 1119-1120; *OR*, 2, 900-902; Holman e-mail.

6. Perryville Driving Tour pamphlet.

7. "Battle of Perryville" http://kyclim.wku.edu/factsheets/thbattleperryville.html (accessed December 2, 2011).

8. Wide Awake films; Noe, *Perryville*, 15-16.

9. Wide Awake Films.

10. Wide Awake Films; Noe, *Perryville*, 143; *OR*, 1, 16, 49-50, 89, 124-125, 134-136.

11. William E. Bevens, *Reminiscences of a Private, Company G. First Arkansas Regiment Infantry May, 1861 to 1865*, (1914).

12. Watkins, *Aytch*, 141; Holman e-mail.

13. *OR*, 1, 16, 1024-1025; Holman e-mail.

14. Ibid.; Sanders, 1862, 10.

15. Ibid.

16. Opposing Forces at Perryville, *B & G*, 29-30.

17. Sanders, 1862, 8; *OR,* 1, 16, 1023-1024.

18. *OR,* 1, 16, 1103.

19. "15th Kentucky," fifteenthkentucky.com/perryville3.htm; W. H, Davis, "Recollections of Perryville," *C.V.* 24, no. 12: 554; "Battle of Perryville" kyclim. wku.edu

20. *OR,* 1, 16, 1103; Holman e-mail.

21. Ibid., 660; Opposing forces, 30; Wide Awake Films; Noe, *Perryville,* 214.

22. *OR,* 1, 16, 660.

23. Ibid., 1087.

24. Davis, Recollections, 554.

25. Wide Awake Films; Sanders, 1862, 24; *OR,* 1, 16, 1119; Noe, *Perryville,* 171-72; Holman e-mail.

26. John Kennedy Street, Letter to "Dear" August 8, 1862 http://antiquemll. hypermart.net/jkletters7.htm

27. Watkins, *Columbia (TN) Journal,* May 30, 1900.

28. James T. Searcy, Letter, October 25, 1862, LPR 78 Box3 Folders 14 & 15, Alabama Department of Archives and History.

29. Lt. Col. James M. Shanklin, *The Soldier of Indiana in the War for the Union,* Vol. I (Indianapolis: Merrill and Company, 1866), 620; Capt. S. F. Horrall, "Word from the other side," *C.V.* 17, no.12: 556; Spillard F. Horrall, *History of the Forty-Second Indiana Volunteer Infantry,* 1892; George W. Landrum, The George W. Landrum Letters MSS.543, Western Reserve Historical Society Library. Cleveland, Ohio, n.d.

30. Sanders, 1862, 13-14; Opposing forces, 29-30.

31. Opposing forces, 30; Noe, *Perryville,* 369; Holman e-mail.

32. Landrum Letters.

33. Ibid.; Wide Awake Films; Sanders, 1862, 14; Holman e-mail.

34. Thomas H. Malone, *Memoir of Thomas H. Malone: An Autobiography written for his children,* 1928.

35. A. J. West, Unidentified newspaper article dated October 16, 1892, Perryville Battlefield State Historic Site archives.

36. James D. Jordan, *Reminiscences of the Boys in Gray 1861-1865,* ed. Mamie Yeary, (1912).

37. Brig. Gen. Daniel S. Donelson, "Report of the part taken in the Battle of Perryville by the 1st Brigade, 1st Div., Rt. Wg. Army of the Miss," October 27, 1862, William P. Palmer Collection of Civil War Manuscripts, Western Reserve Historical Society, Cleveland, OH. (Hereinafter cited as Donelson Report, Western Reserve).

38. Wide Awake Films; Noe, *Perryville,* 185; Burnett, Alf. *Humorous, Pathetic, and Descriptive Incidents of the War.* Cincinnati: R. W. Carroll & Co. 1864. 18-20.

39. Noe, *Perryville,* 185; Sanders, 1862, 15.

40. Noe, *Perryville,* 186; Wide Awake Films; Opposing Forces, 30.

41. Noe, *Perryville,* 469; Wide Awake Films.

42. *OR*, 1, 16, 43; Sanders, 1862, 15.

43. Ibid.

44. Ibid.; Wide Awake Films.

45. Davis, Recollections, 554.

46. *OR*, 1, 16, 1060; Noe, *Perryville*, 374; Sanders, 1862, 16.

47. *OR*, 1, 16, 1064-1065, 1113, 1157; Noe, *Perryville*, 207, 209-210; George Early Maney, "Report of the Action near Perryville, Ky. October 8th, 1862," October 29, 1862, William P. Palmer Collection of Braxton Bragg Papers, Western Reserve Historical Society.,Cleveland, OH; Holman e-mail.

48. Albion W. Tourgee, *The Story of a Thousand, Being a history of the service of the 105th Ohio Volunteer Infantry, in the War for the Union from August 21, 1862 to June 6, 1865*, (Self published, 1896).

49. *OR*, 1, 16, 1046, 1155; Wide Awake Films; Sanders, 1862, 17.

50. Marcus B. Toney, *The Privations of a Private*, (Self Published, 1905).

51. Ibid.; Watkins, *Aytch*, 123.

52. Judge L. B. McFarland, "Maney's Brigade at the Battle of Perryville," *C.V.* 30, no. 12: 468.

53. Wide Awake Films; Sanders, 1862, 16; Holman e-mail.

54. Davis Biggs, "Incidents in battle of Perryville, Ky," *C.V.* 33, no. 4, (April 1925): 141; Holman e-mail.

55. Stuart W. Sanders, "Battle of Perryville: 21st Wisconsin Infantry Regiment's Harrowing Fight," http://www.historynet.com/battle-of-perryville-21st-wisconsin-infantry-regiments-harrowing-fight.htm (accessed December 2, 2011); Holman e-mail.

56. T. A. Head, *C.V.* 5, no. 8, (August 1897): 435.

57. Wide Awake Films; Sanders, 1862, 17.

58. Opposing Forces, 30; Holman e-mail.

59. Wide Awake Films; Sanders, 1862, 18; Noe, *Perryville*, 374.

60. Wide Awake Films; *OR*, 1, 16, 1114, 1116.

61. Joseph Cross, *Camp and Field. Papers from the Portfolio of an Army Chaplain* (Self published, 1864).

62. "Perryville," http://www.kentuckyliving.com/article.asp?articleid=458& issueid=89 (accessed December 2, 2011).

63. Wide Awake Films; Thomas Lawrence Connelly, *Army of the Heartland*, (Louisiana State University Press, 1967), 254; *OR*, 1, 16, 1041.

64. *OR*, 1, 16, 1046, 1117, 1156; Sanders, 1862, 19; Noe, *Perryville*, 256; Holman e-mail.

65. Spillard F. Horrall, *History of the Forty-Second Indiana Volunteer Infantry*, (Self published, 1892), 150-151; Holman e-mail.

66. George Morgan Kirkpatrick, *The Experiences of a Private Soldier of the Civil War*, (self published, 1924).

67. William G. Putney, Memoir transcript, William L. Clements Library, University of Michigan.

68. Opposing forces, 29; S. F. Horrall, *History*, 150-151; Holman e-mail.

69. Shanklin, 623.
70. Capt. S. F. Horrall, "Word from the other side," *C.V.* 17, no. 12: 556.
71. Noe, *Perryville*, 271.
72. Shanklin, 624.
73. Horrall, Word, 556.
74. "Correspondence to Buell's Army," *Princeton (IN) Clarion*, October 17, 1862.
75. Opposing forces, 30; Sanders, 1862, 19.
76. Robert S. Cameron, *Staff Ride Handbook for the Battle of Perryville*, (8 October 1862, reprint Fort Leavenworth, KS: Combat Studies Institute Press, 2005): 216-217; *OR*, 1, 16, 1056.
77. Sanders, 1862, 44; Opposing forces, 29-30; Noe, *Perryville*, 371, 373.
78. Wide Awake Films; Sanders, 1862, 44; Harry Smeltzer, "Squire Bottom Founds a Confederate Cemetery," *Civil War Times* 49, no. 3, (June 2011): 27; Holman e-mail.
79. Sanders, 1862, 44-45; Opposing forces, 30; Noe, *Perryville*, 372-374.
80. W. C. Gipson, "About the Battle of Perryville," *C.V.* 8, no. 9: 433.
81. Col. Curran Pope, Letter to the editors, *Louisville Journal*, October 19, 1862.
82. Noe, *Perryville*, 374; *OR*, 1, 16, 1058.
83. Smeltzer, 27-28.
84. Ibid., 28; Burnett, 16; *OR*, 1, 16, 1126; Sanders, 1862, 45.
85. Pope, Letter.
86. Opposing forces, 29-30.
87. Gipson, 433.
88. Noe, Perryville, 376; A. C. Bruce, "Battle of Perryville, KY, as told in an old letter by J. A. Bruce," *C.V.* 10, no. 4: 177.
89. John Beatty, *The Citizen Soldier*, (Self published, 1879).
90. Wide Awake Films; Sanders, 1862, 46; Noe, *Perryville*, 161; Holman e-mail.
91. Dr. Jefferson J. Polk, *Autobiography of Dr. J. J. Polk*, (1867).
92. Sanders, 1862, 46; Noe, *Perryville*, 372; Holman e-mail.
93. Wesley S. Poulson, Letter to the *Cadiz Republican*, Spring 1863.
94. John H. Nichols, *Proof of the pudding: Autobiography of John Harmon Nichols*(Self published, 1913).
95. Duncan C. Milner, Letter to editor, October 10, 1862. Printed in *National Tribune*, September 27, 1906.
96. Ibid.
97. Ibid.; Wide Awake Films.
98. Wide Awake Films; Noe, *Perryville*, 374.
99. Sanders, 1862, 47; *OR*, 1, 16, 1079, 1159.
100. Sanders, 1862, 47; Wide Awake Films.
101. Stuart W. Sanders,"Literally Covered with the Dead and Dying," http://www.civilwar.org/battlefields/perryville/perryville-history-articles/polksanders.html (accessed December 2, 2011).

102. Wide Awake Films.

103. Sanders, 1862, 47; Perryville Battlefield State Historic Site, Kentucky Department of Parks, June 2007; Charles Gilbert, "On the field of Perryville," *B & L.* 57; Holman e-mail.

104. *Confederate Military History,* (Atlanta: Confederate Publishing Company, 1899): 143.

105. Wide Awake Films; Clairborne, 226-227.

106. Joseph Wheeler, "Bragg's Invasion of Kentucky," *B & L.* 17.

107. Gilbert, 59.

108. J. P. Cannon, *Inside of Rebeldom: The Daily Life of a Private in the Confederate Army,* (Self Published, 1900); Luke W. Finlay, "Fourth Tennessee Infantry," *Military Annals of Tennessee. Confederate* (Nashville, 1886), 213.

109. Poulson.

110. Davis, *Recollections,* 554.

111. *The Daily Dispatch,* October 22, 1862; Lowell Harrison, "Death on a dry river," *Civil War Times Illustrated* 28, no. 2 (May 1979): 47; Holman e-mail.

112. Davis, *Recollections,* 554.

113. Harrison, "Death," 47; Sanders, "Battle of Perryville: 21st Wisconsin Infantry Regiment's Harrowing Fight." http://www.historynet.com/battle-of-perryville-21st-wisconsin-infantry-regiments-harrowing-fight.htm (accessed December 2, 2011).

114. Noe, *Perryville,* 369, 373; Perryville Battlefield pamphlet.

115. Noe, Perryville, 373-374; Perryville Battlefield pamphlet; Sanders, "Battle."

116. Perryville Battlefield pamphlet.

117. Henry Villard, *Memoirs of Henry Villard,* (1904); Cannon, *Inside,* 1900.

118. George W. Morris, *History of the Eighty-First Regiment of Indiana Volunteer Infantry in the Great War of the Rebellion 1861-1865* (1901).

119. Joseph Cross, *Camp and Field. Papers from the portfolio of an Army Chaplain,* (Self published, 1864).

120. Morris, *History;* Burnett, *Humorous.*

121. Biggs, Incidents, 141.

122. Watkins, *Columbia Journal;* Orren Benson, "Dear Friends" *Woodstock Sentinel,* October 15, 1862, Accessed via Perryville Civil War Battlefield Web site; George T. Simonson, Scott Cantwell Meeker, ed., Deep Vee Productions, February 20, 2005; *Daily Dispatch,* October 22, 1862; David Urquhart, "Bragg's Advance and Retreat," *B & L.* 603.

123. "The Tenth Regiment," n.d.

124. Perryville Battlefield pamphlet; Wide Awake films; Kenneth W. Noe, "Remembering Perryville: History and Memory at a Civil War Battlefield," http://www.perryvillereenactment.org/html/more_history.html (accessed December 2, 2011).

125. George Morgan Kirkpatrick, *The Experiences of a Private Soldier of the Civil War,* (Self published, 1924).

126. J. S. Newberry, "The Battle of Perryville." http://www.battleofperryville. com/san_com55.html (accessed December 2, 2011).

127. A. W. Reed, "The Battle of Perryville." http://www.battleofperryville.com/ san_com55.html (accessed December 2, 2011).

128. Ibid.

129. Edward Ferguson, "The Army of the Cumberland under Buell," *Military Order of the Loyal Legion of the United States, Wisconsin Commandary*. vol. 1. (December 5, 1888).

130. Thomas C. Crawford, "The Battle of Perryville," *C.V.* 40, no. 7, (July 1932): 263.

131. Malone; Kenneth A. Hafendorfer, ed. *Civil War Journal of William L. Trask*, (Louisville, KY: KH Press, 2003), 78.

132. *Daily Dispatch*, October 22, 1862.

133. Mead Holmes, *Soldier of the Cumberland: Memoir of Mead Holmes, Jr. Sergeant of Company K, 21ˢᵗ Regiment Wisconsin Volunteers*, (Boston: American Tract Society, 1864).

134. Smeltzer, 28; Noe, Remembering.

135. Crawford, 263.

136. *Update*, 40; Smeltzer, 28; Perryville Battlefield pamphlet.

137. Perryville Battlefield pamphlet; *Update*, 40; "Group donates 54 acres of Perryville Battlefield," *The Civil War Courier* 25, no. 3. (July 2010): 1, 8; Holman e-mail.

138. Sherman Cahal, "American Byways: Perryville Battlefield," http://www. americanbyways.com/index.php?catid=67 (accessed December 2, 2011).

139. "Rantings of a Civil War Historian," http://civilwarcavalry.com/?p=824 (accessed December 2, 2011).

140. Perryville Battlefield Preservation Association pamphlet. n.d.; "Perryville named Preserve America community," http://www.civilwarbuff.org/ NewsLetters/2005/feb05.htm (accessed December 2, 2011).

141. Perryville Battlefield State Historic Site pamphlet, n.d.

142. Perryville Battlefield Walking Trail Guide, Kentucky Department of Parks.

143. "Perryville," www.kentuckyliving.com.

144. Stuart Sanders, "The Cost of War: Centre College and the battle of Perryville," http://www.centre.edu/web/library/sc/special/perryville/index.htm (accessed December 2, 2011).

Chapter Eleven

1. John Hunt Morgan Trail pamphlet.

2. Ibid.

3. Basil W. Duke, *History of Morgan's Cavalry* (Cincinnati: Miami Printing and Publishing Company, 1867): 156, 160.

4. Ibid., 160.

5. Ibid.; Tim Asher, "John Hunt Morgan's Christmas Raid," n.d.

6. Duke, 160.

7. Ibid., 158, 160; *OR*, 1, 20, 154.

8. Duke, 160.

9. John Allen Wyeth, "Morgan's Christmas Raid, 1862-1863," Robert Lanier, ed. *Photographic History of the Civil War: Armies and Leaders* (New York: Random House Publishing, 1983): 145.

10. Duke, 158; *OR*, 1, 20, 154.

11. John Weatherred, *The Wartime Diary of John Weatherred*. www.jackmasters.net/9tncav.html (accessed December 2, 2011).

12. Duke, 160.

13. Ibid.

14. *OR*, 1, 20, 154; Weatherred.

15. *OR*, 1, 20, 154.

16. Ibid.; Duke, 161.

17. *OR*, 1, 20, 148, 154.

18. Ibid.

19. Duke, 161.

20. *OR*, 1, 20, 148.

21. Ibid., 148-49.

22. Ibid., 154-55.

23. Duke, 161.

24. *OR*, 1, 20, 148-49.

25. *OR*, 1, 20, 155.

26. Ibid.

27. Ibid.; Duke, 161-62.

28. *OR*, 1, 20, 155.

29. Ibid.

30. Duke, 162.

31. *OR*, 1, 20, 155.

32. Duke, 162.

33. Darrell Bird, "Christmas Raid surprised Union outposts," *News Enterprise,* December 26, 1992.

34. *OR*, 1, 20, 155.

35. Ibid.; Duke, 162.

36. Ibid.

37. Ibid., *OR*, 156.

38. Ibid.

39. Ibid.

40. Ibid.

41. Ibid., Duke, 163.

42. *OR*, 1, 20, 156.

43. Duke, 163.

44. *OR*, 1, 20, 156;

45. http://www.trailsrus.com/morgan/etown.html (accessed December 2, 2011); Duke, 163.

46. *OR*, 1, 20, 156.
47. Duke, 163.
48. Ibid.; *OR*, 1, 20, 156.
49. Ibid.
50. Ibid.; http://www.trailsrus.com/morgan/etown.html.
51. Ibid.
52. Darrell Bird, "Burning of Bridges a spectacular success," *News Enterprise,* January 2, 1993.
53. *OR*, 1, 20, 153.
54. Ibid., 156; Duke, 163.
55. *OR*, 1, 20, 156.
56. Ibid., 138.
57. Weatherred.
58. Morgan's Raid Driving Trail pamphlet.
59. *OR,* 1, 20, 139.
60. Ibid.
61. Ibid., 157.
62. Ibid., 139.
63. Ibid., 165.
64. Ibid., 139.
65. Duke, 165.
66. Ibid.
67. http://www.trailsrus.com/morgan/bardstown.html (accessed December 2, 2011).
68. Ibid.
69. *OR*, 1, 20, 157; Duke, 165.
70. *OR*, 1, 20, 139, 157.
71. Ibid.; http://www.trailsrus.com/morgan/newhaven.html (accessed December 2, 2011).
72. *OR*, 1, 20, 157.
73. Ibid.
74. Ibid.; http://www.trailsrus.com/morgan/springfield.html (accessed December 2, 2011).
75. Weatherred.
76. *OR*, 1, 20, 157-58.
77. Ibid., 158.
78. Ibid.
79. Ibid.
80. Duke, 167.
81. Asher, 4; Darrell Bird, "Elizabethtown Welcomes General Morgan," *News Enterprise,* (December 28, 1992).
82. http://www.trailsrus.com/morgan/bardstown.html; http://www.trailsrus.com/morgan/ethtown.html.
83. http://www.trailsrus.com/morgan/springfield.html (accessed December 2, 2011).

84. http://www.trailsrus.com/morgan/campbellsville.html (accessed December 2, 2011); http://www.campbellsvilleky.com/historical.html (accessed December 2, 2011).

85. http://www.trailsrus.com/morgan/pr-704.html.

86. Lebanon Tourist and Convention Commission, 2006.

Chapter Twelve

1. Hall Allen, "Chief Paduke: was he real or just a legend?" n.d.; Hall Allen, "Chief Paduke Legend dates back to 1886," n.d.; Hall Allen, "Henderson family has Paduke story," n.d.

2. Hall Allen, "Five-dollar deed Paducah forerunner," n.d.; "Primitive Pekin Becomes the city of Paducah," *Paducah Life* (Summer 1992): 7.

3. "Primitive."

4. http://www.markethousemuseum.com/FAQ (accessed December 6, 2011).

5. "Significant dates in Paducah history," *Paducah Life* (Summer 1993): 60.

6. http://www.markethousemuseum.com/FAQ; http://www.civilwaralbum.com/misc11/paducah1f.htm (accessed December 6, 2011).

7. http://www.civilwaralbum.com/misc11/paducah1f.htm; Hall Allen, "Yankee saviours," (n.d.), 1.; "Grant Takes Possession of Paducah during Civil Strife," *Paducah Life* (Summer 1992): 12.

8. "Louis Kolb, Sr., clearly recalls the Battle of Paducah fought 63 years ago this 25th of March," *New Democrat*, March 25, 1927.

9. "Grant"

10. Allen, "Yankee," 1.

11. "Grant"

12. Allen, "Yankee," 1.

13. Ibid.; Allen, "Yankee," 1; http://www.markethousemuseum.com/FAQ.

14. Shirley M. Beauchamp, "The Battle of Paducah," (n.d.), 1.

15. *Harper's Weekly*, October 26, 1861.

16. Ibid.

17. Ibid.; Beauchamp, 3.

18. Allen, "Yankee," 2.

19. "The true story of Sister Mary Lucy Dosh," http://www.markethousemuseum.com/node/177 (accessed December 6, 2011).

20. "Louis Kolb."

21. "Importance of Paducah stressed by researcher," n.d.

22. "Paducah Fortifications," n.d.

23. "North and South clash at Fort Anderson," *Paducah Life* (Summer 1992).

24. Hall Allen, "Company B."; Shelley Byrne, "Fighting for Freedom," *Paducah Sun*, March 23, 2005.

25. Wyeth, *Life*, 325-26.

26. Ibid., 326.

27. J. V. Greif, "Forrest's Raid on Paducah," *C.V.* 5, no. 5 (May 1897): 212.

28. Ibid.; Lonnie E. Maness, *An Untutored Genius: The Military Career of*

General Nathan Bedford Forrest, (Oxford, MS: The Guild Bindery Press, 1990), 224; John E. L. Robertson, *Paducah 1830-1980,* (Paducah, KY: Image Graphics, n.d.).

29. Greif, 212; Hall Allen, "Battle of Paducah," n.d.

30. Ibid.

31. "The Battle of Paducah," http://kyclim.wku.edu./factsheets/thebattlepaducah.html (accessed December 6, 2011); Hall Allen, *Center of Conflict,* (Paducah Printing Company, 1961), 163.

32. Allen, "Battle"; "Louis Kolb."

33. Jonathan Oliver, "Civil War research brings Michigan to Paducah," *Paducah Sun,* July 7, 1996; *Daily Dispatch,* April 4, 1864.

34. Wyeth, *Life,* 329; "Civil War Service Carved A Place in History For a Paducah Lawyer," *Paducah Sun Democrat,* July 27, 1956.

35. Jordan and Pryor, 411.

36. Ibid., 411; "Paducah Lawyer."

37. Jordan and Pryor, 412.

38. Ibid., 409.

39. Ibid., 410; Allen, *Center,* 164.

40. "Paducah Lawyer."

41. Wyeth, *Life,* 330.

42. Ibid.

43. Ibid.; Allen, *Center,* 164; "Paducah Lawyer."

44. "Good Friday '64 General Forrest Raided Paducah," March 25, 1910; North and South; Fred G. Neuman, *The Story of Paducah,* (Paducah, KY: Young Printing Company, 1920), 43.

45. "Fighting and Feasting," *C.V.* 2, no. 1 (January 1894): 14.

46. Greif, 212.

47. Frank Moore, *The Civil War in Song and Story.*

48. Henry George, *History of the 3rd, 7th, 8th, and 12th Kentucky, C.S.A.* (Paducah Library Special Collections, 1911), 76.

49. Hall Allen, "It has been 100 long years since 'Battle of Paducah.'"; "Civil Paducah Lawyer."

50. "Good Friday"; Greif, 212; Neuman, 43; "Colonel Crossland," *C.V.* (August 1911): 366.

51. "Good Friday."

52. Moore.

53. *OR,* 1, 32, 607; "Paducah Lawyer."

54. "Captain McKnight," *C.V.* 18, no. 1 (January 1910): 37.

55. Jordan and Pryor, 413.

56. Neuman, 43; Allen, *Center,* 164-65; Robertson, 60.

57. Neuman, 43; *OR,* 1, 32, 609; "North and South."

58. "Paducah Lawyer."

59. Greif, 213.

60. George, *History,* 78.

61. *The Illustrated London News* 44, no. 1253 (April 16, 1864): 359.

62. "Paducah's Col. Hicks: It was a case of lose lips creating loss of horses," http://www.thekentuckycivilwarbugle.com/2009-4Qpages/fortanderson.html (accessed December 6, 2011).

63. *Update,* 63.

64. Paducah, Kentucky Downtown Civil War Walking Tour pamphlet, Paducah/ McCracken County Convention and Visitors Bureau; The Lloyd Tilghman House and Civil War Museum pamphlet.

Chapter Thirteen

1. "Welcome to Cynthiana, Kentucky," http://www.cynthianaky.com (Accessed November 29, 2011).

2. Cynthiana-Harrison County Chamber of Commerce. "The Battles of Cynthiana." a study by Gray and Pape, Inc. of Cincinnati (July 19, 2005): vii.

3. "Morgan's Men Association." Cynthiana, Kentucky Tour signs.

4. Gray and Pape, Inc., 26.

5. Basil W. Duke, *History of Morgan's Cavalry* (Cincinnati: Miami Printing and Publishing Company, 1867): 522-523.

6. "The Battle of Cynthiana." http://kyclim.wku.edu/factsheets/ thebattlecynthiana.html (accessed November 30, 2011).

7. Gray and Pape, Inc., 30; G. D. Ewing, "Morgan's Last Raid into Kentucky," *C.V.* 31, no. 7 (July 1923): 254.

8. Ewing, "Morgan's," 255.

9. Gray and Pape, Inc., 32; William A. Penn, *Rattling Spurs and Broad-Brimmed Hats: The Civil War in Cynthiana and Harrison County, Kentucky.* (Battle Grove Press, 1995), 107.

10. Gray and Pape, Inc., 34; Penn, 107-8.

11. Penn, 108.

12. Ibid., 108-9.

13. Ibid., 110; Lewis Collins, *History of Kentucky,* (Covington, KY.: Collins & Co., 1874), 324; Gray and Pape, Inc., 36.

14. Duke, History, 527.

15. Ewing, 255.

16. Ibid.

17. Ibid.

18. *Cynthiana Democrat,* June 1896, 8.

19. Ibid.; "The Second Battle of Cynthiana." http://www.geocities.com/ morgansraid/history.html?200912; Penn, 110-11.

20. *Cynthiana Democrat,* June 1896, 8.

21. Collins, *History,* 324.

22. Ibid.; *Cynthiana Democrat,* June 1896, 8.

23. Ewing, 256.

24. Ibid.

25. "The Second Battle of Cynthiana."

26. *Cynthiana Democrat*, June 1896, 8.

27. Ibid.

28. "The Second Battle of Cynthiana."; Ewing, 256.

29. Ewing, 256; *Cynthiana Democrat*, June 1896.

30. Ewing, 256; Collins, 325.

31. Ewing, 256.

32. Collins, 325; *Cynthiana Democrat*, June 1896.

33. Ewing, 256.

34. "The Second Battle of Cynthiana."; Duke, 528.

35. Mrs. W. T. Towler, "Capt. W. J. Stone—In Memorium," *C.V.* 31, no. 7 (July 1923): 246; "Comrade W. J. Stone," *C.V.* 7, no. 5 (May 1899): 232.

36. http://mayhouse.org/perry/oldhouse5.html (accessed December 6, 2011); Samuel and Susan Sizemore Allen, n.d., HCHS.

37. "Battle Grove Cemetery." http://www.bluegrasskentucky.com/roots-a-resting-places (accessed December 6, 2011).

38. Morgan's Raids at Cynthiana, KY Civil War Driving Tour pamphlet, Cynthiana-Harrison County Chamber of Commerce, n.d.

39. *Update*, 24; "Cynthiana, Kentucky," http://www.trailsrus.com/civilwar/region4/ cynthian.html (accessed December 6, 2011).

BIBLIOGRAPHY

Abbreviations
B & L: Battles and Leaders of the Civil War
BORA: Battle of Richmond Association
C.V.:   Confederate Veteran
HCHS: Hart County Historical Society
MCPL: McCracken County (Kentucky) Public Library
PKPL: Paducah Kentucky Public Library
TSL&A: Tennessee State Library and Archives

Adkins, Ray. Battle of Barboursville, Kentucky. 2d ed., n.d.
Allen, Hall. "Battle of Paducah," Vertical file. MCPL, n.d.
————. Center of Conflict. Paducah Printing Company, 1961.
————. "Chief Paduke Legend dates back to 1886." Vertical file. PKPL, n.d.
————. "Chief Paduke: was he real or just a legend?" Vertical file. PKPL, n.d.
————. "Company B." Vertical file. PKPL, n.d.
————. "Five-dollar deed Paducah forerunner." Vertical file. PKPL, n.d.
————. "Henderson family has Paduke story." Vertical file. PKPL, n.d.
————. "It has been 100 long years since 'Battle of Paducah.'" Vertical file. PKPL, n.d.
————. "Yankee saviours." Vertical file. PKPL, n.d.
Asher, Tim. "John Hunt Morgan's Christmas Raid." n.d.
Baker, James. Letter to his father, January 21, 1862. History of Newaygo County Michigan Civil War Veterans. 1894.
Barati, Justine. "Former Army property becomes a Civil War Interpretive Center." Blue Grass Army Depot, Richmond, Kentucky, October 2, 2008.
Barfield, Lt. Castillo. Letter. n.d. Abraham Lincoln Museum, Lincoln Memorial University, Harrogate, TN.
Barnett, James. "German's hollow square repelled Texas Rangers in Kentucky fight." Lockland (Ohio) Mill Creek Valley News, December 21, 1961.
————. "Munfordville in the Civil War." The Register of the Kentucky Historical Society (October 1971): 339-60.
Barry, Craig L. "Richmond, Kentucky." Civil War Courier 12, no. 10 (October 2008): 5.

Basler, Roy P., ed. *Abraham Lincoln Speeches and Writings: 1859-1865.* Library of America, 1989.

"A Battle at Munfordville, Ky." *Daily Ledger.* Dec. 18, 1861. HCHS.

"The Battle for the Bridge." July 16, 1994. HCHS.

"Battle for the Bridge—Munfordville, KY." www.waymarking.com/waymarks/WM57QK_Battle_for_the_Bridge. Accessed September 25, 2009.

Battle for the Bridge and Battle of Munfordville Driving Tour. n.d.

"Battle Grove Cemetery." http://www.bluegrasskentucky.com/history/attractions.aspx?id=453. Accessed September 12, 2009.

Battle, J. H., W. H. Perrin, and G. C. Kniffin. *Kentucky, a History of the State.* Louisville, KY: F. A. Battey Publishing Co., 1885.

Battle of Camp Wildcat brochure. United States Department of Agriculture Forest Service, Southern Region, Daniel Boone National Forest, 2006.

"The Battle of Chaplin Hills." *Louisville Journal,* October 17, 1862.

"The Battle of Cynthiana." http://kyclim.wku.edu/factsheets/thebattlecynthiana.html. Accessed December 6, 2011.

"The Battle of Fishing Creek." *Daily Avalanche,* January 28, 1862.

"The Battle of Mill Springs." *Harpers Weekly,* March 8, 1862.

"The Battle of Mill Springs." *New York Herald,* January 25, 1862.

"The Battle of Mill Springs, and other interesting tidbits." serene-musings.blogspot.com/2007/01/battle-of-mill-springs-and-other.html. Accessed September 18, 2009.

"Battle of Munfordville." *C.V.* 17, no. 2: 85.

"The Battle of Munfordville." http://kyclim.wku.edu/factsheets/thebattlemunfordville.html. Accessed December 6, 2011.

"The Battle of Paducah." http://kyclim.wku.edu/factsheets/thebattlepaducah.html. Accessed December 6, 2011.

"The Battle of Perryville." http://kyclim.wku.edu/factsheets/thbattleperryville.html. Accessed December 6, 2011.

Battle of the Rolling Fork driving tour. Stop 15.

"Battle of Rowlett's Station."http://kyclim.wku.edu/factsheets/thebattleofrowlett.html. Accessed December 6, 2011.

"Battle of Sacramento Driving Tour" pamphlet, McLean County (KY) Historical Society.

The Battles of Cynthiana. A Study by Gray and Pape, Inc. Cincinnati. July 19, 2005.

Beatty, John. *The Citizen Soldier.* Self published, 1879.

Beauchamp, Shirley M. "The Battle of Paducah." Unpublished paper, Vertical file. PKPL, n.d.

Becker, Robert L. "The Battle of Munfordville." HCHS, n.d.

Bennett, B. Kevin. "The Battle of Richmond, Kentucky." *Blue and Gray* 25, no. 6, (2009).

Benson, Orren. "Dear Friends." *Woodstock Sentinel,* October 15, 1862. Accessed via Perryville Civil War Battlefield Web site.

Bevens, William E. *Reminiscences of a Private, Company G. First Arkansas Regiment Infantry May, 1861 to 1865.* Published by William E. Bevens, 1914.

Biggs, Davis. "Incidents in battle of Perryville, Ky." *C.V.* 33, no. 4, (April 1925): 141-42.

Binford, James R. *Recollections of the Fifteenth Regiment of Mississippi Infantry, C.S.A.* Henry Patrick Papers, Mississippi Department of Archives and History.

Bircher, William. *A Drummer Boy's Diary: Comprising Four years of Service with the Second Regiment Minnesota Veterans Volunteers, 1861-1865.* St. Paul Book & Stationery Company, 1889.

Bishop, Judson W. *The Story of a Regiment—Service of the Second Regiment, Minnesota Veteran Volunteer Infantry.* 1890.

Bird, Darrell. "Burning of Bridges a spectacular success." *News Enterprise.* January 2, 1993.

———. "Christmas Raid surprised Union outposts." *News Enterprise.* December 26, 1992.

———. "Elizabethtown Welcomes General Morgan." *News Enterprise.* December 28, 1992.

Blackburn, James K. P. "Reminiscences of the Texas Rangers." *Southwest Historical Quarterly,* 22, (1918-1919): 38-77, 143-179.

Blakemore, Maj. W. T. *C.V.* 5, no. 6: 249.

Blanton, Capt. J. C. "Forrest's old regiment." *C.V.* 3, no. 2 (February 1895): 41-42.

Blueandgraytrail.com/event/James_Garfield. Accessed September 9, 2009.

Blueandgraytrail.com/site/mill_springs_battlefield. Accessed October 18, 2009.

Boggs, William. *Military Reminiscences of General William R. Boggs, C.S.A.* Durham, NC: The Seeman Printery, 1913.

Bond, Octavia Zollicoffer. *C.V.* (February 1902): 100.

The BORA Bulletin 10, no. 2, (2d Quarter 2011).

Boyles, Margaret. "Gen. F. K. Zollicoffer." *C.V.* 15, no. 1 (January 1907): 28.

Brent, Joseph E. "Barbourville Civil War Interpretive Park." *The Knox Countian* 19, no. 3 (Fall 2007): 1, 52-54.

Bruce, A. C. "Battle of Perryville, KY, as told in an old letter by J. A. Bruce." *C.V.* 10, no. 4: 177.

Bryson, John H. *C.V.* 5, no. 3 (March 1897): 108.

Burnett, Alf. *Humorous, Pathetic, and Descriptive Incidents of the War.* Cincinnati: R. W. Carroll & Co., 1864.

Bush, Bryan. "Morgan's Christmas Raid of 1862." http://civilwargazett.wordpress.com/2011/01/30/morgan-1862. Accessed June 4, 2011.

Button, Charles W. "Early engagements with Forrest." *C.V.* 5, no. 9 (September 1897): 479-80.

Byrne, Shelley. "Fighting for Freedom." *Paducah Sun,* March 23, 2005.

Cahal, Sherman. "American Byways: Perryville Battlefield." http://www.americanbyways.com/index.php?catid=67. Accessed September 12, 2009.

Calhoun Driving Tour pamphlet. McLean County (KY) Historical and Genealogy Museum. n.d.

Calhoun Walking Tour pamphlet. McLean County (KY) Historical and Geneaology Museum. August 8, 1992.

"The Campaign in Kentucky." *New York Times*, November 1, 1861.

Campbell, D. A. "The Battle of Munfordsville" *Jackson (MS) Clarion*, n.d. HCHS.

Cannon, J. P. *Inside of Rebeldom: The Daily Life of a Private in the Confederate Army*. Self published. 1900.

"Captain McKnight." *C.V.* 18, no. 1 (January 1910): 38.

Carroll, Capt. C. W. Letter to his wife. December 19, 1861. HCHS.

Carter, Samuel P. *A Biographical Sketch*. Library of Congress. n.d.

Catton, Bruce. *Terrible Swift Sword*. Garden City, NY: Doubleday and Co., Inc., 1963.

"Chalmer's Great Blunder at Munfordville." *C.V.* 17, no. 5 (May 1909): 221-222.

Chase, John A. *History of the Fourteenth Ohio*. Toledo, Ohio. 1881.

Chatfield (Minnesota) Democrat, n.d.

Cincinnati Enquirer, February 12, 1862.

———. August 29, 1862.

Cist, Henry M. *The Army of the Cumberland.* New York: Charles Scribner's Sons, 1882.

"City, county now own battle site." *Calhoun (KY) McLean County News*, April 18, 2002.

The Civil War Battle of Richmond, Kentucky pamphlet. Richmond Tourism and Main Street Department, n.d.

"Civil War Service carved a place in history for a Paducah lawyer." *Paducah Sun Democrat,* July 27, 1956.

Clairborne, Col. Thomas. "Battle of Perryville." *C.V.* 18, no. 5: 225-227.

Clark, Thomas A. *A History of Laurel County*. The Laurel County Historical Society, London, KY, 1989.

Coffin, J. S. *C.V.* 8, no. 3 (March 1900): 122.

Collins, Lewis. *History of Kentucky*. Covington, KY: Collins & Co., 1874.

"Colonel Crossland." *C.V.* 19, no. 8 (August 1911): 366.

Comer, Diane. "Public meeting about Bloedner Monument, the oldest Civil War Monument in the U.S., will be September 23 in Louisville." August 28, 2009 www.heritage.ky.gov/news/bloednermonmtg.htm. Accessed September 8, 2009.

"Comrade W. J. Stone." *C.V.* 7, no. 5 (May 1899): 232.

Confederate Brig. General Patrick R. Cleburne. BORA.

Confederate Brig. General Thomas James Churchill. BORA.

"A Confederate Cavalry Regiment engaged in the unfortunate War Between the States." *New Birmingham Times.* n.d. www.terrytexasrangers.org/newsclippings/new_birmingham_times/1892_04_09.html. Accessed August 17, 2010.

Confederate Major General Edmund Kirby Smith. BORA.

Confederate Military History. Atlanta: Confederate Publishing Company, 1899.

"Confederates invade Union Home Guard training camp." *The Southern Star.* aotn.homestead.com/Barbourville.html. Accessed September 14, 2009.

Connolly, James A. *Three Years in the Army of the Cumberland: The Letters and Diary of Major James A. Connolly*. Edited by Paul M. Angle. 1959.

Cooper, James L. "Diary." *C.V.* 33, no. 1: 16.

———. *Memoirs*. TSL & A.

"Correspondence to Buell's Army." *Princeton (IN) Clarion*, October 17, 1862.

Crawford, Thomas C. "The Battle of Perryville." *C.V.* 40, no. 7: 262-64.

Cromie, Alice Hamilton. *A Tour Guide to the Civil War*. Chicago: Quadrangle Books, 1965.

Cross, Joseph. *Camp and Field. Papers from the Portfolio of an Army Chaplain*. Self published, 1864.

Cull, Robert J. "Battle of Munfordville called highly significant Civil War event." *Kentucky Explorer*, (January 1996): 82-85. HCHS.

Cutter, O. P. *Our Battery*. Cleveland: Nevins' Book & Job Printing Establishment, 1864.

"CWPT Most Endangered Battlefields." *Civil War Courier* 25, no. 3, (July 2010): 6-7.

Cynthiana Democrat, June 1896.

"Cynthiana, KY." http://www.trailsrus.com/civilwar/region4/cynthian.html. Accessed September 12, 2009.

Richmond (VA) Daily Dispatch, October 22, 1862.

———. April 4, 1864.

———. October 2, 1861.

———. December 25, 1861.

Daily Ledger, December 18, 1861.

Daily Ohio Statesman, September 7, 1862.

Daily Toledo Blade, October 26, 1861.

———. October 29, 1861.

Daniel, Larry J. *Days of Glory: The Army of the Cumberland, 1861-1865*. Baton Rouge: Louisiana State University Press, 2004.

Dashiel, Mastin. Letter n.d. *Indianapolis Daily Journal*, February 6, 1862.

Davidson, W. H. Letter to Mr. George D. Seymour. June 9, 1932. HCHS.

Davis, Jefferson. *The Rise and Fall of the Confederate Government*.Vol. II, New York: D. Appleton and Company,1881.

Davis, W. H. "Recollections of Perryville." *C.V.* 24, no. 12 (December 1916): 554-55.

Deaderick, Inslee. Letter to "Dear Father." September 20, 1861. *The Knox Countian*, 19, no. 1 (Spring 2007): 23.

DeBerry, D. H. "Kirby Smith's Bluegrass Invasion." *America's Civil War* 10, no. 1 (March 1997):54-60, 88-90.

"The Diary or Register of David Anderson Deaderick, Esq." David Anderson Deaderick Papers, Manuscript Division, Library of Congress.

Diary of David A. Fately. Indiana State Library. Indianapolis, IN. n.d.

Doak, Henry Velvil. *Memoirs*. Tennessee State Library and Archives, Nashville, TN, n.d.

Donelson, Brig. Gen. Daniel S. "Report of the part taken in the Battle of Perryville by the 1st Brigade, 1st Div., Rt. Wg. Army of the Miss." October 27, 1862, William P. Palmer Collection of Civil War Manuscripts, Western Reserve Historical Society, Cleveland, OH.

Douglas, Lucia R., ed. *Douglas's Texas Battery, C.S.A.* Tyler, TX: Smith County Historical Society, 1966.

Drake, Lemuel F. Letter to editor. January 29, 1862. *Perry County Weekly.* New Lexington, OH.

Duke, Basil W. *History of Morgan's Cavalry.* Cincinnati: Miami Printing and Publishing Company, 1867.

Durfee, Joseph G. *Geauga County (OH) Jeffersonian Democrat,* February 2, 1862.

Eckels, Lt. Oliver. Letter from camp near Somerset, KY. January 1, 1861. geocities.com/Pentagon/Quarters/1864/eckelsltr.htm?200919. Accessed September 19, 2009.

"The Engagement at Munfordville, Ky." *Louisville Journal,* September 16, 1862. HCHS.

Engerud, Col. "Munfordville." n.d. HCHS.

———. "Remarks." Presented at the Munfordville Civil War Centennial Observance, HCHS, September 15, 1962.

Engle, Stephen D. "Success, Failure, and the Guillotine: Don Carlos Buell and the Campaign for the Bluegrass State." *The Register of the Kentucky Historical Society* 96 (Autumn 1998).

Evans, Mark L. Letter to wife. December 19, 1861. *C.V.* 12, no. 2 (February 1905): 61-62.

Ewing, G. D. "Morgan's Last Raid into Kentucky." *C.V.* 31, no. 7 (July 1923): 254-56.

Ewing, George W. "General Bragg's Kentucky Campaign." *C.V.* 34, no. 6 (June 1926): 214-15.

"Exciting news from Kentucky: A skirmish at Green River!—Brilliant Exploits of the Texas Rangers—Death of Col. Terry." *Nashville Union and American,* December 19, 1861. www.terrystexasrangers.org/newsclippings/nashville_union_and_american/1861_12_19.html. Accessed August 17, 2010.

"Face-lift for the Bloedner Marker." *Civil War Times,* (December 2009): 14.

Faw, Walter Wagner. Letters. TSL&A, Nashville, TN.

"Federal Brig. General Charles Cruft." BORA. n. d.

"Federal Brig. General Mahlon Manson." BORA. n.d.

"Federal Brig. General William 'Bull' Nelson." BORA. n.d.

Ferguson, Edward. "The Army of the Cumberland under Buell." *Military Order of the Loyal Legion of the United States, Wisconsin Commandery* 1 (December 5, 1888).

"15th Kentucky." http://www.fifteenthkentucky.com/Perryville3.htm. Accessed September 17, 2009.

"The Fight at Barboursville." *Barbourville (KY) Knox Countian.* (Spring 2007): 22-23.

"The Fight at Woodsonville." *Richmond Daily Dispatch*, December 25, 1861.

"Fighting and Feasting." *C.V.* 2, no. 1 (January 1894): 14.

Filbeck manuscript, Lilly Library., Indiana University, Bloomington, IN. HCHS.

Finlay, Luke W. "Fourth Tennessee Infantry." *Military Annals of Tennessee, Confederate* (1886).

"Fishing Creek Battle." *Memphis Daily Avalanche*, January 28, 1862.

"Fishing Creek Battle." *Memphis Daily Avalanche*, January 30, 1862.

Flynn, Diana. June 14, 1997. http://files.usgwarchives.org/ky/ky-footsteps/1997/vo1-112.txt. Accessed September 18, 2009.

"Forrest's First" pamphlet, n.d.

Francisco, Darleen. "Munfordville, Kentucky's Civil War Heritage." http://www.historynet.com/munfordville-kentuckys-civil-war-heritage-nov-96-americas-civil-war-feature.htm. Accessed September 8, 2009.

Frierson, Robert M. "Gen. E. Kirby Smith's Campaign in Kentucky." *C.V.* 3, no. 10: 295.

"Funeral Obsequtem of the Intrepid Patriot, Col. B. F. Terry." *Nashville Union and American*, December 19, 1861. www.terrystexasrangers.org/newsclippings/nashville_union_and_american/1861_12_19a.html. Accessed August 17, 2010.

Garrett, Jill K. trans. *Confederate Diary of Robert D. Smith*. Columbia, TN: Captain James Madison Sparkman Chapter, United Daughters of the Confederacy, 1975.

George, Henry. *History of the 3rd, 7th, 8th, and 12th Kentucky, C.S.A.* Paducah Library Special Collections, 1911.

Gilbert, Charles C. "On the field of Perryville." *B & L*: 52-59.

Giles, L. B. *Terry's Texas Rangers*. Austin: Von Boeckman-Jones Co., 1911. www.terrystexasrangers.org/histories/giles_lb/chapter2.htm. Accessed August 17, 2010.

Gipson, W. L. "About the Battle of Perryville." *C.V.* 8, no. 9: 433.

"Good Friday '64 General Forrest Raided Paducah," March 25, 1910, Vertical file. PKPL.

"Grant Takes Possession of Paducah during Civil Strife." *Paducah Life*, (Summer 1992): 12.

Greif, J. V. "Forrest's Raid on Paducah." *C.V.* 5, no. 5 (May 1897): 212-13.

"Group donates 54 acres of Perryville Battlefield." *Civil War Courier* 25, no. 3 (July 2010): 1, 8.

Guerrant, Rev. Edward O. "Marshall and Garfield in Eastern Kentucky." *B & L*: 393-97.

Hadden, Clint. "Sacramento is preserving its heritage." *McLean County News*. Calhoun, KY. n.d.

Hafendorfer, Kenneth A. *Battle of Richmond, Kentucky*. Louisville: KH Press, 2006.

——. *The Battle of Wildcat Mountain*. Louisville: KH Press, 2003.

——, ed. *Civil War Journal of William L. Trask*. Louisville: KH Press, 2003.

——. *Mill Springs: Campaign and Battle of Mill Springs, Kentucky*. Louisville: KH Press, 2001.

Hancock, Richard. *Hancock's Diary.* Nashville, TN: 1887.

Hapley [happy], John. "Battle of Fishing Creek." *Memphis Daily Avalanche,* January 31, 1862.

Harper's Weekly, February 25, 1860.

———.October 26, 1861.

Harrison, Jon P. "Tenth Texas Cavalry." *Military History of Texas and the Southwest* 22 (n.d.).

Harrison, Lowell. "Death on a dry river." *Civil War Times Illustrated* 28, no. 2 (May 1979): 4-9, 44-47.

Harrison, Lowell H. PhD. "Should I surrender? A Civil War Incident." *The Filson Club History Quarterly* (Louisville, Kentucky) 40, no. 4: 297-306. HCHS.

"Hart County Facts." www.mykcntuckygenealogy.com/ky-county-hart.html. Accessed September 26, 2009.

Head, T. A. *C.V.* 5, no. 8 (August 1897): 435.

Hensley, Tammy. "Battle of Munfordville on National Register of Historic Places." n.d. HCHS.

Henry, Robert Selph. *Nathan Bedford Forrest: First with the Most.* New York: Smithmark Publishers, 1991.

Hill, Bob. "Hart County's fields bear witness to war." *Courier Journal,* July 3, 1978. HCHS.

"The Historic Brown-Lanier House Bed and Breakfast" pamphlet. n.d.

"History." HCHS.

"The History of the Orphan Brigade." *C.V.* (July 1898): 317.

"A History of the Pleasant View House and Farm." BORA. n.d.

"A History of the Rogers House." BORA. n.d.

Hodges, Glenn. "Confederate general used legendary tactic for 1st time in McLean." *Messenger-Inquirer,* April 20, 1992. McLean County Historical Society.

———. "Kentucky Belle warned rebels of nearing troops." *Messenger-Inquirer.* n.d. McLean County Historical Society.

Holman, Kurt. E-mail to Randy Bishop. August 2, 2011.

Holmes, Mead. *Soldier of the Cumberland: Memoir of Mead Holmes, Jr. Sergeant of Company K, 21st Regiment Wisconsin Volunteers.* Boston: American Tract Society, 1864.

Horrall, Capt. S. F. "Word from the other side." *C.V.* 17, no. 12: 556.

Horrall, Spillard F. *History of the Forty-Second Indiana Volunteer Infantry.* Self published, 1892.

"How did Paducah get its name?" http://www.markethousemuseum.com/FAQ. Accessed April 9, 2010.

http://breckinridgegrcys.org/history html. Accessed September 7, 2009.

http//:www.civilwaralbum.com/misc11/paducah1f.htm. Accessed September 12, 2009.

http://www.civilwardiscoverytrail.org/location/detail.php?SiteID=500. Accessed September 7, 2009.

http://civilwar.molrganco.freeservers.com/ajmay.htm. Accessed July 30, 2010.

http://kccserv1.estb.wku.edu/factsheets/civilwar/ivymountain.html. Accessed September 7, 2009.

http://kyclim.wku.edu/factsheets/thebattlerrichmond.html. Accessed September 7, 2009.

http://mayhouse.org/perry/oldhouse5.html. Accessed July 30, 2010.

http://members.tripod.com/cornelius_carroll/id33.htm. Accessed July 30, 2010.

http://visitorcenter.madisoncounty.ky.us.htm. Accessed May 24, 2011.

http://www.battleofrichmond.org/ContactUs.htm. Accessed May 24, 2011.

http://www.bencaudill.com/documents_msc/5th.html. Accessed May 24, 2011.

http://www.campbellsvilleky.com/historica.html. Accessed December 16, 2010.

http://www.cityofbarbourvillekentucky.org/index.html. Accessed October 21, 2009.

http://www.friendsofmiddlecreek.org. Accessed December 16, 2010.

http://www.markethousemuseum.com/FAQ. Accessed April 9, 2010.

http://www.mt.net/mtsysdev/civilwar/history.htm. Accessed July 30, 2010.

http://www.prestonburgky.org/visit_info_details.php?id=121. Accessed August 15, 2010.

http://www.prestonburgky.org/visit_info_details.php?id=22. Accessed August 15, 2010.

http://www.trailsrus.com/morgan/bardstown.html. Accessed December 16, 2010.

————./campbellsville.html. Accessed December 16, 2010.

————./etown.html. Accessed December 16, 2010.

————./newhaven.html. Accessed December 16, 2010.

————./pr-704.html. Accessed December 16, 2010.

————./springfield.html. Accessed December 16, 2010.

http://www.uky.edu/KentuckyAtlas/ky-barbourville.html. Accessed October 21, 2009.

http://www.usafuneralhomesonline.com. Accessed September 8, 2009.

Hughes, Nathaniel C. with Connie W. Moretti and James M. Browne. *Brigadier General Tyree H. Bell, C.S.A.* Knoxville: University of Tennessee Press, 2004.

The Illustrated London News 44, no. 1253, (April 16, 1864): 358.

"Importance of Paducah stressed by researcher." Vertical file. PKPL. n.d.

Indianapolis Daily Journal, October 25, 1861.

————. October 26, 1861.

————. October 29, 1861.

————. November 5, 1861.

————.December 19, 1861

————. February 6, 1862.

Isom, William H. *Reminiscences of the 17th Tennessee Volunteers.* n.d.

Ivy Mountain Battlefield interpretive marker, n.d.

Ivy Mountain Battlefield obelisk, n.d.

Jessee, Gordon. "The Battle of Middle Creek, Kentucky." Unpublished article, n.d.

John Hunt Morgan Trail pamphlet, n.d.

Johnson, Brig. Gen. Adam R. *The Partisan Rangers of the Confederate States Army.* Louisville, 1904.

Johnston, William Preston. *The Life of Albert Sidney Johnston.* New York: D. Appleton and Company, 1879.

Jordan, Gen. Thomas and J. P. Pryor. *The Campaigns of Lieut.-Gen. N. B. Forrest, and of Forrest's Cavalry.* Dayton, OH: Press of Morningside Bookshop, 1977.

Jordan, James D. *Reminiscences of the Boys in Gray 1861-1865.* Edited by Mamie Yeary, 1912.

Jorgensen, Kathryn. "Middle Creek Battlefield in Kentucky Open in July." *Civil War News* 28, no. 6 (July 2004).

———. "Richmond, Ky. battlefield will soon open a visitors and heritage center." *Civil War News* 32, no. 9 (October 2008): 5.

"Judge John H. Rogers." *C.V.* 19, no. 5 (May 1911): 241.

Kelly, R. M. "Holding Kentucky for the Union." *B & L.* New York: Castle Books, 1956, 372-92.

Kennedy, Robert C. "Governor Magoffin's Neutrality."

"Kentucky battlefield named to national 'Most Endangered' list." *Daily Times,* March 24, 2004. HCHS.

Kentucky Counties. Kentucky Images, Lexington, Kentucky, n.d.

Kidd, Dan. "Grant Awarded to Munfordville group." n.d. HCHS.

Kinslow, Gina. *Glasgow Daily Times,* n.d.

Kirkpatrick, George Morgan. *The Experiences of a Private Soldier of the Civil War.* Self published, 1924.

Knox Countian(Barbourville, KY) 19, no. 3 (Fall 2007).

Kolk, Mary. E-mail to Randy Bishop. May 13, 2010.

Lambert, D. Warren. "The Decisive Battle of Richmond, Kentucky." The Battle of Richmond Association, Richmond, KY, n.d.

Landrum, George W. The George W. Landrum Letters. MSS.543. Western Reserve Historical Society Library, Cleveland, Ohio, n.d.

Lebanon Tourist and Convention Commission, Lebanon, KY, 2006.

Lewis, Richard B. "Felix Zollicoffer and the Zollie Tree." n.d.

Lexington Kentucky Statesman, September 17, 1862.

Lindsley, John B. *Military Annals of Tennessee—Confederate.* Nashville: J. M. Lindsley & Co., 1886. Reprinted by Broadfoot Publishing Company, Wilmington, NC, 1995.

The Lloyd Tilghman House and Civil War Museum pamphlet.

Logsdon, Myra J. "The Battle of Munfordville as remembered by a young girl." *Filson Clubs History Quarterly* 14, no. 3 (July 1940). HCHS.

"Louis Kolb, Sr., clearly recalls Battle of Paducah fought 63 years ago this 25th of March." *New Democrat,* March 25, 1927. Vertical file. PKPL.

Louisville Courier-Journal, April 6, 1878.

———. September 29, 1933.

Louisville Daily Democrat, September 25, 1861.

———. October 24, 1861.

———. January 3, 1863.

Louisville Daily Journal, October 7, 1861.

———. October 24, 1861.

———. October 29, 1861.

———. September 16, 1862.

Macon, Edna Shewcraft. "A ride into history." n.d. McLean County Historical Society.

Malone, Thomas H. *Memoir of Thomas H. Malone: An Autobiography Written for His Children.* 1928.

Maness, Lonnie E. *An Untutored Genius: The Military Carrier of General Nathan Bedford Forrest.* Oxford, MS: The Guild Bindery Press, 1990.

Maney, George Earl. "Report of the Action near Perryville, Ky. October 8th, 1862." October 29, 1862. William P. Palmer Collection of Braxton Bragg Papers, Western Reserve Historical Society, Cleveland, OH.

Mathes, Capt. J. Harvey. *General Forrest.* New York: D. Appleton and Company, 1902.

McCullaugh, J. B. Letter to Sen. R. J. White. March 10, 1878. *Lexington Herald-Ledger,* August 30, 1957. Somerset, KY. 1999.

McFarland, Judge L. B. "Maney's Brigade at the Battle of Perryville." *C.V.* 30, no. 12: 467-69.

McKinney, Mrs. Anna. "F. K. Zollicoffer First & Last Battle." *C.V.* 17, no. 4 (April 1910): 161-63.

McMurray, W. J. *History of the Twentieth Tennessee Regiment Volunteer Infantry.* Nashville, 1904.

Manship, Luther. "Burial Place of Robert A. Smith." *C.V.* 17, no. 11: 476.

Manson, M. D. Letter to State Sen. R. J. White of Kentucky. *Louisville Courier-Journal,* April 6, 1878.

Martin, Philip. "General Zollicoffer's Bracelet." *C.V.* 12, no. 13 (March 1902): 78.

May family photos. http://mayhouse.org/family/trees/may/photos/JT1828DM. html. Accessed June 10, 2011.

Mehr, Andreas. Letter to the *Louisville Anzeiger.* October 13, 1862.

Memphis Daily Avalanche, January 28, 1862.

———. January 31, 1862.

Middle Creek Driving Tour pamphlet, n.d.

Mill Springs Battlefield Association pamphlet, n.d.

Mill Springs Driving Tour Guide, n.d.

Milner, Duncan C. Letter to editor. October 10, 1862. *National Tribune,* September 27, 1906.

Mint Jelep & the Old General. "Forrest fights his first battle." *The Civil War Courier,* 25, no. 3 (July 2010): 17-19.

Mitchell, Charles Reed. cityofbarbourvillekentucky.com. Accessed October 21, 2009.

"Monument to Gen. Zollicoffer was unveiled before thousands." *Somerset (KY) Times,* October 28, 1910.

Moody, Robert C. "The Battle of Big Hill." Friends of the Richmond Battlefield, 2008.

Moore, Frank. *Civil War in Song and Story*. P. F. Collier, 1889.

———. *Rebellion Record*. New York: G. P. Putnam, 1864.

Morgan's Men Association. Cynthiana, Kentucky Tour signs, n.d.

Morgan's Raids at Cynthiana, KY Civil War Driving Tour pamphlet, Cynthiana-Harrison County Chamber of Commerce, n.d.

Morris, George W. *History of the Eighty-First Regiment of Indiana Volunteer Infantry in the Great War of the Rebellion 1861 to 1865*. Self published, 1901.

Morris, Roy. "Battle in the Bluegrass." *Civil War Times Illustrated* 27, no. 8 (December 1988): 14-23.

Nashville Banner, October 30, 1861.

Nation, Garry D. "Alvis Duncan Hicks in the Civil War." pages.suddenlink.net. Accessed September 7, 2009.

National Tribune, July 5, 1883.

———. October 5, 1861.

———. October 5, 1899.

———. December 3, 1903.

Nelson, John A. "Following Zollicoffer." *Pulaski Week*, October 31, 1991.

Neuman, Fred G. *The Story of Paducah*. Paducah, KY: Young Printing Company, 1920.

New Albany Daily Ledger, October 24, 1861.

Newberry, J. S. "The Battle of Perryville." www.battleofperryville.com/san/com55.html. Accessed September 12, 2009.

New Birmingham Times, 1891.

New York Times, November 1, 1861.

Nichols, John H. *Proof of the pudding: Autobiography of John Harmon Nichols*. Self published, 1913.

Noe, Kenneth W. *Perryville: This Grand Havoc of Battle*. Lexington: The University Press of Kentucky, 2001.

———. "Remembering Perryville: History and Memory at a Civil War Battlefield." http://www.perryvillereenactment.org/html/more_history.html. September 14, 2009.

"North and South clash at Fort Anderson." *Paducah Life* (Summer 1992). Vertical file: PKPL.

"Old Letter Describes Battle of Rowlett's Station." *Hart County News,* October 17, 1974. HCHS.

Oliver, Jonathan. "Civil War research brings Michigan man to Paducah." *Paducah Sun*, July 7, 1996. Vertical file. PKPL.

"The Opposing forces at Perryville, KY." *B & L.*, 29-30.

"Paducah Fortifications." n.d. Vertical file. PKPL.

Paducah, Kentucky Downtown Civil War Walking Tour pamphlet. Paducah/McCracken County Convention and Visitors Bureau.

"Paducah's Col. Hicks: It was a case of lose lips creating loss of horses." http://

www.thekentuckycivilwarbugle.com/2009-4Qpages/fortanderson.html. Accessed April 9, 2010.

Parker, Morgan. Letter to wife. *Detroit Daily Tribune*, February 4, 1862.

"Particulars of the Munsfordville [sic] Fight." *Indianapolis Daily Journal*, December 19, 1861. HCHS.

Partin, Winfred. "Contesting Cumberland Gap." *America's Civil War* 4, no. 2: 26-32.

Patrick, Bethanne Kelly. "Maj. Gen. James Garfield." www.military.com/Content/ moreContent?file=ML_Garfield_bkp. Accessed September 13, 2009.

Peake, Mikel. "Baptism of fire at Rowlett's Station, Kentucky." www.oocities.com/ ind32infantry/bfrs.html. Accessed September 8, 2009.

———. "1st German, 32nd Indiana News Update." Pamphlet, n.d. HCHS.

———. "Oldest Civil War Monument in the Nation Rediscovered in Kentucky." www.Kentuckyliving.com/article.asp?articleid=458&issueid=89. Accessed September 8, 2009.

Penn, William A. *Rattling Spurs and Broad-Brimmed Hats: The Civil War in Cynthiana and Harrison County, Kentucky.* Battle Grove Press, 1995.

"Perryville." www.kentuckyliving.com/article.asp?article=458&issueid=89. Accessed September 8, 2009.

The Perryville Battlefield Preservation Association pamphlet, n.d.

Perryville Battlefield State Historic Site, Kentucky Department of Parks, n.d.

Perryville Battlefield State Historic Site pamphlet, n.d.

Perryville Battlefield Walking Trail Guide, Kentucky Department of Parks, n.d.

"Perryville named Preserve American Community." www.civilwarbuff.org/ NewsLetters/2005/feb05.htm. Accessed September 23, 2009.

Polk, Dr. Jefferson J. *Autobiography of Dr. J. J. Polk.* Louisville: John P. Morton, 1867.

Pope, Colonel Curran. Letter to the editors. *Louisville Journal*, Oct. 19, 1862.

Potter, Thomas C. Letter to his sister. January 24, 1862.

Poulson, Wesley S. Letter to the *Cadiz Republican.* Spring 1863.

"Preservation of oldest Civil War Memorial: Bloedner Monument moved from Cave Hill National Cemetery." www.cem.va.gov/hist/BloednerMon.asp. Accessed September 8, 2009.

"Primitive Pekin Becomes the city of Paducah." *Paducah Life* (Summer 1992): 7.

"Proposed Statue to General Forrest." *C.V.* 4, no. 2 (February 1896): 41-44.

Putnam, Captain J. H. *A Journalistic History of the Thirty-First Regiment.* Louisville, KY: John P. Morton & Co., 1862.

Putney, William G. Memoir transcript. William L. Clements Library, The University of Michigan.

Quisenberry, A. C. "The Battle of Richmond, Kentucky." *Register of Kentucky Historical Society* (September 1918).

"Rantings of a Civil War Historian." http://civilwarcavalry.com/?p=824. Accessed September 12, 2009.

Reed, A. W. "The Battle of Perryville." www.battleofperryville.com/san_com55. html. Accessed September 12, 2009.

"Report from the 1st Michigan Engineers and Mechanics." *Marshall (MI) Statesman,* January 29, 1862.

"Report of Capt. Schwarz." n.d. HCHS.

Richmond, Kentucky pamphlet. Richmond Tourism & Main St. Dept., Richmond, KY., n.d.

"Richmond, Ky., battlefield to receive grant." *Civil War Courier* 20, no. 7 (September 2009): 10.

Richmond, Kentucky Driving Tour, n.d.

Ridley, B. L. "Chat with Col. W. S. McLemore." *C.V.* 8, no. 6 (June 1900): 262-63.

Rietti, John C. "The Robert A. Smith Monument." *C.V.* 4, no. 8 (August 1896): 279.

Robertson, John E. L. *Paducah 1830-1980.* Paducah, KY: Image Graphics, n.d.

Rosser, R. W. E-mail to Randy Bishop. December 15, 2009.

Roth, Dave. Richmond, Kentucky maps. *B & G.* 25, no. 6 (2009).

"Rowlett's Station." Unpublished article, n.d. HCHS.

"Rowlett's Station Battlefield." Unpublished article, n.d. HCHS.

Samuel and Susan Sizemore Allen. Undated sheet. HCHS.

Sanders, Stuart W. "America's Civil War: Battle for Kentucky." www.historynet. com/americas-civil-war-battle-for-kentucky.htm. Accessed September 11, 2009.

———. "Battle of Perryville: 21st Wisconsin Infantry Regiment's Harrowing Fight." www.historynet.com/battle-of-perryville-21st-wisconsin-infantry-regiment's-harrowing-fight. Accessed September 11, 2009.

———. "The Cost of War: Centre College and the battle of Perryville." www. centre.edu/web/library/sc/special/Perryville/index.htm. Accessed September 12, 2009.

———. "The 1862 Kentucky Campaign and the Battle of Perryville." *Blue and Gray Magazine* 22, no. 5 (Holiday 2005): 6-20, 44-65.

———. "Honor and Ego at Munfordville." *Civil War* 63 (n.d.):18-25. HCHS.

———. "Literally Covered with the Dead and Dying." www.civilwar.org/battlefield/ perryville/perryville-history-article. Accessed September 12, 2009.

———. "Surrender at bridge based on foe's word." http://goliath.ecnet.com/ coms2/gi_01993245079/surrenderatthebridgebasedonfoesword. Accessed September 26, 2009.

"Schoepf turns back Zollicoffer's Rebel at Camp Wildcat!" *Southern Star* (Laurel County), October 21, 1861. http://aotn.homestead.com/wildcat.html.

Searcy, James T. Letter. October 25, 1862. LPR 78 Box 3 Folders 14 & 15, Alabama Department of Archives and History.

"The Second Battle of Cynthiana." http://www.geocities.com/morgansraid/history. html?200912. Accessed September 12, 2009.

Sellers, Carol. Letter to author. June 4, 2011.

Seyfrit, Phillip. E-mail to author. July 22, 2011.

———. "Nelson only Naval officer to become major general." http://www. kentuckycivilwarbugle.com/bullnelson.html. Accessed February 10, 2010.

Shanklin, Lt. Col. James M. *The Soldiers of Indiana in the War for the Union.* vol. 1. Indianapolis: Merrill & Company, 1866, 620-24.

Shaw, W. L. "Hard Fighting—Franklin—Munfordville." *C.V.* (n.d.): 221-22. HCHS.

Sievers, Capt. William. Letter to Editor. *Louisville Anzeiger,* December 1861.

"Significan dates in Paducah history." *Paducah Life* (Summer 1993): 60.

Simonson, George T. Scott Cantwell Meeker, ed. A film by Deep Vee Productions. Feb. 20, 2005.

Sisco, Scott. "Civil War buffs want battlefield preserved." *Daily News,* March 4, 2004. HCHS.

"A sketch of Judge Rogers." *C.V.* 11, no. 6 (June 1903): 262.

"The skirmish at Sacramento." *Louisville Democrat,* January 3, 1862.

Smeltzer, Harry. "Squire Bottom Founds a Confederate Cemetery." *Civil War Times* 49, no. 3 (June 2011): 27-28.

Smith, Byron. "Battle of Richmond, Kentucky." *C.V.* 30, no. 8 (August 1922): 297-98.

Smith, Kirby. Letter to Cassie Smith. August 29, 1862. Kirby Smith Papers, Southern Historical Collection, University of North Carolina Library.

"A soldier's 1861 Letter from Munfordville." *Hart County News,* February 15, 1974. HCHS.

The Somerset Times 4, no. 37 (October 28, 1910).

Sparkman, Faron. "5th Kentucky Voluntary Infantry (Original) Brief History." http://www.bencaudill.com/documents_msc/5th.html. Accessed July 30, 2010.

Speed, Capt. Thos. *The Union Regiments of Kentucky.* http://www.mt.net/ mtsysdev/civilwar/history.htm. Accessed July 30, 2010.

Spence, Col. Philip B. "Campaigning in Kentucky." *C.V.* 9, no. 1 (January 1901): 22-23.

Steele, A. L. *C.V.* 2, no. 10 (October 1895): 315.

Stewart, Charles D. "A Bachelor General." *Wisconsin Magazine of History* 12 (1933): 131-54. HCHS.

Stewart, George. Letter of Recollections. November 30, 1915. HCHS.

Stier, William J. "Fury takes the field." *Civil War Times* (December 1999): 41-48.

"The Story of Camp Dick Robinson." *Courier-Journal,* 1895. http://kentuckyexplorer. com/nonmembers/3-camps.html. Accessed December 8, 2011.

Street, John Kennedy. Letter to "Dear." August 8, 1862. http://wehaveneatstuff. com.streetpapers.htm. Accessed September 22, 2009.

Suhr, Robert Collins. "Kentucky Neutrality Threatened." *America's Civil War* 5, no. 2 (July 1992): 22-28.

Swindler, Samantha. http://www.thetimestribune.com/features/local_story_2550 85107.html. Accessed September 19, 2009.

Sykes, E. T. "An Incident of the Battle of Munfordville, KY." n.d. HCHS.

Talley, Spencer B. "The Battle of Fishing Creek." geocities.com/Pentagon/ Quarters/1864/talley.htm?200919. Accessed 9-19-2009.

Tarrant, Sergeant E. *The Wild Riders of the First Kentucky Cavalry.* Louisville, 1894.

Taylor, Robert B. "The Battle of Perryville, October 8, 1862. *The Register of the Kentucky Historical Society* 60, no. 4 (October 1862).

"The Tenth Regiment." n.d.

"Texas Historical Commission Nears Fundraising Goal to Dedicate Texas Civil War Monument." January 2008. www.txnp.org/Articles?press.asp?ArticleID=8093. Accessed September 19, 2009.

"Texas Monument is Dedicated at 1862 Battlefield in Richmond, Ky." August 2009. www.civilwarnews.com/archive/articles/09/august/richmond_08??. Accessed September 13, 2009.

"Texas 'silent Sentinel' dedicated at Battle of Richmond." *Civil War Courier,* 24, no. 4 (July 2009): 1, 22.

"32nd Indiana Casualties." www.ulib.iupui.edu/Kade/peake/casualties_list.html. Accessed August 17, 2010.

"32nd Indiana Infantry (1st German)." www.geocities.com/ind32ndinfantry/monument.html. Accessed September 8, 2009.

"32nd Indiana Monument." www.lib.iupui.edu/Kade/peake/p31.html. Accessed September 8, 2009.

Thomas, Bill. "Old Forts, Monuments at Munfordville Reminders of Bloody Civil War Fighting in Battle of Bridge." *Park City (KY) Daily News,* June 23, 1957. HCHS.

Toledo Daily Herald and Times, October 26, 1861.

Toney, Marcus B. *The Privatations of a Private.* Self published, 1905.

Tourgee, Albion W. *The Story of a Thousand, Being a history of the service of the 105th Ohio Volunteer Infantry, in the War for the Union from August 21, 1862 to June 6, 1865.* Self published, 1896.

Towler, Mrs. W. T. "Capt. W. J. Stone—In Memoriam." *C.V.* 31, no. 7 (July 1923): 246-47.

Tps.cr.nps.gov/nhl/defail.cfm?ResourceId=2110&ResourceType=site. Accessed September 9, 2009.

"The true story of Sister Mary Lucy Dosh." http://www.markethousemuseum.com/node/177. Accessed April 9, 2010.

"Union Commander at Battle of Big Hill." Friends of the Richmond Battlefield, Inc., n.d.

Update to the Civil War Sites Advisory Commission Report on the Nation's Civil War Battlefields. U.S. Department of the Interior, National Park Service, American Battlefield Protection Program, Washington, D.C., October 2008.

Urquhart, David. "Bragg's Advance and Retreat." *B & L.:* 600-609.

Usafuneralhomesonline.com/usnationalcemeteries/national. Accessed September 8, 2009.

Van Der Linden, Frank. "General Bragg's Impossible Dream: Take Kentucky." www.civilwar.org/battlefields/Perryville/Perryville-history. Accessed September 12, 2009.

Villard, Henry. *Memoirs of Henry Villard.* 1904.

Wake, Norrie, ed. *The Zollie Tree* (Official Publication of the Mill Springs Battlefield Association) 11, no. 7 (Winter 2007).

Walden, Geoffrey R. "Disaster on the Cumberland: The Battle of Fishing Creek, Mill Springs, Kentucky." *C. V.* 4(1998): 38-41.

————. "What's in a Name?" geocities.com/Pentagon/Quarters/1864/name. htm?200919. Accessed September 19, 2009.

War of the Rebellion, Official Records of the Union and Confederate Armies. National Historical Society, Gettysburg, PA, 1972, Reprint.

Ward, John K. "Forrest's First Fight." *America's Civil War* 6, no. 1 (March 1993): 50-57.

Ward, Ken. "The battle of Sacramento." Historical Commentary, HCHS, July 11, 1991.

————. "The 31st Indiana Infantry: Drilling and Disease." *McLean County News,* May 4, 2000.

"Was Paducah the site of a Civil War battle?" http://www.markethousemuseum. com/FAQ. Accessed April 9, 2010.

Washington National Tribune, March 8, 1894.

————. April 4, 1898.

————. April 19, 1894.

————. April 28, 1904.

————. May 10, 1894.

Watkins, Col. Sam R. *Columbia (TN) Journal,* May 30, 1900.

————. *Co. Aytch Maury Greys, First Tennessee Regiment, or, A Side Show of the Big Show.* Watkins, 1882.

Weatherred, John. *The Wartime Diary of John Weatherred.* www.jackmasters. net/9tncav.html. Accessed December 17, 2010.

The Weekly Lancaster Gazette, November 7, 1861.

"Welcome to Cynthiana, Kentucky." http://www.cynthianaky.com. Accessed November 30, 2010.

West, A. J. Newspaper article. October 16, 1892. Perryville Battlefield State Historic Site archives.

Western Christian Advocate, n.d.

The Western Star, November 7, 1861.

Wheeler, Joseph. "Bragg's Invasion of Kentucky." *B & L.:* 1-25.

Wheeler, Linda. "Richmond Museum finds a home in the Bluegrass." *Civil War Times* (December 2009): 14.

Whittaker, Dr. Fred. "The Battle of Rowlett's Station, Kentucky." n.d. HCHS.

————. *America's Civil War* 13, no. 5 (November 2000): 8, 60-61.

Wide Awake Films. *The Battle of Perryville: The Invasion of Kentucky.* 2007.

Wilder, Gen. John T. "The Siege of Munfordville: A paper read before the Ohio Commandery, M. O. L. Legion in 1902." HCHS.

Wilder, J. T. Letter to My Dear Pet. September 12, 1862. HCHS.

William E. DeMoss Letter. October 30, 1861. TSL & A, Nashville, TN.

"William James Rogers." *C. V.* 16, no. 3 (March 1908): 137.

Williams, Samuel C. *General John T. Wilder.* Bloomington, IN: 1936.

Wilson, Dan. "The Battle of Perryville." http://webpages.charter.net/danwilly/ perry.htm. Accessed September 12, 2009.

Wilson, Don. "The Boys from Calhoun." February 2008. McLean County Historical Society.

———. "The Boys that never left Calhoun." n.d. McLean County Historical Society.

Wilson, Gilbert. E-mail to Randy Bishop. July 27, 2011.

Worsham, W. J. *The Old Nineteenth Tennessee Regiment. C.S.A.* Knoxville: 1902.

www.americanbyways.com/index.php?catid=359. Accessed September 9, 2009.

www.aotn.homestead.com/richoob.html. Accessed September 14, 2009.

www.battleofbarbourville.com. Accessed September 7, 2009.

www.battleofrichmond.org/preservation.htm. Accessed September 9, 2009.

www.battleofrichmond.org/HistoryBattle.htm. Accessed September 9, 2009.

www.battleofrichmond.org/virtual.htm. Accessed September 9, 2009.

www.battleofsac.com/History.htm. Accessed September 14, 2009.

www.battleofsac.com/sacramento.htm. Accessed September 14, 2009.

www.breckinridgegreys.org. Accessed October 1, 2009.

www.cem.va.gov/cems/nchp/cavehill.asp. Accessed October 1, 2009.

www.cem.va.gov/cems/nchp/millsprings.asp. Accessed October 1, 2009.

www.cityofrichmondkentucky.org/index.html. Accessed September 12, 2009.

www.civilwardiscoverytrail.org/location_detail.php?SiteID=103.   Accessed September 13, 2009.

www.civilwar-pictures.com. Accessed September 7, 2009.

www.civilwartraveler.com/WEST/KY/east-KY.html. Accessed September 22, 2009.

www.fs.fed.us. Accessed September 7, 2009.

www.geocities.com/Pentagon/Quarters/1964/frierson_letter_htm.   Accessed September 13, 2009.

www.geocities.com/rlperry.geo/DesperateFight.html. Accessed September 13, 2009.

www.geocities.com/rlperry.geo/UnionAssault.html. Accessed September 13, 2009.

www.kyclim.wku.edu/factsSheets/MillSprings.html. Accessed October 1, 2009.

www.middlecreek.org/foundation.htm. Accessed October 2, 2010.

———/history.htm. Accessed October 2, 2010.

———/location.htm. Accessed October 2, 2010.

———/participants.htm. Accessed October 2, 2010.

———/plans.htm. Accessed October 2, 2010.

———/welcome.htm. Accessed October 2, 2010.

www.morningsidebooks.com. Accessed September 17, 2009.

www.psci.net/hatch/31hist.html. Accessed October 1, 2010.

www.researchonline.net/generals/crittendongb.htm. Accessed September 18, 2009.

www.scv1817tn.com. Accessed September 7, 2009.

www.thssite.tripod.com. Accessed September 22, 2009.

www.trailsrus.com/civilwar/region4/richmond.html. Accessed September 7, 2009.

www.waymarking.com/waymarkets/WMPKE. Accessed November 3, 2009.

www.wildcatbattlefield.org. Accessed September 7, 2009.

www.wildcatreenactment.org. Accessed September 15, 2009.

Wyeth, John A. *Life of General Nathan Bedford Forrest.* Dayton, OH: Press of Morningside Bookshop, 1975.

Wyeth, John Allen. "Morgan's Christmas Raid, 1862-1863." Edited by Robert Lanier *Photographic History of the Civil War: Armies and Leaders.* New York: Random House Publishing, 1983.

Young, Gen. Bennett. "Address." *C.V.* 18, no. 12 (December 1910): 567-72.

Index